SHAME

The Underside of

Narcissism

SHAME

The Underside of

Narcissism

Andrew P. Morrison

AP THE ANALYTIC PRESS

1989   Hillsdale, NJ   Hove and London

Published by The Analytic Press, Hillsdale, NJ.

Distributed solely by

Lawrence Erlbaum Associates, Inc., Publishers
365 Broadway
Hillsdale, New Jersey   07642

Library of Congress Cataloging-in-Publication Data

Morrison, Andrew P., 1937-
        Shame, the underside of narcissism / Andrew P. Morrison.
        P. cm.
        Includes bibliographical references.
        ISBN 0-88163-082-9
        1. Narcissism. 2. Shame. I. Title.
        RC553.N36M67 1989
        616.85'85—dc2O   89-37655

                                                            CIP

Printed in the United States of America
10 9 8 7 6 5 4

To Amy and Rachel Morrison
and
To the memories of
Sidney Levin and Helen Block Lewis

Contents

Part II
CLINICAL APPLICATIONS

Acknowledgments

I want to express special thanks to my editors and colleagues at The Analytic Press, who have been helpful, encouraging, and supportive throughout the process of preparing this manuscript. My thanks and admiration go especially to Dr. Paul E. Stepansky, who, as Editor-In-Chief, has set a tone of scholarly professionalism, quiet encouragement, and the rigorous ideal of preparing the best manuscript I could manage. Making helpful and challenging suggestions from the beginning, he also expected that I would strive and work to clarify, structure, and improve the several drafts I sent his way.

Also helpful at TAP was Eleanor Starke Kobrin, whose careful manuscript editing assisted enormously in shaping my thoughts and lending some grace to craggy and obscure phrases. She also advised and "problem-solved" on many matters. Through the good offices of TAP, Dr. Joan Lang read various versions of the manuscript and helped me to sharpen and clarify concepts and the shape of their presentation. Kathryn M. Scornavacca has been most responsive and professional in preparing the final format, design, and anticipated marketing approach of the book as we have moved along in production. To these capable and friendly women I extend my gratitude and respect. Mr. Lee Fischer, of *Fine Print* in Cambridge, was exacting and professional in helping with the final tasks of proofreading and preparation of the indices. Thanks too to Shirley Allison for her endless revisions at the Compaq.

Along the way, many others have helped as I struggled to clarify and present my ideas about shame. I want to acknowledge and thank Dr. Michael Basch, who early invited me to Chicago to discuss my ideas with the self psychology study group; Dr. Arnold Goldberg, who made clear where my ideas deviated from those of Heinz Kohut and stimulated me to take responsibility for those differences; Dr. Jason Aronson, who first planted the idea that I write my own book on shame; Dr. Silvan Tomkins, who patiently and thoroughly corresponded about similarities and differences between our views on shame; and, finally, the members of the Eastern Division of the National Council on Self Psychology (in particular, Dr. Frank Lachmann), who helped me crystalize and elaborate ideas relating shame and defense. I especially want to greet my analyst, to whom I returned for what I thought would be merely some "fine tuning." In fact, she provided a wise and affirming environment that enabled the unfolding of my own particular transferences; encouraged me as I pursued my own personal and theoretical thoughts about shame; and reminded me – with force, when necessary – of the importance as well of conflict and "The Oedipus." I feel sure that she knows of my gratitude.

As Helen Block Lewis noted, there is a devoted group of us "shameniks" who tend to be, as we like to think, not only bright and articulate, but also uncommonly supportive of, and nice to, one another! I have had the good fortune to swap ideas with many of them, and I want to note here and express appreciation to this group of clinicians and theoreticians, who include: Frances Broucek, James Gilligan, Sidney Levin, Helen Block Lewis, Nancy Morrison, Donald Nathanson, John O'Leary, Silvan Tomkins, Fred Wright, and Leon Wurmser. Others, of course, have contributed to our understanding of shame, and I hope that they will forgive me for not including them in this list of people with whom I have communicated more directly. It is a club of which I am proud to be a member.

Inevitably, writing a book is a difficult undertaking for a full-time clinician. People often ask, "Where did you find the time?" A good question. The answer, alas, is that the time comes out of evenings, weekends, and summers, many of which might have been spent relaxing with family and friends. For the many hours "stolen" from my family I want to express particular thanks (I have already expressed the apologies!) to my wife, Amy, and my daughter, Rachel. Their support, humor, and, at times, direct expression of frustration and annoyance have humanized this difficult task. I expect that now they will share with me the relief that it is finally over!

Preface

As with most interests that captivate us, my curiosity about shame evolved from an attempt to make sense out of my own personal experience. I think that that experience first drew my attention to psychoanalysis and, within the analytic framework, to the differences between the writings and emphases of Freud and Alfred Adler. In high school I wrote my senior "source theme" on the development of psychoanalysis. In college, one of the most engrossing papers I toiled over was a comparison of Adler and Freud entitled, as I recall, "Adler and Freud: The Ego and Id of Psychoanalysis." My emphases would be different now, but I think—as I mention in the text of the present book—that I was responding to the sensitivity of Adler to issues relating to shame (and, incidentally, to their relative paucity in Freud's writings).

Having acknowledged my recognition of shame sensitivity in my own personal makeup, I want to note the relative absence of discussion of shame in psychoanalytic writings prior to 1971 (with Helen Block Lewis's epic book). Since that time, and particularly in the last decade, papers and books have begun to appear about shame. It is as though this long-neglected affect has finally been taken "out of the closet" by psychoanalytically informed writers and therapists, after its

neglect during the dominance of drive/defense psychology in traditional psychoanalytic thought. As I try to demonstrate in the body of
this book, I believe that such a change is due to a broadening of
psychoanalytic theory to include the study of narcissism and the self,
and due as well to the assumption of a braver stance by therapists. This
new stance allowed them to examine the searing, painful experience of
shame, which goes beyond the more familiar guilt feelings of intrapsychic conflict. As it did with me, in my practice as psychoanalyst
and therapist, work with shame may begin with encounters with
patients, but it inevitably leads to a confrontation by the therapist with
his or her own shame, which frequently follows different paths from
those uncovered in personal analyses or therapies.

It seemed for me personally a daunting experience to contemplate
writing my own book, and I gave the matter serious consideration
before beginning such an undertaking. At first, I planned to collect
some previously published papers on shame, writing some pithy
introductions, and leaving elaboration of the subject to the voices of
others. As a matter of fact, I interrupted the process of work on this
book to edit such a volume of published papers about narcissism, in
part, I think, to move away from the challenge of committing my own
voice to the subject of shame. However, as Nathanson notes in his
Preface to *The Many Faces of Shame*, each approach is somewhat different
from the other – capturing a piece of the elephant – leaving the author
confused and vaguely dissatisfied with the completeness of his own
discussion. Some of the papers on shame that caused such vague
feelings of incompleteness were my own, but I feel that my understanding of shame has become clearer and been sharpened as I have
thought about and responded to the challenge of preparing this book.

In a work about an affective experience like shame, it is not easy
to determine how much attention should be paid to clinical theory.
However, as I became interested in shame, I searched for relevant
theoretical discussions and found these to be few. Many of the readings
were interesting although not directly related to the theory of shame,
but my conceptualizations about shame began to come together
around these preliminary theoretical readings. In fact, my own introduction to self psychology and the work of Kohut came about through
my investigation of shame. As I proceeded to work on early drafts of
this book, I determined that a focus on, and a review of, relevant
theoretical perspectives was necessary to provide a lens through which
to view and consider the clinical manifestations of shame.

My conceptualization of the theory of shame boils down to three
fundamental areas: those relating to the *self*, to the *ideal*, and to *narcis-*

sism. Although much has been written about these areas, many of the seminal papers speak not at all, or very little, about shame. Thus, I found that I had to piece together, for example, the relationships to shame of the ego ideal, of primary narcissism, of the hypothesized supraordinate self or selfobject, and of empathic failure. Other writings included shame in their discussions of these constructs, but sometimes in ways different from those in which I understood the relationship, sometimes almost parenthetically as they focused on other factors. It seemed to me that the shame literature had not clearly and systematically succeeded in relating relevant theoretical contributions about self, ideal, and narcissism to an understanding of shame.

Part One of this book, then, is devoted to such a presentation. Throughout its first five chapters, I attempt to relate my own understanding of shame to Freud's thoughts about shame and narcissism; to those of the ego psychologists and their edification of the ego ideal; to primitive object relations and narcissism; and to later approaches to narcissism, ending with the thinking of Heinz Kohut. In the Introduction, I offer some guiding questions and issues to delineate our excursion into shame, and I attempt throughout to consider these issues as I annotate others' theoretical work. I try to present a roadmap to the understanding of where such thought leads in relation to our own considerations about shame.

In Part Two, I turn to clinical matters, beginning with a case presentation and theoretical considerations deriving from ego psychology, object relations, and, finally, self psychology. I then review shame-related clinical manifestations, which are subsequently reframed as the shame defenses (that is, anger and rage, contempt and envy, and depression), or what Kohut has considered as adaptive defensiveness. The following chapters consider in greater detail shame in narcissistic characters, in more structured (neurotic) characters, and, finally, shame in manic-depressive psychosis.

In the Epilogue, I return full circle to a more anecdotal, expository example of an imaginary experience which I, as author, might have experienced; let me here acknowledge that any relation of this "shame fantasy" to the writing of the present book is far from imaginary! This final chapter also considers shame in the broader contexts of philosophy and literature, societal issues, suicide, and the differences between men and women. More, I am sure, could have been included, but other authors will have to respond as I have to the incompleteness and to questions arising from my particular vision of shame in comparison with their own.

I invite you, the reader, then, to follow my review of previous theoretical considerations as they relate to shame; of clinical examples of shame and its treatment in patients with varying clinical conditions; and of clinical factors that relate to, or defend against, shame. I hope that you will find this journey worthwhile and stimulating and that you will recognize elements of shame that relate to your own clinical work with patients and, inevitably, to your own experience.

1

Introduction and Overview

We have all felt shame. We have all suffered feelings of inferiority, inadequacy, incompetence; known a sense of defect and flaw, of failure; been scorned by others–such feelings are among the most painful we can experience. We hide them from ourselves and from others. Yet, shame has, until very recently, been little explored in the psychoanalytic literature.

My own interest in studying shame began a few years ago with a patient of mine, a man of my own age who had suffered from several episodes of severe depression and mania. He had never fulfilled the promise of his early talents or reached the pinnacles of achievement expected by his parents. The son of two concert musicians, he was "supposed" to reach great artistic heights; instead, he had become a middle-level technocrat in a business concern. He had married, but his wife and two children had left him following a manic episode. During treatment he gradually uncovered deep feelings of shame, mortification, and humiliation at his failures to attain his (and his parents') goals or to form lasting and intimate human relationships. This sense of failure was pervasive and reflected profoundly narcissistic expectations and vulnerabilities. Yet because of the deep pain these feelings caused, it was difficult to ferret them out and examine them in psychotherapy.

He hid his shame both from himself and from me, his therapist, behind a wall of lethargy and depression, with occasional outbursts of mania to express his defensive grandiosity. This patient, then, introduced me to the ravages of shame. It was no accident that I found him likable, that I readily identified with the issues of his age and gender, and with his artistic aspirations. The shame of patients interacts with that of their therapists, and it was through my own identification with his goals and pain – a recognition of elements of my own shame feelings – that I was able to understand to the importance of shame in his life experience. For this man, the experience of shame was embedded in his narcissistic vulnerability and manic-depressive illness. (For an exploration of the relationship of shame to narcissism and to manic-depressive illness, see chapter 11.)

My work with this patient alerted me to shame in other patients. And, indeed, I found it in most of the people I was treating – men and women, neurotic as well as psychotic and character- disordered. In fact, as Wurmser (1981) has pointed out, hardly an analytic or therapeutic session goes by without the appearance of some expression or manifestation of shame, humiliation, embarrassment, mortification, despair, or disgrace. These shame phenomena are sometimes openly and consciously experienced at the heart of human unhappiness but at other times are hidden from experience because they are so painful. As Levin (1971) has noted, shame frequently causes one to hide, to avoid interpersonal contact as a protection against rejection, and to conceal the affective experience from one's own awareness. As guilt invites confession and forgiveness (Thrane, 1979), shame generates concealment out of a fear of rendering the self unacceptable (Morrison, 1983). Throughout this book, I will be exploring manifestations of the tendency to hide, to protect the self from rejection – a social manifestation – and from self-loathing – an intrapsychic, internal one.

Yet, as obvious as these observations may seem, I have been struck by the surprise and novelty they elicit from most clinicians. In discussions or presentations on shame to various groups of therapists, I have noted a common response: they acknowledge the relevance of shame to their practices, but then they remark that "Somehow I never thought about it in that way" or "It hadn't occurred to me as an important focus." How can we account for this seemingly paradoxical situation, in which a clearly relevant and significant human experience is so frequently relegated to the psychological "back burner" in clinical practice?

First, we must consider why shame for so long has been paid so little attention in the psychoanalytic and psychotherapeutic literature.

As the clinical vignette described earlier showed, shame is a central affective experience of narcissism (Broucek, 1982; Kinston, 1983; Morrison, 1983). In *On Narcissism*, Freud (1914) introduced the concepts of the ego ideal and self-regard, both of which are central to my perspective on shame. Freud described the ego ideal as that intrapsychic agent (later to be associated with the superego) which contains values and ideals. Had he gone further with this concept, Freud might well have proceeded to an investigation of shame and its relationship to conflicts and failures in the attainment of the perfection of the ego ideal. In the next chapter, I examine in more detail Freud's views on shame, but for now let me suggest that he left the ego ideal and self-regard essentially unexamined after his 1914 work, choosing instead to pursue guilt as a response to oedipal conflict, the intrapsychic tension between ego, id, and superego, between wish and defense.

Schafer (1960) has noted this distinction by referring to the ego ideal as "the loving function" of the superego in contrast with its "punitive function." It was the punitive superego, however, that dominated the conflict-drive psychology of Freud's seminal work, as he turned from narcissism, the ego ideal, and self-esteem to the neuroses in evolution of the structural theory. Wurmser (1981) has made a similar point. Thus, signal anxiety, oedipal conflicts, repression, and the drives were taken as the cornerstones of psychoanalytic theory, with guilt and anxiety underscored as the manifestations of conflict between the intrapsychic components. Shame was not readily assimilated into psychoanalytic conflict theory as it might have been had Freud pursued a fuller elaboration of narcissism. It was not until the more recent developments of ego psychology that interest returned to the study of narcissism and the self, and with this an opening to the understanding of shame emerged.

Why did Freud not significantly pursue his study of narcissism and its rich manifestations as sketched in his 1914 paper? Certainly, second guessing motivation about such a historical turn is at best hazardous. The manifest fruit of Freud's labors may be justification enough to explain the direction of his interests. Yet, from the perspective of one interested in shame and narcissism, the question remains intriguing, and a sociopolitical answer suggests itself. It seems likely that Freud's relative lack of interest in shame might have been an unintentional but inevitable outcome of the historical evolution of psychoanalysis.

For example, Freud's attention to libidinal manifestations, their repression in response to intrapsychic conflict, and their representation in the unconscious—the essence of his conceptualization of psychoanalysis – is known to have reflected his defense of these discoveries against dilution by premature incursions from ego psychology, conscious mental phenomena, and social interaction. Protecting "the gold of psychoanalysis," he may well have shown less interest in the elaboration of such other phenomena as narcissism and its manifestations. This historical evolution may have related also to Freud's conflict with Alfred Adler, whom Freud had expelled from the psychoanalytic movement in 1911.

In a scholarly review of the development of Adler's theories, and Adler's relationship to Freud in the organization of the Vienna Psychoanalytic Society, Stepansky (1983) has elucidated the course of the inevitable split between the two men. Without elaborating here the details of Adler's thinking outlined in that study, we can summarize Adler's theory as focusing on "organ inferiority," leading to generalized inferiority feelings; resultant "masculine protest" as a manifestation of an aggressive drive to deal with these feelings; and the universal wish to defend against the feminine and assert the masculine ("psychic hermaphroditism"). While Freud accepted for some time Adler's contributions as supplementary to psychoanalytic principles, he ultimately rejected them as antagonistic to the theory of libido and repression and spent subsequent years elaborating the content of unconscious processes and the structure and defenses of the mental apparatus.

One need not fully endorse Adler's formulations to see how close they come to a framework that would allow for shame and its manifestations (although, interestingly, Adler himself never did so). Organ inferiority and inferiority feelings, masculine protest and aggression (which have been viewed as typical reactions instigated by shame; see Gilligan, 1976); and femininity (related by Freud to passivity and passive longings, discussed with regard to shame by Lewis, 1971, and Anthony, 1981) – each may be viewed as a major expression of, or defense against, the experience of shame. Seen from a different perspective, these qualities relate also to the attributes of primary and secondary narcissism, with libidinal cathexis of the ego, the beginnings of internalized object relations, and elucidation of the ego ideal and self-regard, which Freud (1914) described in "On Narcissism." However, the relationship of these constructs to Adler's "Individual Psychology" (Adler, 1907, 1912, 1929) may well have consolidated Freud's subsequent turn away from narcissism as he built the edifice of psychoanalysis. It was not that Freud explicitly denied the importance of shame in psychic development, but rather that he turned elsewhere to develop a system that was clearly differentiated from those of his various detractors. Thrane (1979) has made a similar point with regard to Adler.

Whether or not we fully accept this speculative hypothesis about the influence of historical forces on the direction of Freud's theoretical foundation for psychoanalysis, the conclusion is clear: Freud's structural theory emphasized the importance of guilt rather than shame as a central dysphoric affect, clearly related as it was to intrapsychic conflict. This emphasis assured a delay in attention to shame as an important focus of study until the structural theory itself was modified and opened up by the next generation of analysts. (This process of theoretical change will be considered in chapters 2 through 5, following a consideration of shame in Freud's writings.) I believe, however, that there are also additional explanations for the low profile of shame.

Building upon the values of psychoanalysis propounded by Freud, guilt was viewed as the more *worthy* affective experience compared with shame. Guilt is the result of *activity,* a transgression against a superego barrier (Piers, 1953), and a response to intrapsychic conflict. Palliation comes through confession and forgiveness. Shame, on the other hand, reflects *passivity,* a failure or defect of the whole self. Shame has been viewed as the developmentally more primitive affect (Jacobson, 1964), a product of oral need and anal failure (in contrast to oedipal longings); Tomkins (1962–63) even included shame as one of the innate, inborn emotions. Others have viewed shame disparagingly as inevitably embedded in a social matrix, in contrast to the intrapsychic origins of guilt. Each of these factors has, I believe, influenced the feeling among psychoanalysts that shame is somehow more superficial, and thus less worthy of attention, than guilt. Such assumptions will be considered later, for they certainly play a part in the relatively distant place accorded shame in most clinical considerations.

I have already suggested that shame induces hiding and concealment, thus making it more difficult to ferret out in clinical work. Patients recoil from facing their shame – and the failures, senses of defect, inferiority, and passivity that engender it. Patients often express, instead, defenses against, and displaced manifestations of, shame – certain depressions, mania, rage, envy, and contempt (see chapters 8 and 9). Because shame is so often unspoken, many therapists have not appreciated its importance in analytic and therapeutic work. Frequently it is hidden behind the clearly defensive manifestations of distress, and these are usually investigated alone – often from the perspective of intrapsychic conflict and related dynamics – without appreciation of the underlying or accompanying shame.

Moreover, the shame of patients is contagious, often resonating with the clinician's own shame experiences – the therapist's own sense of failure, self-deficiency, and life disappointments. Painful countertransference feelings may thus be generated in the analyst/ therapist, feelings that he or she, like the patient, would just as soon avoid, feelings that not infrequently lead to a collusion, preventing investigation of the shame experience. Frequently the therapist's own analysis or psychotherapy will not have explored shame, and thus both patient and therapist share various methods of concealment, blind spots unavailable to analytic exploration. As Levin (1971) also noted, then, the pain of shame, and the fear of rejection and abandonment, may affect the therapist as well as the patient.

In order for shame to gain prominence within psychoanalytic study, elaboration of the structural theory was necessary. Hartmann's (1939) contributions to ego psychology amplified and enriched classical psychoanalytic theory; he (Hartmann, 1950) again examined narcissism, defining it as "the libidinal cathexis not of the ego but of the self" (p. 85). Hartmann and Loewenstein (1962) detailed the construct of the ego ideal within the superego. Jacobson (1964) regarded the self as an experiencing entity more global than the intrapsychic structures; she introduced *self-* and *object* representations (that is, the symbolic, internalized personae of external reality) into ego psychology. Finally, more recent recognition of *narcissism* by Kohut (1971, 1977, 1984), Kernberg (1975), and others has opened a path for the optimal investigation of shame, as indicated by many recent contributions to the shame literature (Thrane, 1979; Broucek, 1982; Kinston, 1983; Morrison, 1983).

With this brief historical review of some of the salient themes in psychoanalysis that inform my approach to the study of shame, we come to some principal questions about shame to which we will return again and again in this book. These questions reappear and shape various portions of the Theoretical and Clinical Sections (though not necessarily in tidy fashion.) I will restate them in the Epilogue and will there reconsider them on the basis of material that, by then, will be familiar to the reader.

GUIDING QUESTIONS

1. **Is shame to be viewed as a defense against exhibitionism/ grandiosity (and other drive manifestations), or is it best understood as an affect?** Freud (1895, 1896, 1900, 1905) was ambiguous on this point. He viewed shame as a reaction formation against the wish

for genital exhibitionism and expression of other sexual impulses and perversions; saw shame as socially useful, directing sexual energy away from the self and toward tasks necessary for the preservation of the species. Lowenfeld (1976) has made a similar point about the potential utility of shame in preserving the mores of society. Freud also considered shame to be a result of anxiety, which is "objective" and social, reflecting fear of rejection and disapproval by others.

Thus, shame can be viewed as a defense, a reaction formation against the wish/drive to exhibit. Interestingly, Kohut's position on shame (see chapter 5) was in many ways similar to Freud's. Kohut (1971, 1972) considered shame to be a reflection of what he called the "vertical split," in which the ego is in danger of being overwhelmed by unbridled grandiosity. Hence, shame protects against the breakthrough of grandiosity and consequently serves a defensive function. For Levin (1967, 1971) also, shame is a signal, alerting the ego, through anticipatory shame anxiety, to the danger of future shame if action is not taken to protect the self.

Clearly, though, shame is also a painful affect, even when viewed as a signal to modify behavior, to repress wishes, or to hide. As indicated earlier, Tomkins (1962–63) viewed shame as one of the basic affects, generating its own set of facial expressions (see chapter 4). Many authors (for example, Piers, 1953; Lynd, 1958; Lewis, 1971; Thrane, 1979) have stressed the relationship between shame and guilt. I have suggested elsewhere (Morrison, 1983, 1984a, b) that shame is a painful feeling central to narcissistic disorders and plays a role analogous to that which guilt plays in neurosis.

Are these viewpoints contradictory, or can shame be seen simultaneously as a painful affect, as a signal of danger from underlying grandiosity and exhibitionism, and as a defense against these (and other) phenomena and drive derivatives? I consider this matter further in chapters 2, 7, and 8.

2. **Can shame be fully understood within the context of structural (conflict-defense) psychology, or must a broader psychology of the self and its deficits be invoked?** Here the controversy is joined about whether self-psychology adds anything new to conflict theory, or whether it is really old wine in a new bottle. Certainly the early discussions of shame were from a classical, ego-psychological perspective. Piers (1953) defined shame as a reflection of tension between the ego and the ego ideal, representing a failure to attain a goal of the ego ideal. One manifestation of this tension is the negative comparison of the self and its body parts to others, which comparison leads to feelings of inferiority; the relationship of this perspective to Adler's (1907) "organ inferiority" is obvious. Feldman

(1962) postulated a drive "to be the center of attention" (p. 382), analogous to Freud's thoughts about exhibitionism. Thus, Feldman introduced the role of external reality as a source of conflict with id drives leading to the shame response. As noted earlier, even Kohut (1971) originally viewed shame from the perspective of a conflict model, although shame was seen not as the result of the failure of the ego to meet the demands of a rigid ego ideal, but as the response of the ego flooded by unneutralized grandiosity, with the ego ideal standing as guardian and protector against grandiosity. Wurmser (1981) also considered an exhibitionistic drive as he underscored the relationship of shame to a defensive need to hide (a reaction formation) and its reflection in patients' feelings of unlovability. Annie Reich (1960) related shame to narcissism by noting oscillations of feelings from grandiosity to worthlessness and dejection, alternations that reflect wide shifts in self-esteem for certain narcissistic patients. Reich believed that objects are used by such patients in an attempt to stabilize self-esteem, leading to fluctuation of idealization and contempt toward self and others.

Clearly, then, the consideration of shame by many psychoanalytic thinkers has been rooted in the structural model, but, I suggest, these formulations are limited in their scope. A different, wider pathway to viewing shame derives from Erikson's (1950) elaboration of autonomy and shame and doubt. Lynd (1958) related shame to the search for identity, and Lewis (1971) further contended that shame reflects feelings about the whole self. Thus, with a consideration of identity and the self as central to the experience of shame, I believe that the analytic emphasis shifted from structural conflict to problems of narcissism. Certainly there remains much disagreement within the psychoanalytic community about the relationship of conflict and drives to narcissism (Morrison, 1986a), but most people would agree that some construct of "self" is essential in considerations about narcissism. It is a major contention of this book that shame is a crucial dysphoric affect in narcissistic phenomena. If this is so, can shame best be explained within the framework of drive-defense (conflict) theory, or is a separate emphasis on the self and its vicissitudes necessary?

Kohut (1966) introduced the concept of a separate developmental line for narcissism, but even in 1971 he was attempting to work within the parameters of conflict-drive theory. However, in his paper on narcissistic rage (Kohut, 1972), he moved away from the concept of drives toward a view of rage as a response to narcissistic injury. I have already noted that Kohut continued to view shame exclusively from the perspective of overwhelming grandiosity or empathic failure by selfobjects, minimizing the relationship of failure in relation to an ego ideal. The challenge to integrate an ego ideal (or ideal self) concept into a psychology of shame and self will be evident throughout this volume. I will try to show, however, that the more recent papers on shame have included a perspective on narcissism, identity, and the self (for example, Thrane, 1979; Broucek, 1982; Kinston, 1983; Morrison, 1983). So, we must continue to evaluate the usefulness of competing frameworks in the integration of shame and narcissism—a conflict-drive theory or a theory that incorporates the self and its vicissitudes. Further, we must explore whether these theories have to be seen as mutually exclusive, or whether they can usefully be integrated. Our consideration of shame, then, arrives at the heart of one of the most engrossing issues facing psychoanalysis today: the relationship between intrapsychic conflict and self- deficit.

3. **Can shame arise in isolation as an internal experience (as a manifestation of intrapsychic/exhibitionistic drives, grandiosity, or failure with regard to a goal or ideal), or must it be seen in a social context (that is, as a product of comparison with others, the presence of an audience, or as a reflection of active shaming, leading to feelings of inadequacy, inferiority, or unlovability)?** I believe that this question is encompassed even in Freud's preliminary observations about shame (for example, 1896, 1898, 1900). For instance, if shame is viewed as a reaction formation against an exhibitionistic drive—an urge to "show off," to display—it is an intrapsychic defense mechanism. On the other hand, exhibitionism itself implies an audience, a social group of one or more who view what is being exhibited. Wurmser (1981) emphasized the visual element of shame, which, again, calls attention to the viewing "other." He also equated shame with a feeling of "unlovability," underscoring the interpersonal context of shame. Nathanson (1987) asserted that with shame, there is always a shamer. I have suggested earlier that shame was underemphasized in psychoanalytic writings because it was viewed as essentially social and environmental, and thus less relevant to intrapsychic processes. Even Lewis (1971), while relating shame to the whole self, viewed it in terms of field dependency, which she equated with social investment and attachment.

Alternatively, shame may be viewed as an affective response to the self alone, the self experienced relatively independent of its social matrix. For instance, while identity formation certainly involves identifications and object internalizations, the emphasis is on a core experience of selfhood, an orientation inward that can, I suggest, be separated from a social context. Shame reflecting failure of the self to attain the goals of its ego ideal can be seen as essentially intrapsychic and nonsocial, representing internalized ideals that are the products of a relatively well-formed self.

This view of shame as an internal, intrapsychic manifestation underscores shame's relationship to narcissism, and particularly to the contributions of Kohut. One of the major issues in the study of narcissism has been that of the relationship of the object to narcissistic phenomena – that is, to what degree is functional impairment of the self independent of configurational objects and the interpersonal surround? Kohut (1966) took an extreme position on this question, suggesting that object relations theory is essentially a "social psychology" and that narcissism has a developmental line independent of object love. Thus, grandiosity to Kohut – and the shame that results from it – may be totally independent of a social context and is a truly intrapsychic phenomenon. The Kohutian concept of the *selfobject* is relevant here in defining whether shame occurs intrapsychically (in social isolation) or whether, indeed, it functions within the broader matrix of self-selfobject relations. This matter will be explored in chapter 5. I believe that Kohut's perspective on grandiosity differs from Freud's concept of exhibitionism, which requires the presence of a viewing or experiencing other and hence is more interpersonal.

So, to Kohut, grandiosity reflects a developmental failure of self-cohesion from inadequate selfobject mirroring, and the shame it engenders (by threatening to overwhelm the self) is essentially independent of a social context. I will develop this theme in chapter 5, but here I suggest simply that failure to reach the goals and values of the ego ideal (or, as I prefer to view it, the ideal self) also generates shame and that this shame reflects both internal and nonsocial, as well as interpersonal elements.

We have, then, contrasting perspectives on shame with regard to its social (interpersonal) or internal (intrapsychic) context. That shame can be experienced interpersonally is beyond doubt. The real question is whether or not shame can exist independent of a social context. I have implied above that, indeed, it can be; this question will recur throughout the remainder of our study.

4. What is the relationship of shame to guilt? Are they separate affects, or are they inexorably intertwined through an inevitable cycle or alternation? Which is the more primitive affect, and which lends itself more easily to psychotherapeutic intervention? I have noted that Freud turned from elaboration of the ego ideal toward the structural theory and the superego, and, with this orientation, to an emphasis on guilt in response to oedipal conflict. Piers

(1953) differentiated guilt from shame by relating guilt to transgression of a superego barrier, leading to the danger of annihilation and dismemberment (castration). Shame, on the other hand, results from a tension between the ego and ego ideal, reflecting failure to meet a goal of the ego ideal, which failure leads to a threat of rejection and abandonment. Thrane (1979) reiterated the relationship of shame to identity, and hence to the experience of the self (or "failure of the whole self," as Lewis [1971, p. 40] has phrased it). Guilt over an action, a transgression, can be felt abstractly, as "alien" to the self; by contrast, shame always has an immediate, personal, searing quality. Wurmser (1981) emphasized that guilt is always a reflection of action toward, "hurting," another, and thus refers to an expression (and abuse) of power, whereas shame reflects a failure of the self, and thus an absence, a withholding of power.

What is the developmental difference between guilt and shame? Which is the earlier to develop, the more primitive, the less differentiated? Most authors consider shame to be developmentally the earlier affect, with guilt requiring the evolution of a differentiated superego for its full expression. Tomkins (1962–63) described shame as one of the nine affects present at birth. By contrast, guilt was described as a more complex feeling, differentiated out of the earlier shame matrix. This perspective is logical developmentally, in that it emphasizes an early experience of the "self-as-entity," with later differentiation of self from other, and triadic differentiation awaiting the development of oedipal configurations and the superego. However, this viewpoint does not imply that primitive shame is necessarily replaced by guilt. In fact, Wurmser (1981) stated that "the complex affect of shame – in contrast to shame anxiety, its core – always involves the superego" (p. 73). Thus, primitive shame (or shame anxiety) evolves into a propensity for more differentiated shame with superego development and refinement of the ego ideal (or ideal self). This evolution of shame implicitly occurs independent of, but concomitantly with, the generation and refinement of guilt.

But are shame and guilt so easily differentiated from one another? Piers (1953) described a guilt-shame cycle as a useful conceptualization by which guilt and shame interact and can be interchanged. According to Piers, an id impulse (that is, libidinal or aggressive) is inhibited (guilt), leading to passivity (shame), and subsequent overcompensation and reactive impulse expression, which again leads to guilt and inhibition of the impulse. Thus, the two affects can be integrated, and their mutual (or simultaneous) expression understood, minimizing the reductionistic tendency in attempting to keep them entirely separate.

Wurmser (1981, p. 206) spoke of a "dialectic" between shame and guilt, in which the two affects oscillate rapidly, reflecting an action and its inhibition. I (Morrison, 1984a) have suggested that shame in neurotic patients frequently reflects inhibition of competitive, oedipal strivings out of guilt and feared retaliation, in favor of less threatening passivity and the resultant shame (see also chapter 10).

There seems to be, then, a meaningful difference between shame and guilt and a potential for an oscillating dialectic between them in clinical situations. Hartmann and Loewenstein (1962), however, doubted this distinction (see chapter 2, this volume). Nonetheless, shame appears to predominate in narcissistic states, whereas guilt is more clearly experienced in the neuroses. This contrast will inform a more detailed examination of shame in chapters 9 and 10.

5. **Is shame a manifestation of passivity, dependency, and, therefore, of inherent femininity (as suggested by Freud, and by several recent authors), or does this formulation reflect an outmoded notion of femininity?** Shame is a reflection of feelings about the whole self in failure, as inferior in competition or in comparison with others, as inadequate and defective. As such, shame relates to low self-esteem, to faulty identity-formation. Just as guilt is a manifestation of harmful action, a transgression, shame can be experienced as a result of inaction, of passivity. Lewis (1971, 1987) equated shame with passivity, femininity, and what she had studied as "field dependence" – that is, individual concern about the surround, with self-esteem dependent on feedback from the social environment. Guilt, on the other hand, tends more to be a function of activity, masculine identification, and "field-independence" (that is, independence of the social context).

While the sources of shame in passivity – and in feelings of inferiority, inadequacy, deficiency, and low self-esteem – are clear and consonant with the view of shame I have been developing, what is to be made of the equation of these qualities with femininity? Historically, Freud (1933) early equated shame with femininity and with genital inferiority – that issue (i.e., penis envy) which has been so heartily contested by students of female development. Freud stated, "Shame, which is considered to be a feminine characteristic par excellence but is far more a matter of convention than might be supposed, has as its purpose, we believe, concealment of genital deficiency. We are not forgetting that at a later time shame takes on other functions" (p.132). In so stating, Freud indicated that this equation of shame with femininity is "a convention" and that it later "takes on other functions." Freud might well have elaborated on these points, but here he was certainly equating shame with female genital inferiority.

Anthony (1981) spoke of secondary shame in women, which

produces passivity, secretiveness, and a predominantly preoedipal cast to their analyses, as a result of prolonged and complex attachment to the mother. He suggested that the "identity theme" imprinted on the girl is one of shame, leading to prolonged analyses of paranoia and depression which relate to shame. Lewis (1981) also discussed shame as a field-dependent mode of functioning that predominates in women, because of their unchanging, same-sex anaclitic identifications. She also related shame to depression, a conclusion with which I agree. Lewis suggested that the superego of narcissistic patients is shame prone, representing the relation of the self to another in unrequited love and reflecting attempts to restore these lost attachments.

Thus, for these authors, the connection between femininity and shame goes beyond Freud's "genital inferiority" hypothesis and relates more to feminine concern with intimacy, attachments, and object relatedness. This approach seems to reflect Wurmser's (1981) view of shame's relationship to feelings of "unlovability," as well as to Gilligan's (1982) work on female moral development. I think that current changes in women's views of themselves should have significant impact on field dependence and self-esteem, and undoubtedly will influence these factors in relation to shame. Thus, Freud's (1933) comment about the "matter of convention" takes on added significance in contemporary society. In addition, I believe that the equation of activity, field independence, and guilt with maleness is an oversimplification. I am not impressed that the majority of shame experiences are to be found in women, as suggested by Anthony (1981), but I will attempt to demonstrate that shame – in relation to narcissistic phenomena and retreat from oedipal and sexual feelings – exists equally strongly in men and women. Similarly, as men experience elements of themselves as "feminine" – needing intimacy and attachment, recognizing and expressing feelings in general – they are likely to struggle with pangs of shame.

6. **What is the relationship of shame to anger/rage, contempt, envy, vulnerability, and humiliation?** Before we consider these affects and feelings about the self, it should be noted that shame itself can be expressed as several related feelings, such as mortification, humiliation, despair, remorse, apathy, embarrassment, and lowered self-esteem. Some authors believe that these represent separate feelings. I suggest, however, that they each express some element of shame, with variations in the object, aim, or intensity of the affective experience. In subsequent discussions, it will be seen that different patients may experience one or another of these shame equivalents as being most descriptive of their own feeling state.

I believe that underlying many expressions of *rage* is a feeling of shame—a feeling that reflects a sense of failure or inadequacy so intolerable that it leads to a flailing out, an attempt to rid the self of the despised subjective experience. Kohut's (1972) view of narcissistic rage as a response of the vulnerable patient to narcissistic injury—echoing a need for absolute control over an archaic environment—is relevant here. Kohut's formulation of rage, and its contrast with that of Kernberg (1975), will be discussed later. For now, however, it is worth considering the possibility that shame's role in generating rage has been overlooked because of the tendency to hide from shame in the transformation of passive to active, from self- hatred to outward expression of hatred and anger. I differ from Kohut in that I believe that rage frequently reflects shame over self-failure and inferiority, not only as a response to injury from another (for example, from the selfobject).

Contempt represents, I suggest, an attempt to "relocate" the shame experience from within the self into another person, and, thus, like rage, it may be an attempt to rid the self of shame. Wurmser (1981) stated that "contempt [is] the form of aggression intrinsic to shame affects" (p. 18). I argue (chapter 7) that this attempt to reestablish self-esteem through relocation of shame into contempt for others occurs through the process of *projective identification.* Nathanson (1987) referred to this process as "affect broadcasting." In essence, subjective shame, over failure, inferiority, or defect, is disavowed or repressed and is "placed" into another, who must then "accept" and "contain" the projection. Therefore, the object of contempt must bear a certain similarity to the subject, at least with respect to the source of the projected shame, and must also be willing to interact with the subject on the basis of the implicit contempt. From this perspective, then, contempt can be seen as an interactive externalization of the shame experience, and thus, ultimately, as a defense against it.[1]

Shame vulnerability, like shame anxiety, is a sensitivity to, and readiness for, shame. As Levin (1967) has shown, shame anxiety is a signal of impending shame, evoking the defenses of hiding and withdrawal to protect against imminent rejection and abandonment. Wurmser (1981, pp. 82–84) has made a similar point. Levin elaborated his views on shame and shame anxiety from the perspective of ego psychology. I suggest that shame vulnerability is closely related to narcissistic vulnerability and, again, underscores the inevitable relationship of shame to narcissism. Narcissistic vulnerability is the "underside" of exhibitionism, grandiosity, and haughtiness—the low self-

---

[1]See Dinnerstein (1976) for her exposition of this mechanism as embedded in our culturally determined, gender-specific arrangements.

esteem, self-doubt, and fragility of self-cohesion that defines the narcissistic condition. I believe that shame is the principal ubiquitous affect that accompanies and defines that condition. Shame vulnerability is, then, the readiness and sensitivity to experience shame and is a frequent affective counterpart of narcissistic vulnerability. Just as shame anxiety relates to intrapsychic conflict and structural theory, shame vulnerability represents an affective component of narcissism and its clinical manifestations.

Finally, humiliation deserves a special place in this overview of shame. Humiliation specifically reflects the social, interpersonal manifestation of shame, or internalized representation of the "humiliator." In the presence of humiliation, there must be someone who humiliates or who has, at some time, humiliated. Humiliation is that manifestation of shame which is the product of *action* perpetrated against the self by someone else. As I have noted elsewhere (Morrison, 1984a), ". . . humiliation represents the strong experience of shame reflecting severe external shaming or shame anxiety at the hands of a highly cathected object 'a significant other' " (p. 488).

Rothstein (1984) has made a similar point with regard to humiliation. Embarrassment is another manifestation of shame in a social context, but it differs from humiliation in intensity and in the activity necessary for its generation. Embarrassment is a less searing, less intense form of shame that is more readily acceptable to most people and that, therefore, may more readily be acknowledged in psychotherapy or analysis. Also, to experience embarrassment, there need not necessarily be an "embarrasser," but rather the presence at least of a social context, one or more observers of the self in weakness or failure. Embarrassment underscores the special relationship of the visual–seeing and being seen–to shame. Alternatively, Miller (1985) has related embarrassment to the emergence of hidden sexual longings.

This discussion of humiliation and embarrassment calls attention again to the question of the "social embeddedness" of the shame experience. As noted earlier, many authors believe that shame occurs only in an interpersonal context, as the reflection of an active shamer or observer, or representing the danger of "unlovability" or abandonment by a significant object who views the personal shortcomings. On the other hand, from the vantage point of Kohut's (1971) formulation regarding "overwhelming grandiosity," or the demands or goals of a strict ego ideal (the ideal self), shame can be appreciated as an essentially intrapsychic, internal experience. Of course, internalization of objects and their representations in the formation of the ego ideal and ideal self, along with the need for the selfobject function in self-development, ultimately puts these intrapsychic structures into an interpersonal, or intersubjective, framework. But this is true as well for all human development, including the identifications that generate the superego and lead ultimately to guilt as well as to shame, with inevitable reflections of an object-filled environment.

7. **Finally, what is the explicit relationship of shame to narcissism?** I will attempt to examine this question thoroughly because I believe that shame and narcissism do coexist and define each other, emerging together in what I shall describe as the Dialectic of Narcissism (see chapter 4). I have already commented on shame in the context of narcissistic vulnerability and manic-depressive illness; on the importance of the ego ideal and self-regard – first articulated by Freud (1914) – to my conceptualization of shame; on the lack of psychoanalytic interest in both shame and narcissism until relatively recently; and on the relationship of shame to various experiences of defect in the self. Most recent works on shame have related it, in one way or another, to narcissistic phenomena. This is especially true of the work of Kohut (1971, 1977), who suggested a separate line of narcissistic development and for whom shame represented experiences of overwhelming grandiosity and repeated selfobject failure to meet (age-appropriate) self-needs. (These points will be covered in detail in chapters 4 and 5.)

I implied in question 4 that shame may be experienced alone, in isolation, as an intrapsychic rather than an interpersonal phenomenon and that, as such, it touches on a core of narcissism. This relationship between shame and narcissism seems firmly established, but whether shame is the sole cause of narcissistic distress must remain an open question at this time. To phrase it differently, can there be narcissism or its manifestations without the presence of shame? Might not other dysphoric affects – for example, depression, anxiety, or guilt – be at the center of narcissistic distress?

SUMMARIZING REMARKS

In this introductory overview, I have considered some of the broad themes that recur throughout the discussions that follow. These themes fall into place as contrasts and ambiguities that have accompanied previous writings on shame and that reflect subtleties inherent in it. Is shame a defense, or is it an affect? Can it be understood within the framework of structural (conflict-defense) psychology, or is a theory of the self and developmental arrest more useful? Can shame arise exclusively as an intrapsychic phenomenon, or must a social context be invoked to explain its presence? Does shame differ from guilt, and, if it does, how do they relate to one another? Is shame related to passivity, dependency, and femininity? From another perspective, might "femininity" be viewed as reflecting an outmoded "convention," as implied even by Freud (1933)? I have suggested a relationship between shame and several other key phenomena, including rage, contempt, shame vulnerability, humiliation, and, especially, narcissism.

In addition to these guiding themes and questions, our perspective on shame inevitably brings into focus some of the major issues currently confronting psychoanalytic psychology. These include, most importantly, whether or not Kohut's contributions and the self-psychological perspective are a significant addition to classical psychoanalytic theory, or whether these observations can better be integrated into existing theory. What is the role of the drives (including exhibitionism) in human existence? Can an individual ever be viewed primarily as an isolated organism, or must he or she inevitably be seen in a broader social context? What are the implications of shame for the our current interest in narcissism? Finally, what are the implications for treatment in this emphasis on shame? More pointedly, has shame been overlooked in traditional work with patients, and, if so, how can this failure be addressed?

Obviously, I raise some of these questions rhetorically. I believe that shame has conspicuously been overlooked and underemphasized, and I shall try to demonstrate how it can be, and ought to be, worked with clinically. I also believe that Kohut's contributions are significant additions to the classical perspective. Many of the other questions remain ambiguous, recurring throughout the subsequent chapters of our study of shame—the underside of narcissism.

PART I

A THEORETICAL FRAMEWORK

In this section, I shall consider some closely related areas of psychoanalytic theory and their ultimate relationship to shame. An integration of previous psychoanalytic contributions will provide a framework for our understanding of shame.

The theoretical issues to be considered include creations and fantasies of the *ideal* (and the structures that "contain" them – the *ego ideal* and *ideal self, primitive object representations and object relations*; and *narcissism*. We will see that shame plays a varyingly important role in the thinking of the authors to be reviewed. I will be building on their formulations to show that shame is the central response to *failure* with respect to the ideal, to flaws in the experience of self. Failures in early object relationships – either because of active, humiliating attacks or as a result of disruptions in empathic attunement by the significant selfobject – lead to shame sensitivity in the later construction of the self.

These considerations inevitably generate formulations about *narcissism*, which will be examined throughout this volume but are the explicit focus of chapters 4 and 5. Narcissism has been viewed in different ways by the authors to be considered, but, I suggest, we can organize these various approaches in terms of dialectics: between feelings of inferiority and (defensive) grandiosity, between the ideal of autonomy and self-sufficiency and merger with the fantasied, omnipotent "other." Kohut (1966, 1971) suggested a separate line of self-development for narcissism, independent of that of object love and the ego ideal, which relies heavily on the sustaining function of the (mirroring and idealizable) selfobjects. As we progress, I will try to demonstrate that shame is the principal experienced affect of narcissism, from whichever perspective the dialectic is approached.

This review of previous writings on the ideal, primitive object relationships and narcissism will provide the foundation for a discussion of shame informed by clinical perspectives. I will try to relate my understanding of shame to the work of earlier contributors. In Part II, I will offer my own understanding of shame's varied clinical manifestations (including its relationship to resistance and defense) and its relevance to manic-depressive psychosis and will present clinical material on the treatment of shame in neurotic and narcissistic patients.

2

Some Theoretical Perspectives
on Shame

Freud's passing attention to shame was alluded to in chapter 1. Here I will review his writings on shame in greater detail, relying especially on the analysis of Wurmser (1981), who delineated Freud's view of shame's relationship to scopophilic and exhibitionistic drives. I then will attempt to relate Freud's thoughts on narcissism, self-regard, and the ego ideal to the perspective on shame elaborated in this volume. Because of the central place of the ego ideal in my conception of shame, the work of various authors on this subject will then be reviewed in some detail, particularly from the perspective of psychoanalytic ego psychology. While most of these authors did not emphasize the relationship of shame to the ego ideal, I will underscore the relevance of this relationship. In the next two chapters, I will turn to a consideration of the work of two authors (A. Reich, 1953, 1960; Jacobson, 1964) who did deal with shame's place in the framework of primitive narcissism, early object relations, and the ego ideal. I will then consider other contributions on shame from the perspective of object relations and narcissism.

FREUD'S VIEWS ON SHAME

In 1895, Freud (1892–1899) first wrote about shame in Draft K of a letter to Fliess, which outlined his thoughts about the neuroses of defense and was written at the same time as his famous "Project for a Scientific Psychology" (Freud, 1895). In his letter to Fleiss, shame, along with morality and disgust, was proposed as a cause of repression of sexual experiences (p. 222) and thus was seen to function as a *defense*. Interestingly, in this passage Freud equated the absence of shame with masculinity. Elsewhere in the letter, in discussing puberty, Freud suggested that girls, by contrast, are "seized by a non- neurotic sexual repugnance," which may account for "the flood of shame which overwhelms the female at that period . . ." (p. 270). In "Further Remarks on the Neuro-Psychoses of Defense," Freud (1896) linked shame with conscientiousness and self- distrust as primary symptoms of defense (p. 169), explicitly with regard to obsessional symptoms (p. 178).

In discussing the return of the repressed, Freud (1892–1899) wrote in Draft K of "self-reproach" being transformed into other affects, which, in addition to anxiety, hypochondria, and delusions of persecution, included shame (p. 224). In letter 66 to Fliess, Freud later mentioned "an interesting dream of wandering about among strangers, totally or half undressed and with feelings of shame and anxiety" (p. 258).

Again, in "The Interpretation of Dreams," Freud (1900) described several embarrassing dreams of being naked, and "a distressing feeling in the nature of shame and in the fact that one wishes to hide one's nakedness, as a rule by locomotion, but finds one is unable to do so" (p. 242). Elsewhere, Freud (1898, p. 275) had also equated shame in a young boy with a history of bed- wetting, and the threat by the boy's mother to tell friends and teachers.

Thus, Freud (1892–1899) unequivocally placed shame as an affect within a social context, equating it with "fear of other people knowing about it [the self-reproach]." Similarly, Freud wrote, "I reproach myself on account of an event – I am afraid other people know about it – therefore I feel ashamed in front of other people" (p. 225). One of these "events" was the emergence of sexual feelings in young girls, elaborated in Miller's (1985) view of embarrassment noted in the previous chapter.

From Freud's first mention of shame, then, we note a lack of clarity as he struggled to define the dynamics of defense (and repression, which he equated with defense at that time). Shame was seen (1) as a social (interpersonal) *affect*, linked with being observed, being found out, by another; (2) as a defense against the memory of a source of unpleasure (that is, prepubertal sexual experience or, later, fantasy); and (3) as a symptom analogous to self-reproach for having been discovered in the early commission of a sexual act. This ambiguity (of shame as affect, defense, or symptom) continued throughout Freud's work and in the contributions of authors who followed. We, too, will continue to wrestle with this ambiguity as our study progresses—for example, can one affect serve at the same time as a defense against other, more noxious affects, and, if so, how does this valence get established? Various authors differ in the emphasis they place on these three qualities of shame; I will attempt to underscore the relevant shifts in emphasis as we proceed.

In "Three Essays on Sexuality," Freud (1905) moved from shame as an affective response to being seen, to shame as a defense against the drives. He described two important sexual drives—exhibitionism, and voyeurism (curiosity, ocopophilia)—each of which is visual (seeing and being seen) and is socially embedded in the viewing other. Thus, passive wishes to be seen (exhibitionism) evolve from intense wishes to look (voyeurism) (Wurmser, 1981; p. 147). Freud (1905) introduced shame as a "resistance" against these drives, which "impede the course of the sexual instinct and, like dams, restrict its flow—disgust, feelings of shame, and the claims of aesthetic and moral ideals" (p. 177). Here, shame as affect is linked with another emotion, disgust, and with the more cognitive "ideal" as a defense against drives. These counterforces against the exhibitionistic and scopophilic drives were designated by Freud (1908) as "reaction formations." Nunberg (1955) followed Freud's designation by stating, "Shame is a reaction formation of the ego to the wish to exhibit" (p. 157).

Thus, in his 1905 work Freud's emphasis regarding shame shifted significantly from affective experience to defense. When exhibitionism and voyeurism are restricted to their sexual aims, overcome the defenses erected against them (including shame), and supplant genitality, they become perversions rather than normal components of sexuality (Wurmser, 1981, p. 147). From our perspective on shame, it is particularly interesting to note that Freud (1905) linked "the claims of aesthetic and moral ideals" with disgust and shame as the defenses against these visual drives. I believe that this is an early statement about the function of the ego ideal, which was not to be introduced by Freud until his 1914 paper "On Narcissism" and which plays an important part in my view of shame. This relationship of the ego ideal to the experience of shame is consistent with the ego ideal's role, as part of the superego, in controlling the drives. I will consider later various aspects of the ego ideal and its function in shame.

So far, then, Freud's view of shame had evolved into its role as a defense, a reaction formation against the visual/sexual drives. Earlier, he had described it as an affective experience connected to femininity, passivity, and exposure. Shame had been embedded in a social context, relating to others' *knowing* (as in bed- wetting) or *seeing* (as in nudity) a personal *defect*. Such defects apparently included sexuality and sexual desire. In relation to looking and being looked at, Freud considered shame as both affective experience and defense. Freud conceived of shame as the danger from self-exposure to others and also as a sense of inadequacy (Thrane, 1979, p. 331). Freud (1930) wrote, ". . . man's raising himself from the ground, of his assumption of an upright gait; this made his genitals, which were previously concealed, visible and in need of protection, and so provoked feelings of shame in him" (p. 99n). This statement reflected a reaction to danger and fear, although Freud did not explicitly spell out why the visible genitals provoke shame and thus exemplified shame as an affective response to another affect (that is, fear).[1] Here, one is ashamed of feeling afraid.

Freud (1933) also noted that shame can reflect, and defend against, feelings of inadequacy. As quoted in the previous chapter, he stated, "Shame, which is considered to be a feminine characteristic par excellence but is far more a matter of convention than might be supposed, has as its purpose, we believe, concealment of genital deficiency. We are not forgetting that at a later time shame takes on other functions" (p. 132).

Here Freud noted the relationship between shame and concealment, and genital deficiency, thus highlighting shame's central place in the framework of a social context (that is, being seen), of hiding, and of inferiority feelings, and its inevitable relationship to narcissism and a sense of self-defect. Shame's generation of a wish to hide presumably is aimed at defending the self from rejection, contempt, or loss of love.

Freud's (1914) paper, "On Narcissism," is meaningful here for his views on the ego ideal and self-regard and their relationship with the voyeuristic/exhibitionistic drives. Evolving from his consideration of the instincts, the essay first discussed an agency of mind that was to be the anlage of "conscience," whose function was to *watch* the ego (or self)–again, the visual–and hold it to criteria of behavioral and cognitive control over the drives. This agency, the ego ideal, was to be the

---

[1] I will suggest later that shame frequently is a response to need and desire.

forerunner of the superego in the evolution of Freud's structural model. However, in working toward introduction of this concept, Freud noted the relationship of libidinal instincts to culture and morality in the quest to maintain self-esteem.[2]

Repression, then, is a result of conflict between the libidinal instincts and cultural and ethical values and reflects the formation of an internalized "ideal" based on these values. It represents the internalization of culture – *external* precepts – and formation of ethics – *internal* precepts. In this way, Freud continued to vacillate between external and internal factors, considering shame, along with cultural and ethical ideals, as a source of defense against the drives.

"'On Narcissism" and The Ego Ideal

With these few confounding thoughts, Freud's explicit attention to shame came to an end. Why, then, spend time on the "Narcissism" paper, which did not deal specifically with shame?

1. Because shame is about the self, I believe that an understanding of narcissism in its various forms is essential to an appreciation of the development and manifestations of shame. I have already stated my conviction that shame forms the affective underpinning of narcissistic vulnerability. In "On Narcissism," Freud sketched the outlines of narcissism against which all subsequent considerations of narcissistic manifestations and vulnerability would be measured.

2. Because shame represents failure and defect in relation to culture and ethics and their created and fantasied ideals of behavior, structure, and self- regard, it is important to understand the evolution of thinking about ideals and the psychic structure that "houses" them. In "On Narcissism" Freud first elaborated the ego ideal, which is that structure. Other issues relating to the ego ideal and shame will be considered later in our discussion of other authors.

3. In his movement from narcissism to structural theory, Freud introduced guilt where shame would more appropriately have been placed (for example, with respect to inferiority feelings). This same tendency occurred in later writings as well, and, since Freud's avoid-

---

[2]"We have learnt that libidinal instinctual impulses undergo the vicissitude of pathogenic repression if they come into conflict with the subject's cultural and ethical ideas . . . he recognizes them as a standard for himself and submits to the claims they make on him. Repression, we have said, proceeds from the ego; we might say with greater precision that it proceeds from the self-respect of the ego" (Freud, 1914, p. 93); and "For the ego the formation of an ideal would be the conditioning factor of repression" (p. 94).

ance of the subject of shame influenced subsequent inattention to this feeling, it is relevant here to document his ambiguity regarding shame and guilt.

In "On Narcissism," Freud suggested that the "ideal ego" is invested with narcissism lost from the sense of original perfection emanating from the infantile ego and determines the subjective sense of self-respect (i.e., self-regard, and self-esteem).[3] Here Freud again implied both external and internal sources of this ego ideal as represented by "admonition of others" and by "his own critical judgment." He then proceeded to his well-known formulation of the ego ideal and its relationship to what was to become the superego: "It would not surprise us if we were to find a special psychical agency which performs the task of seeing that narcissistic satisfaction from the ego ideal is ensured and which, with this end in view, constantly watches the actual ego and measures it by that ideal" (Freud, 1914, p. 95).

Freud then explicitly related the ego ideal to self-regard and to its dependence on narcissistic libido. The inability to love, to invest in an object, lowers self-regard (i.e., self-esteem) and leads to feelings of inferiority. Here Freud equated feelings of inferiority with the functions of the ego ideal. Also, at this point in his essay Freud discussed Adler's concept of organ inferiority and resultant overcompensation. He went on to dispute Adler's conclusions, which, as I suggested in the previous chapter, may well have played a part in his neglecting to elaborate further on the ego ideal, narcissism, and a significant study of shame.

Freud ended his essay with a discussion of object love as a means of rediscovering lost narcissism through narcissistic idealization of, and investment in, the libidinal object. He spoke of the liberation of homosexual libido, which is transformed into a sense of guilt out of a fear of the loss of love of the parents, and, later, of the social group (Freud, 1914, pp. 101–102).[4] In "On Narcissism," Freud elucidated the ego ideal, inferiority feelings, and loss of self-esteem, thus paving the way to an appreciation of shame.

From Ego Ideal to Ego

Freud's subsequent writing on the ego ideal, before it "disappeared" into the superego, are of interest in relation to shame. In "Group

---

[3]". . .and when, as he grows up, he is disturbed by the admonitions of others and by the awakening of his own critical judgment, so that he can no longer retain that perfection, he seeks to recover it in the new form of an ego ideal" (Freud, 1914; p. 94).

[4]It seems to me that the "guilt" Freud described in regard to homosexual feelings might more accurately be considered to be shame (i.e., relating to loss of love, rather than to castration).

Psychology and the Analysis of the Ego," Freud, (1921) summarized what he had said previously about the ego ideal, indicating functions including ". . . self-observation, the moral conscience, the censorship of dreams, and the chief influence in repression" (p. 110). The state of being in love may lead to idealization of the love object, through which unattained qualities and perfection of the ego ideal are realized through "overvaluation of the object" in an attempt to regain the lost narcissism (pp. 112–113). Such overvaluation may lead to a substitution of the object for the ego ideal; in this essay, Freud introduced the concepts of identification with, and internalization of, the object. However, in describing this state, he observed that ". . . with this 'devotion' of the ego to the object, *which is no longer to be distinguished from a sublimated devotion to an abstract idea,* the functions allotted to the ego ideal entirely cease to operate" (p. 113, emphasis added).

With this statement, Freud acknowledged that "an abstract idea" (that is, an ethical ideal), as well as an object, may replace the ego ideal. This suggestion allows for the concept of "falling short of ideals" as a source of inferiority feelings and shame, which I will discuss subsequently. For Freud, the shared replacement by a given object for the ego ideals of a collective of individuals defined a primary group (p. 116).

He suggested that euphoria of the ego may result from blotting out the restrictions of the ego ideal or from successfully living up to its demands. But it seems to me, Freud again confounded guilt with shame: "And the sense of guilt (as well as the sense of inferiority) can also be understood as an expression of tension between the ego and ego ideal" (p. 131).

As Freud later explored the functions of the superego, the role of guilt was to be clarified. However, as Piers (1953) has argued, that tension between ego and ego ideal is more accurately seen as the experience of shame. This is probably the equivalent of the "sense of inferiority" noted by Freud.

A final point about Freud's 1921 essay plays a part in my viewpoint on shame, namely, the relationship of the ego ideal and shame to manic-depressive illness (see chapter 11). Freud (1917) had indicated that the ego ideal was involved as a cause of melancholia, through the ego's identification with, and its internalization of, the rejected object. This leads to self-reproaches reflecting condemnation of the internalized object by the ego ideal. In his 1921 work, however, he spoke of mania as a reflection of ". . . the ego and the ego ideal [having been] fused together, so that the person, in a mood of triumph and self-satisfaction, disturbed by *no self-criticism,* can enjoy the abolition of his inhibitions, his feelings of consideration for others, and his *self-reproaches*" (p. 132, emphasis added).

Are not self-criticism and self-reproaches to be viewed as equivalents of shame in relation to manic-depressive illness? Unaware of Freud's statement, I have made this point elsewhere (Morrison, 1983): "I believe that shame is a central affect for the manic-depressive, which the manic flight attempts to hide through fantasied merger with the ideal self" (p. 306n).[5]

With regard to melancholia, Freud (1921) wrote, "It is not so obvious, but nevertheless very probable, that the misery of the melancholic is the expression of a sharp conflict between the two agencies of his ego, a conflict in which the ideal, in an excess of sensitiveness, relentlessly exhibits its condemnation of the ego in delusions of *inferiority* and in self-depreciation" (p. 132, emphasis added). This quote suggests a relationship between shame and depression, in which the latter may also result from failures to live up to the demands of the ego ideal. I will expand upon this point in chapters 5 and 7 in relating the work of Kohut to that of Bibring (see also Morrison, 1983, p. 312).

In "The Ego and the Id," Freud (1923) introduced the concept superego by equating it with the ego ideal and again reiterated guilt (rather than shame, which seems more appropriate) as the result of tension between the ego and ego ideal, with guilt assumed once more to relate to feelings of inferiority (p. 51). However, as this essay proceeded, with delineation of the superego and the relationship of guilt to "repressed impulses" and to the Oedipus complex, Freud's interest in the ego ideal seemed to fade away. In subsequent writings, (for example, 1930) he related guilt to the more familiar aggressive and sexual impulses and the response of the superego, with less mention of "inferiority feelings." Attention to shame and related phenomena was pushed to the periphery of Freud's interest.

Summary

Freud's view of shame was neither consistent nor clearly defined. He did not focus on shame as a principal concern. Instead, he developed the structural theory, with guilt and the Oedipus complex at its center. I have suggested that this relative lack of interest may have stemmed from the proximity of the key concepts of narcissism (inferiority, self-regard, and self-criticism) to the contributions of Adler. Another speculation might be that shame was an affect that struck too close to

---

[5]For a related perspective on the role of self-criticism, see Kris, 1985.

Freud's own personal vulnerabilities and that he eschewed study of it, therefore, in favor of other pursuits.

Nonetheless, Freud did write about shame, early as a painful affect related to audience, discovery, and inferiority, and later as a defense against voyeuristic/exhibitionistic drives and the sense of genital defect in women. These different viewpoints relate to questions I raised in the first chapter, namely, whether shame can be experienced in isolation or only in a social context; and whether shame is to be viewed primarily as affective experience or as defense. Certainly the latter two attributes do coexist, but Freud's emphasis seems to have shifted over time (Hazard, 1969). It seems that, for Freud, affective experience and defense were intertwined, in that a social context is inferred for the painful affect of shame (for example, in conflict with cultural norms), whereas an internal, intrapsychic context is posited for shame as a reaction-formation against the drives (for example, ethical ideals).

In addition, I have suggested that Freud (1914) might have offered a framework for an elaboration of shame had he chosen to do so; that a consideration of shame as a central affect underlying narcissistic phenomena, in combination with Freud's (1914) consideration of the ego ideal and self-regard, might have led to further work on shame.

SUBSEQUENT WORKS RELATED TO SHAME

I have searched in vain for work explicitly devoted to shame prior to the contributions of Piers (1953) and Lynd (1958). For a historical perspective on shame, therefore, we must locate comments about shame embedded in writings, particularly those of the ego psychologists. As suggested earlier, I believe that the limited attention to shame reflected the theoretical direction set by Freud. Shame, however, is mentioned by several authors who concern themselves with feelings of *inferiority* and with the *ego ideal*. It will become apparent that these works relate directly to an evolving interest in the *self* and in *narcissism*, reflecting a resurgence of interest in Freud's "On Narcissism" (1914) and in other issues he had left essentially incomplete.

After discussing several psychoanalytic writers who address shame independently of the ego ideal, I will turn to an assessment of the ego ideal and its relationship to shame, as implied in Freud's 1914 work. Shame takes its place within a matrix of the self and narcissistic vulnerability, particularly in the writings of A. Reich (1960) and Jacobson (1964). A more complete elaboration of shame and narcissism is offered in chapter 4.

Voyeurism and Inferiority Feelings

Abraham's (1913) study of scopophilia (voyeurism) expanded upon Freud's conceptualizations, with scopophilia being transformed into compulsive curiosity and a tendency to brood. Defenses against this drive lead to visual symptoms, neurotic blindness, and thought blocking; shame is not a factor in these transformations. Fenichel (1945) also considered scopophilia, but he introduced shame as a motive for defense against it and against exhibitionism. He related shame to visual stimuli; " 'I feel ashamed' means 'I do not want to be seen' " (p. 139). Therefore, people who feel ashamed hide themselves or at least avert their faces. However, they also close their eyes and refuse to look: "This is a kind of magical gesture, arising from the magical belief that anyone who does not look cannot be looked at" (p. 139). As noted, Nunberg (1955) also stated that "Shame is a reaction formation of the ego to the wish to exhibit" (p. 157).

Fenichel (1945) emphasized as well the relationship between shame and urethral eroticism (as implied in the episode of bed- wetting mentioned by Freud, 1898).

> ". . . failures in urethral cleanliness are usually punished by putting the child to shame – much more so than failures in rectal cleanliness. . . . *shame* is the specific force directed against urethral-erotic temptations. *Ambition,* so often described as an outcome of urethral-erotic conflicts, represents the fight against this shame" [p. 69].

Fenichel's equating ambition and defense against shame is an interesting reversal of Kohut's view of shame as a response to ambition and grandiosity. Here, Fenichel posits shame both as a defense and as a painful affective experience against which ambition serves as the defense; thus, shame may function as an affect that itself generates defense.

Alexander (1938) wrote about the role of inferiority feelings, which he seemed to equate with shame in contrast to guilt. He suggested that inferiority feelings are experienced in comparison with other people, leading to a sense of weakness which itself stimulates competition and aggression.[6] Thus, whereas guilt inhibits aggression, shame unleashes it. Also, according to Alexander, inferiority feelings represent responses to the regressive pull of dependency, leaving one narcissistically vulnerable and ashamed.

THE EGO IDEAL

As suggested earlier, an investigation of ego psychology from our perspective on shame leads inevitably to the reemergence of issues of narcissism and the ego ideal. Freud (1914) viewed the ego ideal as an attempt to recapture the lost narcissism of infancy. For Freud, the ego ideal merged with conscience and ultimately with the superego as he created the structural model. At this point, I will consider certain seminal papers on the ego ideal that raise important issues about shame's genesis but do not specifically bear on the role of shame. Such issues, especially with regard to idealization, will be seen to be relevant in our later consideration of shame. Since the ego ideal is that structure which contains the internalizations, identifications, and creations forming the individual's guiding ideals, failure to attain or to live up to these ideals is the primary source of shame.

Hartmann and Loewenstein

By defining narcissism as "the libidinal cathexis not of the ego but of the self," Hartmann (1950, p. 85) refocused the attention of ego psychology on the relevance of the self and narcissism for psychoanalytic study. Thus, Hartmann distinguished between the ego as structure and the self as referent of "one's own person"–a subjective, experiencing agent. Following Hartmann, we might say that it is the self as experiencing agent, rather than the ego as actor and doer, that feels shame for failures and inferiorities. Hartmann and Loewenstein (1962) attempted to delineate the ego ideal in relationship to the superego. They acknowledged that idealizations occur prior to the evolution of the superego but suggested that the concept of the ego ideal be reserved for those aspects of the superego which originate later, from oedipal conflicts, and thus that it be differentiated from earlier idealizations (p. 59). Quoting Freud's "New Introductory Lectures," they indicated that the superego "is also the vehicle of the ego ideal, by

---

[6]This sequence will be seen to be similar to the guilt–shame cycle of Piers (1953).

which the ego measures itself, toward which it strives, and whose demands for ever-increasing perfection it is always striving to fulfill" (Hartmann and Loewenstein, 1962, p. 60).

We might add that it is the self which is measured and in which failure to attain the ego ideal's dictates and demands for perfection resides.

Hartmann and Loewenstein then suggested that much of the infantile omnipotence is projected onto the parents, thus accounting for parental idealization. The child then identifies with the parents in an attempt to restore the lost narcissism: "Looked at from this angle, the setting up of the ego ideal can be considered a rescue operation for narcissism" (p. 61). They also asserted that the superego gradually integrates the aims of the ego ideal and the restrictions of the moral code, leading to development of a system of "good" and "ought not."

We recall that Piers (1953) stated that shame reflects tension between the ego and the ego ideal when a goal of the ego ideal is not attained. Alluding to this work, Hartmann and Loewenstein questioned whether a distinction between shame and guilt can be made in terms of analytic psychology: "It seems unlikely to us that one can, as these authors assume, distinguish between shame and guilt in terms of outer or inner sanction" (p. 66). They preferred to emphasize connections between "ideal demands" and "ought nots."

Thus, in this central contribution of ego psychology, Hartmann and Loewenstein took several positions with regard to shame and its relation to the ego ideal. First of all, they indicated that early (archaic) idealizations do occur, but that these are to be distinguished from the actual ego ideal, which they positioned closer to oedipal conflicts and the development of the superego. They defined the ego ideal, with Freud, as the vehicle of expectations for perfection within the superego and posited a sequence of projection of infantile narcissism onto, and subsequent identification with, the idealized parents. Their basic position was that the ego ideal becomes integrated into the mature superego, which still maintains separate systems of ideals and prohibitions. Not surprisingly, they then turned to shame, but, because of the fading of the ego ideal into the superego, they denied a meaningful difference between shame and guilt.

This assumption of a blurred distinction between shame and guilt must be refuted on the basis of clinical differences between the two emotions. It seems to me that Hartmann and Loewenstein's position reflected their investment in structural theory and the difficulties inherent in attempts to differentiate superego from ego ideal (see Sandler, Holder, and Meers, 1963). Thus, as they moved from clinical observa tion to explanation derived from structural theory, they confronted Freud's inevitable oedipal perspective on superego development and his turn away from narcissism and the ideal of perfection. We and others have noted the difficulty in assigning a clinical place, or conceptual referent for shame within the oedipally derived superego because of the ambiguity of the ego ideal within this model. One way to deal with this ambiguity is the approach taken by Hartmann and Loewenstein — to maintain that the superego actually encompasses the functions of the ego ideal and that therefore no substantial distinction exists between shame and guilt.

Return to the Ideal

Certain other authors returned to a study of the ego ideal, with (at times almost parenthetical) attention to shame and a continuing attempt to differentiate the functions and structure of the ego ideal from those of the superego. We shall see that these authors were not satisfied with elements of Freud's understanding of the superego, and especially with the degree to which the superego of the structural model swallows up and dedifferentiates the ego ideal. For them, Freud's structural theory tended to recast the developmental factors eventuating in the ego ideal in terms of oedipal issues revolving primarily around guilt and thus failed to delineate adequately specific functions of the ideal, including feelings of shame. For example, Schafer (1960) separated the loving from the hostile functions of the superego. The loving functions, according to Schafer, protect the ego from excessive guilt, from abandonment by significant objects, and facilitate adaptation through identification with the parental superego. These functions also include ideals and pride, through identification with the admired parents. Schafer's viewpoint was similar to mine when he stated, "It is in failing to reach these goals that the ego feels inferior. . . . [inferiority feelings] correspond to feelings of loss of the superego's love, just as guilt corresponds to feelings of the superego's hatred" (pp. 178–179).

Schafer (1967) further considered the development of ideals in relation to the ego ideal and the ideal self. While reviewing in detail the relationship of the ego ideal and ideal-formation to the psychic structures (that is, ego, superego, and id), he moved further into an examination of the *self* and its representations, including ideals and the *ideal self*. These were considered in terms of patients' experience; "An *ideal self-representation* is an image or concept of oneself as one would be if one had satisfied a specific ideal" (p. 15).

Schafer contrasted this view of the self with that of the *"experienced self-representation"* (reflecting a view of the self as one thinks one is) and suggested that one continually aspires to achieve the ideal self. Ideals may be created or internalized through identification with the "perfection" of the parents. Failure to attain the state of the ideal self (or the ego's standards) may lead to various negative feelings (for example, guilt, unworthiness, being unloved and forsaken, helplessness), which might be experienced as shame. This is the only reference to shame in Schafer's paper.

Sandler and his colleagues (1963) were also troubled by inconsistencies in the concept of the ego ideal, beginning first with those in Freud's (1914) writings on the subject. These inconsistencies included an ideal for oneself in an attempt to regain the lost narcissism; an ideal for oneself, combined with conscience; a mental structure synonymous with the superego; and the superego as the vehicle for the ego ideal. Thus Sandler noted Freud's early equation of the ideal with narcissism and the subsequent disappearance of both into the mechanistic ambiguities of the structural superego. Presumably, these authors were dissatisfied with the theoretical and clinical explanatory power of the superego with regard to ideals, found this to be an important limitation, and sought to elucidate a separate structure for them. They also considered later work on the ego ideal, noting Nunberg's 1955 differentiation of it from the superego. For Nunberg, the ego ideal represented internalized love objects, and the superego reflected the internalized hated and feared objects. Annie Reich's (1953) distinction between the two was mentioned: "[T]he ego ideal expresses what one desires to be; the superego, what one ought to be" (p. 146).

As we shall see later, Reich (1960) suggested as well that self- and object representations are magically fused to enable the person to feel "as though he were his own ego ideal" (p. 226). Jacobson (1954) also viewed the ego ideal as integrating idealized self- and object features to gratify the longing for merger between loved self and object.

Like Schafer (1967), Sandler and his co-workers (1963) went on to suggest that the self-representation takes on different "shapes" at different times, one of which is referred to as the "ideal self," "i.e., that which, at any moment, is a desired shape of the self—the 'self-as-I-want-to-be!' "(p. 152–153).

The ideal self would provide the greatest sense of well-being at any given time. The authors viewed the ideal self as being "far more fluid and flexible than the ideals held up to the child by his introjects"

(p. 154).[7] The shape of the ideal self is also influenced by knowledge of the reality of the self's potentialities and limitations and of the environment. But what happens when the actual self fails to conform to the shape of the ideal self? Sandler et al. dealt explicitly with such failure, stating, "If the individual cannot change the shape of his self so as to identify it with his ideal self, then he will suffer the pangs of disappointment, and the affective states associated with lowered self-esteem" (p. 156).

They then suggested that "the affect of shame arises when the individual perceives himself (or believes himself to have been perceived by others) as having failed to live up to ideal standards which he accepts, whereas guilt is experienced when his ideal self differs from that which he feels to be dictated by his introjects" (p. 157). Here, shame was explicitly considered to reflect *failure to approximate the shape of the ideal self*. It is interesting to note that the authors indicated both an internal (self-perception) and an external/social (perceived by others) view of shame.

DISCUSSION

In this consideration of the ego ideal and the ideal self, I have tried to lay the groundwork for a structural understanding of shame and its relationship to ideals. Starting with Freud's (1914) elucidation of primary narcissism, the ego ideal, and self-regard, I moved to Hartmann and Loewenstein's (1962) metapsychological attempt to root the ego ideal in the superego. While these authors posited the ego ideal as a "rescue operation" for narcissism, they did not further elaborate the role of narcissism and its relationship to structural theory. They also failed to find a meaningful difference between shame and guilt from the perspective of psychoanalytic theory. I believe that this lack of distinction between shame and guilt reflected a greater emphasis on theory than on clinical observation. With Schafer's (1967) and Sandler et al.'s (1963) movement toward a more clinical view of the ego ideal, and their ultimate preference for the phenomenological, experience-near notion of the ideal self, a place for shame within the theoretical context of the ego ideal became possible. Since our interest in shame moves toward affective experience, and the ideal self is a clinically relevant subjective experience that attends to the nature and boundaries of failure, shame could then be introduced as *a response to failure in attaining*

---

[7]This view is similar to Schafer's (1967) contention that the ideal self is phenomenologically a more useful concept than the ego ideal.

the shape of the ideal self. Thus, Sandler et al. (1963) attempted to clarify
the ambiguity over the ego ideal evolving from oedipal/structural
emphasis on the superego; they introduced (with Schafer, 1967) an
experiential, "fluid shape of the ideal self" more closely approximating
subjective goals than does the "check-list of internalizations" implied
by the more abstract ego ideal; and they have pointed to the connection
between failure, the ideal self, and shame. Why does this not adequately encompass a theoretical understanding of shame, allowing us
to move on to our clinical consideration of shame and its manifestations? Because, I suggest, these authors stopped short of relating their
observations to narcissistic phenomena and vulnerability, upon which
a more complete understanding of shame must be built. It is to these
considerations we will turn next.

I believe that the ego ideal–and particularly the ideal self–
provides a framework for understanding shame from an *internal* perspective. The values, idealizations, and internalized parental expectations of perfection, which form the content of the ego ideal, have been
structuralized and no longer require the presence of the external object
as guide. The shape of the ideal self is determined by this internal
perspective. It is *failure* to live up to this ideal self–experienced as a sense
of inferiority, defeat, flaw, or weakness–that results in the feeling of
shame. In chapter 5, we will examine the contributions of self psychology, and particularly the role of rupture and failure of the self-selfobject
bond, in understanding that sense of internal failure.

Failure to achieve the ideal may be *defensive,* as I shall consider
with regard to neurotic conflict over libidinal wishes or success in
competition. However, it is the affective *response* to that failure, the
searing shame, that is experienced clinically (even when that failure is
defensive), and that therefore should be the first focus of therapeutic
intervention.

Our consideration of the ego ideal has so far been confined to
classical/structural theory. Certainly, the suggestion that shame and
guilt cannot readily be differentiated psychoanalytically reflects a theoretical emphasis in which the ego ideal is firmly embedded within the
superego. Several authors attempted to differentiate the loving function
of the ego ideal from the punitive, critical functions of the morally
restrictive superego, which threatens criticism and punishment by
internalized objects and leads to guilt. We then saw movement toward
a more phenomenological view of the ego ideal, represented by the
"shape" of an ideal self, creating a clinical place for shame and an
opening toward the self and narcissism.

Shame's relationship to guilt will not form a major part of this book, as it has been considered extensively elsewhere (see, for example, Piers, 1953; Lynd, 1958; Levin, 1967; Lewis, 1971, 1987; Thrane, 1978; and Wurmser, 1981). However, the issue of *diagnostic* and *developmental primitiveness* of shame arises in the nature of its relationship to guilt. These issues played a major role in the thinking of Reich (1960) and, particularly, of Jacobson (1964).

Now we turn to primitive object relations and pathological narcissism, to enrich our understanding of the ego ideal. With these additions, the meaning of shame will come into sharper focus, and I will then consider in greater detail shame's relationship to narcissism.

3

Primitive Object Relations, Early Narcissism, and Shame

In the previous chapter, I reviewed some of the writing on the ego ideal and the ideal self because I believe that these constructs play a central role in the evolution of shame as affective experience. Reflecting experiences of failure, inferiority, and defect, shame must be viewed as the consequence of failure to attain the ideals that one forms for oneself and hence failure to fulfill the mandates of the intrapsychic structures that contain those ideals (that is, superego, ego ideal, and ideal self). However, any attempt to consider ego psychology's view of shame in terms of the ego ideal inevitably shades into concerns about narcissism, primitive object relations, and self-esteem. These issues, and their relationship to the creation of ideals, play a central role in the works of Reich and Jacobson, to which we will turn shortly.

First, we must return briefly to the question of shame as an affective experience, which is relevant to the thinking of these two authors. Many psychoanalytic writers have emphasized the importance of affect and have contributed to its theoretical understanding (for example, Brenner, 1974; Basch, 1976; Emde, 1980; Demos, 1988; Stern, 1988). The significant contributions of Tomkins (1962–63) to a theory of affect are particularly pertinent here because of the importance he placed on shame (chapter 5). Tomkins delineated nine primary affects (including shame), which he described as specific, inborn, biologically determined patterns of physiological response, especially with regard to facial expression. These patterns are innate for each affect, and the quality of each is determined by the intensity (what Tomkins calls the density) of neuronal firings. According to Tomkins, we become aware of our positive or negative affects by attending to our physiological and facial responses. Tomkins postulated that instead of drives determining affective responses, as suggested by classical psychoanalytic theory, affects serve as necessary *amplifiers* of the drives and hence are the source of motivation, cognition, and action. Thus, the nine primary affects are antecedent to all subsequent human development.

Let us now turn to the work of Reich and Jacobson, and study their approach to shame.

REICH AND JACOBSON

In her paper on self-esteem regulation, Reich (1960) noted that a particular kind of narcissist engages in fantasies of self-aggrandizement and believes these to be magically fulfilled, but has only limited interest in reality or in objects (p. 221). Such patients gain heightened self-esteem from fantasies of magnificence and suffer pangs of helplessness, anxiety, and rage at the "narcissistic injuries" resulting when their grandiose wishes, particularly with regard to phallic perfection, are not realized. Thus, for such patients, ". . . eroticized, manic self-inflation easily shifts to a feeling of utter dejection, of worthlessness, and to hypochondriacal anxieties. 'Narcissists' of this type thus suffer regularly from repetitive, violent oscillations of self-esteem" (p. 224).

During the low points of dejection, they look to the omnipotent object for magical fusion and merger and through such idealization participate in the object's "greatness" (p. 227). However, idealization frequently leads to envy and then to aggression, and finally to devaluation and destruction of the object, in a repetitive and self-defeating cycle (splitting). In discussing self-consciousness, Reich elaborated on contempt for the "admiring" object, contempt that is then shifted to the self as a reflection of feelings of inferiority and "shameful exposure" (p. 230).[1] Reich also pointed to the relationship of oscillations of self-

---

[1]The relationship of shame to contempt is discussed in chapters 7 and 8.

esteem to cyclothymic states – which are considered in chapter 11 with regard to narcissism and mania – and suggested that restitution of the positive phase in the cycles of self-esteem occurs through the fantasy of fusion with an archaic ego ideal.

In Reich's view, then, self-esteem in primitive narcissistic personalities oscillates between idealization of, and fantasied merger with, omnipotent objects in one direction, and aggressive contempt for, and envious devaluation of the object in the other. These swings reflect grandiose fantasies of magnificence, alternating with feelings of dejection, helplessness, worthlessness, or shame. The idealization of the object is the product of a harsh, primitive ego ideal, which became magically fused to it. Thus, for such primitively narcissistic patients, shame and the archaic ego ideal – and, at moments of fantasied magnificence, the ego ideal and idealized object – become magically fused. The rapid shifts in self-esteem described by Reich correlate with the surprising suddenness with which shame may strike (Wurmser, 1981; Tomkins, 1987). This is particularly true for shame-prone, narcissistically vulnerable persons.

Murray (1964) also examined the relationship of narcissism to the ego ideal, emphasizing the pathological consequences of a primitive, demanding ego ideal leading to "narcissistic entitlement" at the expense of a mature sense of reality and object attachments. It was the work of Jacobson (1954, 1964), however, that most extensively integrated ego-psychological and object relational perspectives on the ego ideal and narcissism and identified shame as a major manifestation of failure and inferiority. Jacobson used structural theory and intrapsychic conflict to explain shame and guilt, thus placing herself squarely within the camp of ego psychology. Like Schafer (1967) and Sandler et al. (1963), she noted that lowered moral self-esteem evokes guilt or shame and is caused by conflicts between ego and superego. However, Jacobson's (1964) notion of conflict included failure of the self to meet the demands of a narcissistically invested ego ideal, leading to shame:

> [These conflicts] reflect disharmony between (conscious or unconscious) ego-ideal components and the self-representations. . . . Such conflicts develop from discordance between wishful self images which embody the narcissistic goals of the ego and a self that appears to be failing, defective, inferior, weak, contemptible in comparison. These narcissistic conflicts are apt to evoke feelings of inferiority and shame [pp. 154–155].

Thus, like Reich and Murray, Jacobson was particularly interested in feelings of vulnerability and failure in regard to the ego ideal.

These she related to narcissism and destructive early objects. She observed in these patients a proclivity to shame reactions and feelings of inferiority. Her commitment to the structural viewpoint caused her to frame these problems as "narcissistic conflicts," and consequently limited her freedom to explore narcissistic phenomena further. Her wider view of the dynamics of conflict did, however, did enable her to address problems of narcissism, shame, and the self and to carry these beyond the earlier confines of ego psychology.

According to Jacobson (1964), the ego ideal acts as a *bridge* between the ego and superego (p. 187) and thus functions as a separate structure outside of the superego. Containing the grandiose fantasies and ideals, the ego ideal inevitably leads to feelings of shame and inferiority. In taking this position, Jacobson differed from Hartmann and Loewenstein (1962) and demonstrated greater clinical interest in the afflictions of narcissism. While she viewed shame, along with narcissism, within the context of a conflict psychology, that conflict was *intrasystemic* (conflicting views of the self, or ego), rather than *intersystemic* (drive-driven conflicts between ego, id, and superego).

Describing patients fixated at levels of narcissistic object relations and primitive identifications with glorified objects (similar to those considered by Reich), Jacobson suggested that

> Such patients are apt to sustain . . . a proclivity to devastating shame reactions from infantile sources; reactions that may lead to depressive states with occasional brooding about ineradicable memories of shameful or humiliating situations. Some of these patients manifest a strong preponderance of shame over guilt reactions and of social over superego fears [Jacobson, 1964, p. 201].

Jacobson, then, viewed shame diagnostically as a predominantly social/interpersonal manifestation of pathological narcissism and a primitive ego ideal (differentiating it from implicitly more mature guilt/superego reactions), and of more severe psychopathology suggesting borderline or paranoid conditions (p. 208). She suggested that, developmentally, shame originates in exposure – of lack of control, female genital inferiority, and failure. With ego maturation, however, comes internalization of these "self-conflicts," thus moving beyond the traditional view of conflict and guilt to include internally generated shame, which she called "disgrace" (p. 144). Jacobson then moved to a language of narcissism and the self by relating inferiority feelings to "narcissistic defeat" in ego accomplishments and object relations resulting from early narcissistic injuries and failures, which precede castration conflict. It is difficult to see here how a concept of intrapsychic conflict helps in Jacobson's understanding of narcissistic fixation and failure. Shame and inferiority feelings are differentiated from guilt in terms of their relationship to the self and "its power, its intactness, its appearance, and even its moral perfection but not in terms of our loving or hostile impulses and behavior toward others" (p. 146).

Summary

Reich explored the relationship of oscillations of self-esteem and vulnerability to narcissistic injury[2] and the attempts of primitive patients to restore their damaged self-esteem through merger with idealized objects. The resulting object dependency becomes intolerable, however, and leads to contempt for, and distancing from, objects. Reich suggested that such idealized objects are fantasied representations of archaic ego ideals. I shall suggest later that idealized object representation may also be created through projective identification of the archaic ego ideal (or ideal self). Reich's observations about contempt as an alternative to shame will be considered as projective identification of shame into a devalued object (see chapter 7).

Through her emphasis on narcissistic vulnerability and fixation, primitive object relations, and shame, while retaining a perspective on conflict and an independent ego ideal, Jacobson represented a transition in interest from ego psychology to narcissism. Not surprisingly, shame played an important part in her speculations relating to failures and inferiority with regard to the archaic ego ideal. This emphasis on shame became possible, it seems to me, because of her differentiation of ego ideal from the superego. In this way, she took a position that contrasted with Hartmann and Loewenstein's (1962) lack of distinction between shame and guilt. Failures of the self included also faulty relationships with primitive, punitive objects, as Jacobson introduced a developmental timetable for shame sensitivity. She viewed shame *diagnostically* as grossly pathological, as reflecting primitive ego development and, in general, a lack of capacity for guilt. Her shame-sensitive patient was essentially needy, clinging, and not clearly separated/differentiated from the depriving parent.

Anticipating Kohut, Jacobson indicated that shame frequently reflects deficiencies (again, *not* conflicts) that the individual feels incapable of remedying. Masochistic, passive, and dependent tendencies,

---

[2]While she did not address shame per se in detail, these rapid oscillations of self-esteem clearly represent the sudden, overwhelming intrusion of shame which so often accounts for its "searing" quality.

which may lead to ineptitude, evoke shame and inferiority. Jacobson (1964) took the position, which forms the premise of the next chapter of this book, that shame and inferiority feelings indicate narcissistic difficulties:

> [T]he prevalence of shame and inferiority over guilt conflicts after adolescence is mostly indicative of the type of narcissistic disturbances which cause identity problems. . . . feelings of shame maintain an even closer connection with the more primitive types of narcissistic conflicts, which induce feelings of inferiority and humiliation [p. 152].

Interestingly, in relating narcissistic strivings to greed and power in some patients, Jacobson included a footnote calling attention to Adler's (1912) theory of the origin of neuroses in the "power drive," a relationship I noted earlier. She also acknowledged Adler's (1907) concept of "inferiority," while resolving to examine the term "from the standpoint of analytic psychology" (p. 136*n*).

We move on now to a consideration of object relations in our understanding of shame.[3]

A FOCUS ON OBJECT RELATIONS

Freud (1905) viewed shame ambiguously, both as a reaction formation against the drives and as affective experience, a point noted also by other authors (for example, Hazard, 1969; Kinston, 1983). Freud variously commented upon shame both in an external, social/interpersonal context (1900) and as an internal experience (that is, failure and inferiority in relation to the ego ideal, which he misidentified as "guilt" (1921). Freud (1914) then gave thought to the ego ideal, recognizing it as a structure created by the internalization of cultural values, idealized parent representations, and moral precepts to guide the actions and contours of the self. I have suggested that shame is the affective response to failure and inferiority with regard to the ideal. The focus on self that emerges inevitably from consideration of failure and inferiority leads directly to narcissism, or "the libidinal investment of the self," as defined by Hartmann (1950). However, this passage from self to narcissism is incomplete without the object – our earlier recent review of Reich and Jacobson underscored that relationship.

I turn, then, to a consideration of the object relations perspective

---

[3]Other papers from an ego-psychological perspective on shame include those of Feldman, (1962), Grinker, (1955), and Levin (1967, 1971).

and its approach to shame. Here, shame may be regarded in terms of real or fantasied *interpersonal interaction* (with resultant embarrassment, hiding, inferiority feelings, fear of abandonment, and the like) or as *failure* with regard to internalized objects (contemptuous introjects, the ego ideal, and so on). However, shame has been strikingly absent from the writings of most object relations theorists (also noted by Kinston, 1983; Fisher, 1985). Shame is not even indexed in Greenberg and Mitchell's (1983) *Object Relations in Psychoanalytic Theory.*

Two authors in particular do consider shame and object relations, and I will discuss them before turning to narcissism and shame in the next chapter. The writing of each of these authors is informed by Mahler, Pine, and Bergman's (1975) formulation on separation/individuation, and, especially, the rapprochement subphase. (As far as I could discover, though, Mahler herself did not directly address shame.) Spero (1984) suggested that shame evolves from negative ego ideals, which he defined as "those aspects of superego structure which never gain complete internalization" (p. 267). These superego elements he differentiated as introjects and split-object representations, contrasted with internalizations of whole objects attained through identification. From this vantage point, the ego ideal might be viewed as *separate* from the superego, as implied by Jacobson. Spero suggested that shame reflects "unstable self- other boundaries" and negative and devaluing internalized object representations that have remained alien to self-structure. Utilizing a Mahlerian viewpoint, he believed that self-object differentiation is incomplete, leading to the threat of diffusion of the self's boundaries by painful envy of the "observing other," thus impinging on the self's separate identity. For shame-prone personalities, Spero suggested, introjects and part-object representations predominate over true identifications and hence threaten the separate existence of the self. Hence, a sense of shame requires both exposure and audience and also implies more archaic ego development than in persons for whom guilt predominates. Note again the similarity of this view to that of Jacobson.

Like Jacobson, Spero also emphasized the presence of shame during adolescence, when weak self-boundaries and secondary sexual development predominate. He also attributed heightened shame reactions in senescence and terminal illness to a feeling of infirmity and loss of control, leading to a weakened sense of self. Again like Jacobson, but from a more explicitly object relations point of view, he related shame to narcissistic vulnerability, a theme I will develop in the next chapter. Spero concluded that shame-proneness is but one of the many reflections of impaired object relations.

Kinston (1983) also suggested that shame is best understood from the perspective of object relations theory. He indicated that it signals an incipient move from what he called self-narcissism to object narcissism. In an earlier paper, Kinston (1980) had defined self-narcissism as an attempt to maintain an integrated, stable, and essentially positive self-representation. Disturbances in self-narcissism occur when the self-image easily becomes negative, as in states of low self-esteem, which in turn reflect narcissistic vulnerability. Object narcissism, on the other hand, represents a primitive object relationship in which self-object differentiation and boundaries are not easily maintained, leading to an anxious withdrawal from important objects to preserve the integrity of self-boundaries and, with it, the impression of self-sufficiency, denial of need, and indifference toward others. In states of object narcissism, the therapeutic relationship is characterized by confusion or indifference toward the therapist; in states of self-narcissism, by dependence and vulnerability. According to Kinston, narcissistic disturbance reflects early difficulty in differentiating from parents who need to maintain symbiosis.

In a subsequent study of shame, Kinston (1983) questioned the explanatory adequacy of structural and instinctual models. Instead, he considered shame from an object relations model that emphasized the self's attempts at individuation and identity formation. He described shame as a signal experience reflecting painful self-awareness and separate identity (self-narcissism) in the face of difficulty in relating to others. Anxiety from this self-awareness leads to a wish to deny need, dependency, conflicts, meaning, and imperfection. Shame then recedes with the move to "object narcissism" (related to Winnicott's [1965] "false self"), causing a disavowal of independent self-identity and autonomy and leading to replacement of spontaneous self-awareness by stereotyped activity. Kinston held a view of shame similar to Erikson's (1950) equation of shame and doubt, with difficulty in forging and maintaining a separate identity. Developmentally, then, shame relates to "the urge to live up to parental expectations which disregard or violate a unique personal identity; but which offer a sense of closeness, love or approval" (p. 220).

In a paper taking an object relations approach to shame and borderline development, Fisher (1985) also suggested that shame reflects a lack of sharp self-other differentiation and boundary formation, with an unformed sense of self and a split concept of good mother and bad self.

By contrast, Lynd (1958) viewed shame as *resulting* from self-exposure, related to self-knowledge and self-awareness. Thus, for her, shame was a consequence of the sense of an independent self without movement toward satisfying the claims of important objects.

Whereas the ego-psychological perspective on shame emphasized the ego ideal and self-esteem, an object relations orientation introduces concerns with introjects and split-object representations, and unstable self-other boundaries. The shame-prone self (or ego) is seen as unstable, archaic, and undifferentiated with regard to objects, maintaining symbiotic, stilted, or indifferent and unsatisfactory interpersonal relationships. Shame, then, is seen as a manifestation of painful and incomplete autonomy and identity, reflected in a vulnerability to hostile and rejecting significant (internal and external) objects. Thus, Spero and Kinston share Jacobson's pessimistic *developmental* and *diagnostic* viewpoint that shame reflects primitive and archaic developmental experiences with early objects. Spero emphasized the sense of audience in shame, with intrusion of part-objects into the self-experience, reflecting these impoverished or primitive object relations. For Kinston, the process of moving away from painful autonomy and identity (self-narcissism) toward merger with, and acquiescence to, the demands of others (object narcissism) leads to the experience of shame. Shame is resolved when this process, creating a false self, is completed. Implicit in these formulations are fluctuations of self-esteem, shifts from object idealization to contempt, as noted by Reich (1960).

SUMMARY

While it is true that shame has remained relatively hidden in psychoanalytic investigations, particularly in comparison with guilt, it played a part in Freud's early contributions and later in particular applications of ego psychology and object relations theory. I have suggested that shame strains the boundaries of structural psychology (that is, with regard to structural conceptualizations of superego and ego ideal, and the place of inferiority feelings in a theory of conflict), particularly in the work of Jacobson, and forced Hartmann and Loewenstein to minimize the distinction between shame and guilt. The limits of structural psychology will be considered in the following discussion of shame and narcissism, particularly with regard to the work of Kohut.

As to central issues regarding shame, *diagnostic* and *developmental* considerations suggest that most of the writers cited have considered shame as reflecting primitive or archaic conflicts or developmental fixations (that is, qualities of self-experience). These are manifested by overly harsh or perfectionistic criteria imposed by an incompletely structuralized and integrated ego ideal or by critical, rejecting internalized parental representations and early experiences of traumatizing humiliation by significant objects. The question of an "archaic nature" of shame is another guiding issue throughout our inquiry. I will try to show that shame occurs as a significant affect in *all* people, including neurotic patients. Since it may present in a less pernicious and intractable form than in severe narcissistic (primitive) states, the shame experience need *not* be a signal of archaic psychopathology, especially when it appears *as a reaction* to oedipal conflict.

As to whether shame can occur internally or only in an external social context, I have suggested that Freud viewed it from both vantage points at different times (as an intrapsychic reaction formation against the voyeuristic drive and as a response to the experience of being scrutinized publicly in naked vulnerability). When seen as a response to failure regarding the ego ideal (or shape of the ideal self), shame is an internal experience that may occur in social isolation or in response to repeated selfobject failure. (We will consider later with regard to the internal-external issue the role of rupture of a sustaining self-selfobject bond in generating shame.) On the other hand, there is no question that shame can occur in relation to the external object world, as a response to failed self-esteem in the quest for acceptance by an idealized object, a reaction to intrusive audience, or to weakened self-other boundaries.

All the issues raised so far about shame move inevitably toward narcissism. I have suggested the implicit importance of narcissism in the works of Freud, the ego psychologists, and object relations theorists and will turn now to a consideration of shame explicitly from the perspective of narcissism.

4

Shame and Narcissism

Thus far, we have examined shame from the perspectives of the ego ideal and of primitive object relations and have begun to touch on the place of shame in narcissistic phenomena. The experience of shame has been considered an affective response to a cognitive sense of *failure* to attain ideals and fantasied perfection, a reflection of a sense of *inferiority*. I have suggested that shame may be experienced internally and alone, in social isolation, as well as in response to active interpersonal humiliation or to the presence of an observing audience.

Whereas guilt reflects a hurtful thought or action, shame is an affective response to a perception of the self as flawed, and thus inevitably involves narcissism, vulnerability, and their various manifestations. Before we confront the specific relationship between shame and narcissism, however, it will be useful to review some central issues about narcissism itself.

In the introduction to a recent volume of papers on narcissism (Morrison, 1986a), I suggested that the essence of narcissistic concern is a yearning for absolute uniqueness and sole importance to someone else, a "significant other." This yearning, which may be transitory, is signaled in patients by such statements as, "If I am not the only person important to [therapist or another], I feel like I am noth-

48

ing." Such a feeling reverberates with primitive fantasies of symbiotic merger, omnipotence, and grandiosity, what Freud (1914) referred to as primary narcissism. Its emphasis is on the state and status of the self, and yet, paradoxically, it implies as well the presence of an object for whom the self is uniquely special or who offers no competition or barriers to the self in meeting needs for sustenance.

The narcissistic demand for uniqueness is expressed directly, as assertions of entitlement; defensively, as haughty aloofness and grandiosity; or affectively, through dejected or rageful responses to its absence and failure. Inevitably, *shame* follows narcissistic defeat. Patients have described the torment they have suffered from a perceived lack of specialness: "This humiliation is the most painful feeling I have ever experienced." This statement reflects the importance of shame and humiliation in our patients and, again, underscores the paradox of the relative lack of attention paid to shame in the clinical literature. The other paradox, of course, is that such a yearning for uniqueness—by its very nature—can never be satisfied fully or for long.

The literature about narcissism has focused on various of its manifestations: the nature of the ideal (discussed earlier as the ego ideal and ideal self); aspects of internalized and external objects and their representations (previous chapter); the structure and experience of the self (including identity, cohesion, separation/individuation, and self-esteem); and characteristic behavioral patterns.

We have discussed the ego ideal as an ambiguous central construct in structural theory, whose relationship to the superego generated much debate among ego psychologists. Are the ego ideal and the superego to be viewed as two different functions of the same structure, as suggested by Schafer (1960) and others, or as separate entities, as Piers (1953) and Jacobson (1964) maintain? Is it sufficient to regard the ego ideal in structural, instinctual terms, or must it be seen from the broader perspective of narcissism? After all, Freud (1914) first described the ego ideal in his paper on narcissism, and only later did it disappear from Freud's thinking in favor of the superego and the mental apparatus. Sandler et al. (1963), examining some of the confusion about the ego ideal, noted that shame results from the failure of the actual self to approximate configurations of the ideal self (that is, the self's goals, values, and ideals). However, those authors did not explicitly connect shame with narcissism.

In considering the relationship of the ego ideal to narcissism, Hartmann and Loewenstein (1962) defined it as a rescue operation for narcissism. However, they denied a meaningful psychoanalytic distinction between shame and guilt, thus minimizing any explicit relationship between shame, the ego ideal, and narcissism. Other authors have contested this position (for example Kinston, 1983). Reich (1960) discussed narcissism explicitly in terms of oscillating self-esteem and an archaically perfectionistic ego ideal in a particular type of narcissistic patient. She, along with Jacobson (1964), called attention to the inexorable interrelationship between narcissistic phenomena, structural/libidinal psychology, and object relations, evidenced by the narcissistic patients' alternating between grandiosity (especially phallic) and feelings of worthlessness and dejection in their relationship to, and envy of, omnipotent objects. We shall see that Reich's views anticipate the suggestions of Bursten (1973) and of Chasseguet-Smirgel (1985) with regard to fantasied fusion and reunion with the idealized, omnipotent parent (recipient of the projected ego ideal).

Jacobson attended in detail to the relationship of the ego ideal and narcissism from the perspective of conflict/drive psychology. She described the narcissistic elements of discordance between wished-for perfectionistic self images and images of an inferior, failing self, leading explicitly to shame. However, her thoughts about narcissism (like those of Reich) and about the ego ideal seem more descriptive than explanatory, probably reflecting the secondary position of narcissism in an era dominated by ego psychology and structural (intrapsychic) conflict. Historically, however, both Reich and Jacobson clearly anticipated the transition to an interest in narcissism and object relations.

APPROACHES TO THE SHAME-NARCISSISM
RELATIONSHIP

In exploring how shame relates to narcissism, I will first examine several important works that offer distinct views of narcissism and shame. I will then consider in some detail the contributions of two authors, Bursten and Chasseguet-Smirgel, who viewed shame and narcissism in relationship to fantasies of reunion and merger. Finally, I will summarize these contributions in the context of a *dialectic* between shame and narcissism.

Piers

In his ground-breaking psychoanalytic essay on shame, Piers (1953) differentiated the ego ideal from the superego and the ego, and defined as its first attribute "a core of narcissistic omnipotence." By this, Piers meant pathological conditions "with overinflated, grandiose, or perfectionistic ideals that put the ego under unbearable tensions"(p. 26). Here we note that Piers did not describe the defensive quality of narcissistic omnipotence against underlying ego feelings of failure and inferiority (which I will consider later as the *Dialectic of Narcissism*).

Lynd and Levin

Lynd (1958) noted that Freud initially viewed the ego ideal as "a derivative of early narcissism." Lewis (1971) also indicated that "shame is about the self; it is thus a 'narcissistic' reaction, evoked by a lapse from the ego-ideal" (p. 37)

Levin (1982) suggested that intense shame leads to a disruption of narcissistic equilibrium, which is experienced "not only as an unpleasant feeling of shame but also as a feeling of being hurt, accompanied by a feeling of anger and a lowering of self-esteem. We often label such a disruption as a 'narcissistic injury.' "

Wurmser

Wurmser (1981) related shame to the protection of integrity. He described it as a reflection of rampant narcissism; "If 'integrity' is based on controlled, 'normal' sublimated narcissism, and if its violation by drives for power rests on pathological narcissism, then shame is clearly the companion affect to both forms of narcissism" (p. 48).

Thus, the relationship of shame to narcissism is noted in each of these major works on shame, which emphasize divergence from the ego ideal, strains on the ego, lowered self-esteem, and protection of the self's integrity. But that relationship is only adumbrated in these works. I noted earlier that Freud's writing on narcissism, the ego ideal, and self-regard contained all the ingredients necessary for a further exploration of shame, but that his interest had led him to examine guilt within the framework of psychic conflict and his evolving structural theory. Reich and Jacobson went further than other ego psychologists in recognizing the relationship between pathological narcissism and primitive ego ideal components, but their conclusions were, I believe, limited by strict adherence to classical theory. Accordingly, narcissistic reactions, and strong shame propensity, were viewed as primitive fixations reflecting traumatic developmental relationships with objects that did not allow for adequate developmental attainment of intrapsychic (oedipal) conflict. Thus, intrapsychic (oedipal) conflict and guilt must be built upon satisfactory early object relationships. More recent contributions—principally the writings of Kohut—have viewed narcissism from a different vantage point. Kohut's works, which have greatly influenced my own view of shame, are considered in chapter 5.

Lewis

Writing from a phenomenological perspective, Lewis (1981) amplified her earlier contribution on shame and guilt by suggesting that these are "universal affective states which function to maintain and repair lost affectional bonds," rather than serving only as "drive controls" (p. 261). Emphasizing the affiliative nature of shame, Lewis considered it to represent "the relation of the self to another person in unrequited love" (p. 244), reflecting a fear of loss of love based on anaclitic identifications. Shame suggests field dependency, in which a person relies upon and merges with the "surround" in order to establish self-esteem. Lewis concluded that shame-prone people are field-dependent, are likely to be women, and are given to depression; shame itself protects against the loss of boundaries of the self, maintaining a sense of separate identity.[1] Further, she equated the shame-prone superego mode with narcissistic disorders, which she related to a defective sense of self.

According to Lewis, shame and narcissism are closely related and can easily be transformed from one into the other. In this regard, she stated that shame is "an 'implosion' or momentary destruction of the self; narcissism is love of the self" (p. 248). She further asserted that narcissism functions as a defense against self-hatred and shame. In her view of narcissism, however, there seems to be no place for the states of self-vulnerability. Emphasizing the primacy of shame, Lewis viewed narcissism as being subsumed under the construct of shame, as part of it. Considering shame to function in an interpersonal context— "to replace lost affectional ties . . ."(p. 245), Lewis argued that narcissism, shaped by shame, serves defensively to restore the integrity of the self and its esteem. The implicit social interaction in shame states may involve an "internalized other in whose eyes one is proud or ashamed" (p. 249) and who remains beloved at the expense of the self. Lewis further hypothesized that unanalyzed shame reactions (and related self-hatred) are the source of frequent negative therapeutic reactions and failed analyses.

Thus, Lewis viewed narcissism manifestly as love of the self, although she acknowledged that narcissism may defend against failure

---

[1]Note the difference between this view and those of Spero (1984), Kinston (1983), and Lynd (1958).

and low self-esteem. She did not elaborate further on narcissism except to observe that it relates closely to shame (causing the momentary destruction of the self), reflecting a superego mode aimed at maintaining affectionate object ties. More than any other writer on shame and narcissism, Lewis considered shame to be primary, with narcissism playing a secondary, supportive role in coping with shame. Her phenomenology and descriptions of shame are much richer and more detailed than her attention to narcissism. Lewis's position on narcissism was clearly at odds with that of most other writers, and no doubt reflected her long-standing interest in, and emphasis on, shame. She believed that current attention to narcissism is excessive, a position shared by Nathanson (1987) and, paradoxically, by Wurmser (1981), who failed to consider Lewis's writings in his book.

Broucek

In a stimulating paper relating shame to narcissistic developments, Broucek (1982) suggested that shame is the fundamental painful affect encountered in problems of narcissistic personalities – a position with which I totally agree. Expanding on Tomkins's (1962–63) view of shame as a primitive, indwelling affect that reflects interruption of, or negative feedback about, excitement, interest, or joy in the infant, Broucek connected shame with disappointment in the hoped-for response of the parental (caretaking) environment to the infant's communicated pleasurable behavior. It represents as well environmental feedback suggesting incompetence, inefficacy, and the "inability to influence, predict, or comprehend an event which the infant expected . . . to be able to control or understand" (p. 370). Such environmental responses usually occur suddenly, accounting for the abrupt and searing quality generally noted in shame and for the tendency to withdraw and hide.

Broucek then considered Lewis's contributions on the relationship of shame to the sense of self and object-defined self-awareness, and finally shame's place with regard to the ideal and grandiose self – both manifestations of the ego ideal, as we have seen. He contrasted the views of Kernberg (1975) and Kohut (1971) about the grandiose self, noting the striking omission of shame in Kernberg's formulations. Broucek agreed with Kernberg about the nature of the grandiose self; both viewed it as a "pathological" reflection of mental pain in the developing infant leading to compensatory constructions of a fantastic and grandiose nature in formation of the ideal self. Broucek considered shame to play a double role in narcissism and the grandiose self: as an instigator in the (defensive) creation of the grandiose self, and as an ego response to grandiosity, leading to the splitting off of the grandiose self from the core self organization.[2]

In reviewing Kernberg's example of "splitting" in narcissistic personalities, Broucek suggested that the words used – "haughty grandiosity," "shyness," and "feelings of inferiority" – are all shame variants or derivatives, even though Kernberg did not explicate the role of shame in such states. (I shall make a similar point about Kohut's, 1977, descriptions of self pathology.) Broucek further differentiated the "normal" ideal self from the grandiose self, suggesting that narcissistic patients with grandiose self-pathology suffer the greater, self-conscious shame, due to "the greater discrepancy between objectively derived self-observation and the defensively exalted grandiose self" (p. 375).

Quoting Bursten (1973), Broucek observed that narcissistically vulnerable patients with a grandiose self must, through projection, distance themselves from shame. Broucek differentiated an 'egotistical' type from a dissociative narcissistic type: the latter splits off and projects the grandiose self onto an idealized and omnipotent object, maintaining for his or her own self-view the depreciated sense of actual self that accompanies low self-esteem and shame. (This formulation is analogous to Reich's, 1960, conceptualization of oscillating self-esteem noted earlier.)

Broucek, then, examined shame as a response to narcissistic vulnerability and injury, which he related to the infant's incompetence and inability to elicit an expected positive response from the caretaking environment (see Tomkins, 1962–63, and Chasseguet-Smirgel, 1985). Interestingly, Broucek suggested that shame propensity occurs very early in development, since self-object differentiation is present from birth. Contemporary observations of infant-mother interaction (for example, Stern, 1985) support this view. This position differs from that of Mahler (1975) and other object relations authors (for example, Spero, 1984), who related shame to the quality of self-object differentiation (in terms of "boundaries" and "introjects") and to the resultant internalized and external object representations.

Broucek contrasted Kernberg's and Kohut's views of the grandiose self and sided with Kernberg. I tend to agree with Broucek, whose position reflects, I believe, Kohut's problematic dismissal of the relationship of shame to failures in attaining ideals (and, hence, the ego ideal). I will discuss this in greater detail in chapter 5, but it is worth

---

[2]The latter view (shame as an ego response to grandiosity) will be seen to resemble Kohut's notion of the "vertical split" (see chapter 5).

noting now that Kohut is the only author considered so far who denied the relationship of shame to the ego ideal—a position, I believe, that demonstrated his separation of narcissistic and object relational lines of development.

Broucek suggested that shame plays a double role in the grandiose self: as a *stimulus* to reactive narcissistic self-aggrandizement and as an ego *response* to recognition of excessive grandiosity. He followed Bursten in setting up narcissistic character types, but his typology differentiated manifest self-aggrandizement (the egotistical narcissist) from an underlying feeling of unworthiness (the dissociative narcissist). The former devalues the object (through contempt) while aggrandizing the self; the latter idealizes the object (by projection of grandiosity) and scorns the self (through feelings of inferiority). This distinction is contained in what I have called *Narcissistic Dialectic* (to be discussed at the end of this chapter).

Thrane

Thrane (1979) examined shame from the perspective of identity formation and the narcissistic construction of the self. Quoting Sartre (1943), he wrote, "I am ashamed of what I am. Shame therefore realizes an intimate relation of myself to myself. Through shame I have discovered an aspect of my being" (p. 324). Reflecting our interest in the internal or social/external quality of shame—implied as well by Sartre—Thrane also noted shame's dual social and internal nature. He related shame both to the sense of audience implied in facing others and to the presence of internalized ideals, which form a significant part of the self-representation and of moral development. However, he disagreed with the anthropological notion that shame reflects exclusively condemnation by others, which would make it more superficial, less intrapsychic, than guilt. Like Broucek (1982), Thrane indicated that shame always implies self-recognition, or self-consciousness and self-awareness, not only in terms of group identification or wished-for identification, but also with regard to deeply embraced group ideals. As Erikson (1950) noted, shame reflects failure not only to achieve parentally approved behavior, but also to attain the mastery and self-control, or autonomy, that represent internalized, narcissistic expectations of the self. Thus, through both identification and obedience, the child strives for "narcissistic fusion"—internalization of, and merger, with the idealized parents. Failure to achieve this state leads to shame, with the threat of loss of love from, and unity with, the omnipotent parental objects (see the section on reunion and merger in this chapter).

At the same time, identity requires differentiation and individuation from the parental "other," and, in Thrane's view, failure to delimit self boundaries also leads to shame, as occurs frequently during adolescence.[3]Ultimately, then, from Thrane's (1979) perspective on "normal" narcissism, shame may be seen as a natural manifestation of self-development:[4] "The liability to shame is now seen as an inevitable by-product of the loving construction of the self. Identity and individuation are protected by the fear of shame" (p. 339).

Broucek emphasized interactions of shame, the ideal self, and the self's relationship to objects as determinants of narcissism, with shame playing a central role in narcissistic configurations. Thrane, on the other hand, considered identity formation to be a central factor in narcissism, with shame relating to that process. For Thrane, shame was a normal experience, forming part of the narcissistic process of individuation (identity formation), identification with objects, and the establishment of ideals. Consistent with our conceptualization of a narcissistic dialectic, Thrane viewed narcissism both in relationship to the establishment of a separate self and as a means to seek fantasied reunion with parental ideals. Shame occurs in anticipation of inevitable difficulty or failure in the achievement of each of these goals. With regard to failures in identity formation, Thrane's viewpoint is reminiscent of the shame described by Kinston (1983) over the self's autonomous isolation in self-narcissism, although Kinston proposed that shame is experienced at the point of *achieving* a separate identity, while Thrane suggested that shame is a response to *failure* in that quest.

Shame from failure to achieve fantasied merger with parental ideals, as described by Thrane, is similar to failure to attain the internalized ego ideal. He made explicit, however, the dual, internal and external, aspects of the self's relationship to ideals, with respect both to creation of identity (internal) and to the relevance of audience and group membership and norms (external). For Thrane, then, narcissistic elements are central in identity formation and merger, in the self's subjective experience and in its relationship to others. Shame plays an important role in each of these manifestations of narcissism, where it is not necessarily pathological but may be part of the human condition. This "normative" perspective on shame and narcissistic development

---

[3]Note how this view resembles Lewis's (1981) position but differs from that of Kinston (1983), for whom separateness itself may lead to shame.

[4]This view of shame as a normal developmental phenomenon of identity formation, along with that of Lewis (1981), differs sharply from the "pathological," preoedipal/guilt emphasis of Jacobson (1964). I agree with the thrust of Thrane's formulation.

will be seen to resemble Kohut's (1966, 1971) view of a developmental line for narcissism.

SHAME AND MERGER (REUNION)

Bursten

Bursten (1973) has offered a categorization of narcissistic personality types, in which the major challenge for the narcissistic personality is to rid itself of shame. For these patients, "fantasies of humiliation, embarrassment, and mortification are common. Shame is the enemy of the grandiose self and it makes the narcissist feel unacceptable to the omnipotent object. Thus, the task of the narcissistic repair mechanism is to be rid of the shame" (p. 294).[5]

Initially, Bursten had differentiated borderline, narcissistic, and complementary (that is, neurotic) personalities in terms of the nature of their object choices and relationships, attributing to the narcissistic personality a primary life task of "reunion":

> For the person with a narcissistic personality, then, the essential task is that of maintaining and restoring the self-esteem which accompanies the reunion of a grandiose self-representation with an omnipotent object representation. The manner in which these four personality types go about this task is what I call the mode of narcissistic repair – "repair" because their narcissism is so vulnerable that keeping it in repair is a lifetime project [p. 292].

According to Bursten, ridding the self of shame is the lifelong goal of the narcissistic personality, which he classified into the four types: *craving, paranoid, manipulative,* and *phallic.* Dealing with shame is central for the latter three; the craving personality, closely aligned with the borderline syndrome, seems too preoccupied with the danger of fragmentation to deal with shame.[6] Bursten then elaborated on the importance of shame to the paranoid, manipulative, and phallic narcissistic

---

[5]Bursten was in agreement, then, with Broucek's (1972) and with my own position that shame is the central painful affect underlying narcissism, and that the challenge to the narcissistic patient of dealing effectively with shame represents a central narcissistic quandary.

[6]Here, too, I agree with Bursten. Even though shame may be an early, archaic experience, I will suggest later that the experience of shame necessitates a modicum of self-cohesion. When concerns of fragmentation predominate, rather than those of depletion and absence of ideals, patients do not have the luxury to register shame (see chapter 5). This view differs from that of Fisher (1985) and N. Morrison (1987).

personality types, and on the mechanism that each utilizes to deal with
shame as part of attempts at narcissistic repair.

For the paranoid personality, for example, ridding the self of its
shameful self-concept becomes a central goal and a means to gain the
sought-after reunion with the idealized object. Such a person turns "I do
not love him (or her)" and "I am not shameful" into "He (or she) is
shameful," through externalization and projection leading to contempt
for the now scorned "other." Thus, the paranoid personality is
cleansed, and becomes worthy of reunion with the omnipotent other,
through projection of the shameful self onto yet another person.[7]
Bursten then quoted a patient who said, "'I can't drop my contempt
for you. . . . If I do, I'll feel humiliated with my little penis. I'll just be a
shitty little boy.' The danger of loving me made him feel weak,
homosexual and shitty—truly a cripple. It was this shit which he
expelled by projecting (throwing) it onto others" (p. 295).

Similarly, the manipulative personality attempts to "put something over" on someone else, leading to contempt and devaluation
when the deception works. As with the paranoid personality, this
represents "a purging of a shameful, worthless self-image and its
projection onto the victim" (p. 295), leading to the exhilaration of
feeling worthy of the fantasied reunion ("glorified and powerful"). The
phallic narcissist, on the other hand, displays his sense of shame
through identification with a father who is perceived as weak. Thus,
"the shame of being weak is repaired by arrogance, self-glorification,
aggressive competitiveness and pseudo-masculinity" (p. 295). Phallic
narcissists deny their fear of the shame of castration through the
fantasy of having a powerful phallus.

Bursten then considered the value systems of narcissistic personalities, each attempting to deal with the shame and humiliation of
feeling weak and inferior. The particular form of shame and lowered
self-esteem for each narcissistic personality type reflects specific internalized parental values, which in turn determines the specific quality of
the ego ideal and introject for the fantasized reunion.

So, Bursten defined narcissism in terms of a goal of reunion with
the idealized, omnipotent parent, for which the experienced self must
be worthy. While he did not emphasize the role of the ego ideal,
Bursten was clearly among those authors who thought that ideal to
reflect attributes of the fantasized, introjected parents. Thus, his view is
similar to that of the ego psychologists and to that of Chasseguet-

---

[7]I will suggest later that this mechanism, delineated by Bursten (1973), is more usefully
understood as the *projective identification* of shame, turning it into *contempt* for another.

Smirgel (1985), although she located the ideal earlier, in primary narcissism, where the undifferentiated self serves as its own ideal. For Bursten, the major narcissistic impediment to achieving reunion was shame, and the mode of repair for the various delineated narcissistic character types lay in the method selected to deny and eliminate shame. Implicitly, this goal necessitated changing or molding the self to make it acceptable to the idealized object, thus removing the source of shame which "gnaws" at the self.

For each of Bursten's character types, shame is the major affective ingredient of narcissistic vulnerability. Bursten's typology of narcissistic disorders differed from that of Broucek, in that each category combined a particular vulnerability with a mode of repair, rather than distinguishing between those that manifestly express narcissistic grandiosity and those which express underlying narcissistic vulnerability.

Bursten's approach to narcissism expressed that question common to all narcissistic problems, considered at the beginning of this chapter: is narcissism (and grandiosity) to be viewed as a primary *expression* of the state of the self, or is it best understood as a *defense* against particular self-vulnerabilities? Bursten viewed the various expressions of narcissism as *defensive* against the specific nature of self-vulnerability pertinent to each character type, and against the perceived failures and defects that seem to impede the longed-for reunion with the fantasied ideal. For him, shame was the major element preventing such reunion, and thus it had to be eliminated.

Chasseguet-Smirgel

Another writer who explicated the fantasy of narcissistic merger and shame was Chasseguet-Smirgel (1985), who considered the ego ideal from the perspective of the "malady of the ideal." She differentiated the ego ideal from the superego, positing an ongoing dialectic between the instinctual ego and the narcissistic self. She accepted Freud's suggestion that the ego ideal is heir to primary narcissism, as the superego is heir to the Oedipus complex, and thus embedded her understanding of the ego ideal within a context of narcissism. According to Chasseguet-Smirgel, the ego ideal is born of an attempt to regain the lost, infantile sense of primary narcissism, when the infant took itself to be its own ideal. "There was no unsatisfaction, no desire, no loss . . . an example of perfect, unending contentment" (p. 5).

This blissful state ends abruptly and inevitably, with recognition of self-object difference and the simultaneous realization of the self's dependence on the (imperfect) object.

The violent end to which the primary state of fusion is brought by this helplessness obliges the infant to recognize the "not-me." This seems to be the crucial moment when the narcissistic omnipotence that he is forced to give up is projected onto the object, the infant's first ego ideal, a narcissistic omnipotence from which he is henceforth divided by a gulf that he will spend the rest of his life trying to bridge [p. 6].

Again, she stated, "He is involved in a constant quest for that part of his narcissism that was wrested from him at the time of the primary loss of fusion" (p. 7). Thus, the self invests the ego ideal in the idealized, omnipotent object, leading to a lifelong quest for fantasied fusion with that object.

This perspective is very similar to that of Bursten. It illuminates the narcissistic task of seeking reunion with the idealized, powerful object, in whom original narcissistic perfection has been placed (through projection, or, more accurately, through projective identification). Such a goal is seen in the fantasied merger with the archaic, preoedipal mother, and, later, in the boy's resolution of his Oedipus complex through identification with the powerful father. The ego ideal, then, "represents a link-concept between absolute narcissism and object relatedness, between the pleasure principle and the reality principle, because it is itself a product of the severance of the ego from the object" (p. 28).[8]

Chasseguet-Smirgel also believed that the search for fusion with the ideal is always regressive, leading to dependence on the object for self-esteem and a related sense of passivity and shame.

Where does shame fit in this interesting perspective on narcissism? Since narcissism is seen by Chasseguet-Smirgel as linked to the object through the ego ideal, loss of the object's love is a primary source of narcissistic injury, experienced as shame. (This view of shame as a reflection of a sense of unlovableness is similar to that posited by Wurmser, 1981, and Thrane, 1979.) Implicitly, loss of love by the idealized object renders totally futile the fantasy of ultimate merger and reunion, because of the self's assumed unworthiness.

Chasseguet-Smirgel linked exhibitionism with abrupt disappointment in the expectation of homosexual admiration. She saw this as a path leading to narcissistic injury. Shame results from that disappointment in attaining anticipated narcissistic satisfaction from peers (the

---

[8]This conceptualization of the ego ideal (as a link between narcissism and object relatedness) is similar to my own view of the creation of the idealized selfobject as a primitive object representation through projective identification of the ideal self (see chapter 5).

"homosexual double"), who fail to recognize or admire the self. She related this exhibitionism to homosexual longings, blushing, anal exposure, and the resultant need to hide (to disguise these unaccepted longings). This formulation is well exemplified by Bursten's (1973) clinical vignette of the "shitty little boy" cited earlier. Chasseguet-Smirgel suggested that the power of shame and humiliation may be so great as to lead to suicide.[9] "The person who is ashamed is said to be unable to look others in the face, to be unable to face up to them, the hidden anus being now written on his face. One 'dies of shame'; and to claim that ridicule cannot kill is but a denial" (p. 203).

The searing shame that leads to suicide is, then, the true root of *mortification* and, according to Chasseguet-Smirgel, can lead as well to fantasies of murdering those in whose presence one has experienced humiliation.

Chasseguet Smirgel considered the quest for the lost ideal, and the attempt at fusion with it, to be the major source of human misery. Consequently, the ego ideal represented to her that structure which comes into being at the point of the infant's first recognition of separateness from the object and is then relocated in the fantasied object; fusion with this ideal becomes the lifelong quest of individual existence. Born of primary narcissism, the ego ideal is the link between the self (absolute narcissism) and the object, and thus represents the relationship between narcissistic and structural/libidinal themes. The compelling attempt at fantasied union with the ideal expresses human struggle, unhappiness, and, presumably, isolation. In addition, this narcissistic quest is always seen as regressive, for Chasseguet-Smirgel, a longing to regain the ideal state of fusion that also leads to shame, a "feeling about a feeling." In this schema, shame is not only about unworthiness, but also about "regressive longings," and about dependency. I will consider the relationship of shame to other feelings (especially need) in subsequent clinical material.

The major cause of shame, in Chasseguet-Smirgel's view, is fear of loss of love by the idealized (and fantasied) object. However, this loss of love derives from two principal sources: (1) conflicted and unacceptable libidinal longings, particularly homosexual and anal-erotic exhibitionism. With regard to these longings, she harkened back to Freud and other early psychoanalytic theorists about the libidinal source of shame; (2) self-accusation about the *regressive* and *dependent* nature of these libidinal wishes, which would make the self unworthy of the

---

[9]This point is also made by Kohut (see chapter 5), and will be elaborated in the Epilogue.

yearned-for fusion with the fantasied object, leading to the object's lack of approval and to resultant blushing and humiliation. Thus, her notion of the ego ideal and shame was also grounded in the response of the social surround. Chasseguet-Smirgel, like many others whom I have considered, also integrated narcissistic themes with those of structural/libidinal and object relational perspectives. The nature of regressive narcissistic, as well as prohibited libidinal, wishes brings intense shame at recognition of the (flawed) self's unacceptability.

Lest I give the impression that shame's relation to narcissism is essentially *external*, signifying humiliation in the eyes of the omnipotent object, I want to underscore that shame – failure to meet the standards of the ego ideal – often reflects failure to achieve *internalized* values and goals (the shape of the ideal self, as elaborated by Joffe and Sandler (1967). Wurmser (1981) pointed out:

> Not only is much of what we are ashamed of or protect with shame internal, even pertaining to the nucleus of the self – hence by definition "narcissistic" – but also the "eye" to which such aspects of the self are exposed may be internal. In German the common expression, *Ich schame mich vor mir selbst* ("I am ashamed in front of myself") captures this important and frequent experience very well [p. 49].

 Wurmser wrote of the narcissistic quality of shame: ". . . self-images of a wished-for, admirable, even overvalued quality or, on the contrary, to degraded and despised self-images. In other words, inherent in shame is a 'measuring' of the image of the self as it is against the image as it ought to be" (p.70). This view of the internal nature of shame implies a degree of self-cohesion, ego strength, and objective self-awareness adequate to allow for reflection on shame-as-affect and to enable internalization of the ideal against which the actual self can be measured (see Morrison, 1987). The capacity to experience shame might even serve as one fundamental marker of self-other differentiation and objective self-awareness (Broucek, 1982).

THE CENTRAL ROLE OF SHAME IN NARCISSISTIC PHENOMENA

From this review, what can we surmise about the relationship of shame to narcissism? The authors cited demonstrate, I believe, that shame earns its place at the center of narcissistic experience. This assertion about narcissism will be considered further in the next chapter as I discuss Kohut's understanding of narcissistic development and the place of shame in self pathology.

Kinston (1980) suggested two major pathological forms – self-narcissism and object-narcissism. While Kinston did not pursue the role of the ego ideal, his view of self-narcissism included the presence of negative self-images, which we might consider to be equivalent to failure regarding the ego ideal, or to discordance between the shapes of the actual and ideal selves (Sandler et al.,1963). Kinston's view of object-narcissism eliminated the separation of self from object, and even the need for the distinct object. This view of narcissism is inconsistent with the suggestion of a narcissistic longing for fusion with the idealized object (Bursten, 1973; Chasseguet-Smirgel, 1985) and is more congruent with a notion of haughty aloofness and self-sufficiency (for example, Modell, 1975). However, self-narcissism reflects pain experienced at separateness, at identity representation, which is perceived as countering the parental demand for symbiosis. As I understand Kinston, shame occurs when one abandons identity and autonomy in favor of acquiescence to environmental expectations. Neither reunion fantasies nor the ego ideal – internalized or object-related – play a major role in Kinston's schema. His notion of narcissism seems quite distinct from the others we have considered.

Kinston's view of shame and narcissism does, however, underscore the paradox inherent in our consideration of narcissistic phenomena. Does narcissism reflect the self's attempt at identity formation, separateness, and autonomy (with resultant dangers of pathological grandiosity – the "egotistical" narcissist of Broucek), or does it refer to the self's quest for perfection and worthiness for merger with an idealized other (recipient of the projected ego ideal – Broucek's (1982) "dissociative" narcissist)? Failure to attain either goal – autonomous identity or worthiness for merger – will lead to shame and humiliation (see Thrane, 1979). This paradox constitutes the narcissistic quandary and can be resolved only by a state of "good enough" autonomy and identity (for example, approximation of the shape of the ideal self) to merit fantasied fusion with the idealized parent/other.

Spero's (1984) view of shame as a reflection of unclear ego boundaries and intrusive, incomplete, and devaluing introjects leading to weak self-delineation seems closer to a concept of narcissism representing unrealizable yearnings for fantasied merger with an idealized, omnipotent object. Shame, then, would reflect the self's perceived unworthiness for fantasied, metaphorical merger with the idealized object because of these negative introjects. However, Spero's viewpoint does not specifically explicate the nature of idealization or the yearning for reunion with the idealized object.

THE DIALECTIC OF NARCISSISM

While this chapter's review of the relationship between shame and narcissism makes a strong case, I believe, for the intricate intertwining of these two themes of human existence, it has raised many questions about the nature of this relationship. First, it is important to consider various perspectives on narcissism and their relationship to libidinal and object-relational elements (Morrison, 1986a). Can narcissism be considered alone, in the "primary" sense that Freud (1914) suggested, or must it always be seen in the context of drives and objects, whether from the vantage point of voyeurism/exhibitionism, mother-child interaction, audience, or internalized object representations? Perhaps, with recognition of the self's separateness from its surround comes a change in the nature of narcissism and an inevitable dependence on the object world, both internal and external. If so, the self must always be experienced in the context of its object matrix. Kohut, alone, has questioned the inevitable reliance of self on object, through his view of a developmental line for narcissism separate from object love. Paradoxically, Kohut (1984) also suggested that the self is never truly independent of, or separate from its need for the functional relationship with selfobjects, and its embeddedness in the matrix of selfobject relationships. I will consider the implications of this view in chapter 5.

What, then, is the true aim of narcissistic needs? Some (for example, Bursten, 1973; Chasseguet-Smirgel, 1985) have argued that reunion, merger with the fantasy of the idealized object, is the ultimate goal of the self; others (for example, Rothstein, 1979) have suggested that its real aims are autonomy, identity, uniqueness, competence, and perfection. On the other hand, are these two aims truly antithetical, or might they be understood as complementary—each present, in an alternating, figure-ground relationship to each other? I have found it useful to conceptualize this relationship metaphorically as a *dialectic.* With this approach, we can reconsider one of the early, guiding themes—the apparently frequent *alternation* of narcissism and shame between external (object-related) and internal (ideals and defenses surrounding autonomy and independence) factors, each informed and fueled by the fantasy of perfection and omnipotence (Reich, 1960).

While shame seems intimately related to narcissistic elements, the nature of this relationship is not so clear. Some (Bursten, 1973; Reich, 1960) maintain that shame functions ultimately to remind the self of its failure to meet perfectionistic demands for worthiness to attain fantasied merger with its ideal, variously conceptualized as the ego ideal (Chasseguet-Smirgel, 1985) or the shape of the ideal self (Sandler et al., 1963). This unworthiness has been described alternately as defect, libidinal conflict, perversion, failure, or inferiority, depending on the theoretical orientation of the author. Shame has also been viewed as a response to the wish for merger itself—object dependence, selfobject need, regressive yearnings for closeness, and so on. From this latter viewpoint, the goal of the self *is* autonomy, separateness, and independence, and any suggestion that it falls short, through object need, generates shame. "To need," itself, is frequently experienced as shameful. The metaphor of a dialectic seems apt to describe the relationship between these two sources of shame.

Our first guiding theme from chapter 1 questioned whether shame is to be viewed as a *defense* (or signal) that warns the self of unacceptable drives or drive derivatives (for example, exhibitionism, merger wishes, homoerotic feelings, oedipal competition, anal eroticism), or as an *affective experience* that informs the self of its own inadequacy to attain the goals of such drive derivatives. I believe that shame does indeed often serve defensive narcissistic functions, but that, even as defense, it is experienced principally as affect. Thus, our dialectic recurs with regard to meaning—defense or affective self-state—and so underscores a narcissistic focus at a given moment. Similarly, is there a pull toward attachment (including merger, reunion) with an idealized object or its representation (the ego ideal), and, if so, might shame sometimes represent a defensive reaction against that drive itself? Alternatively, shame may reflect the self's failure of worthiness to achieve the longed-for reunion. These, then, are manifestations of an ongoing, dynamic dialectic that illuminates now conflictual elements, now reflections on the state of the self. This dialectical tension signifies, I believe, the nature of the shame-narcissism relationship touched on in our earlier guiding themes: that between guilt (action) and shame, as elucidated in Piers's (1953) guilt-shame cycle, that between passive longings and action, and that between shame and contempt (see chapters 7 and 8).

Finally, what of the dialectical relationship itself between shame and narcissism? Most authors (for example, Bursten, 1973; Lewis, 1971) have suggested a tautology: narcissistic needs or drives, however defined, lead ultimately to a sense of imperfection about the self's worthiness to attain its yearnings. Shame, then, can be viewed as an inevitable feeling about the self for its narcissistic imperfection, for failure, for being flawed. Others (Broucek, 1982; Kinston, 1983; Morrison, 1984) contend that the relationship is the reverse: that the self's experience of shame is so painful that the narcissistic constructions of perfection, grandiosity, superiority, and self-sufficiency are generated to eliminate and deny shame itself.

I suggest that both of these positions are correct—that there is an ongoing, tension-generating *dialectic* between narcissistic grandiosity and desire for perfection, and the archaic sense of self as flawed, inadequate, and inferior following realization of separateness from, and dependence on, objects. Similarly, a metaphorical dialectic exists between the wish for absolute autonomy and uniqueness and the wish for perfect merger and reunion with the projected fantasy of the ideal. Thus, shame and narcissism inform each other, as the self is experienced, first, alone, separate, and small, and, again, grandiosely, striving to be perfect and reunited with its ideal. Uniqueness and specialness may be imagined in terms of total autonomy and independence, or worthiness for merger with the fantasied ideal. The narcissistic dialectic may also be formulated with regard to those tensions occurring within the self—intrasystemic *conflicts* regarding autonomy or merger—about the best means to attain uniqueness.

I shall turn now to a different perspective on narcissism and its relation to shame, in the work of Kohut and his followers in the evolution of self psychology.

5

Shame and Self Psychology

Kohut's Contributions

In chapter 4 I discussed the relationship of shame to narcissism, arguing that shame is a central dysphoric affect of narcissistic phenomena. Following a review of the major role played by the ego ideal and its related manifestations, as articulated by several psychoanalytic authors, I focused on shame with regard to failure and the ideal. Thus, the self's failure to approximate its "ideal shape" as contrasted with the representation of the "actual self" (Sandler et al., 1963) leads to the sense of self-defect and shortcoming that is central to the experience of shame. This sense of defect represents either feelings of unworthiness for merger with the ideal or feelings of dependence and lack of autonomy, resulting in the *need/longing* for merger itself.

In this chapter, I will focus on the work of Kohut and self psychology, in an attempt to locate the place of shame in Kohut's system. I will suggest areas where I think Kohut's system was incomplete and also will suggest ways in which a more detailed understanding of shame and its manifestations might broaden the framework of self psychology. Kohut classified psychopathology in the categories of Guilty Man (dominated by intrapsychic conflict) and Tragic Man (where self-defects and lack of self-cohesion predominate).

Inasmuch as guilt is the dysphoric affect of Guilty Man, I suggest that shame must be considered a central affective experience of Tragic Man.

SHAME IN KOHUT'S EARLY WRITINGS

Kohut's emphasis on the self (and, after 1977, on its "supraordinate" role) is central to his theories and provides a basis for the further understanding of shame. As Kohut (1977) readily admitted, his definitions of self were relatively meager: "a center of productive initiative – the exhilarating experience that I am producing the work, that I have produced it" (p. 18).

Thus, the self as a center of initiative was experienced subjectively, linked to the "exhilarating experience" of action. However, in that work he went no further in attempting to define the self. He stated at the end. "My investigation contains hundreds of pages dealing with the psychology of the self – yet it never assigns an inflexible meaning to the term self, it never explains how the essence of the self should be defined" (p. 310).

He offered a narrow definition of the self as a "specific structure in the mental apparatus" (p. 310) and a broader one, as "the center of the individual's psychological universe" (p. 311). It is in the latter sense, as the center of the subjective, experience-near attributes of individual identity, that "self" assumed its supraordinate status in Kohut's thinking.

In his posthumous book, Kohut (1984) added only that the self is the product of psychic structure, which is laid down via optimal frustration and transmuting internalization. Thus, it

> allows us to speak of the attributes of the self in general terms, without specifying whether we have in mind its cohesion, its strength, or its harmony, [including] . . . such diverse and defining attributes of the self as those given by our abiding experience of being a center of initiative, of being a recipient of impressions, of having cohesion in space and continuity in time [p. 99].

Kohut thus offered a view of the self's structural defects and shortcomings. It is out of one of these – self-depletion – that an understanding of shame emerges. However, before discussing shame and self-depletion, I will briefly review and discuss the self-psychological perspective from which a consideration of shame may proceed.

Issues Relevant to Shame

The *bipolar self* is a central construct in Kohut's framework, encompassing much of what preceded it in the evolution of self psychology. The bipolar self refers to two chances at establishing a healthy, cohesive self.[1]

> The two chances relate, in gross approximation, to the establishment of the child's cohesive grandiose-exhibitionistic self (via his relation to the empathically responding merging-mirroring-approving selfobject), on the one hand, and to the establishment of the child's cohesive idealized parent-imago (via his relation to the empathically responding selfobject parent who permits and indeed enjoys the child's idealization of him and merger with him), on the other [Kohut, 1977, p. 185].

Thus, the first opportunity for development of self-cohesion arises early, usually with the mother; it results from adequately responsive empathic mirroring of the exhibitionistic grandiose self, which Kohut had earlier named the "narcissistic self." The second chance comes later, usually with the father, and requires empathic acceptance of the child's "voyeuristic" idealization and wish for merger. Kohut posited a tension arc, an "action-promoting condition" (p. 190), which integrates *ambitions* (reflecting adequate mirroring by the early selfobject) and goals and *ideals* (derived later in relationship to the empathic, idealized selfobject). Thus, the notion of the bipolar self suggests two opportunities for the development of a cohesive, unfragmented nuclear self; if the mirroring selfobject fails, some of the damage in self-structure may be corrected by the responsive presence of the empathic, idealized selfobject later on. Kohut believed that these two functions do not progress in strictly linear fashion, but interact during self-development.

Clearly, an understanding of the concept of the selfobject is crucial for understanding Kohut; it has been well elaborated in all of Kohut's writings since 1966 and has been amplified in contributions to the further development of self psychology (for example, Tolpin, 1978; Wolf, 1980). For the present purpose, I will emphasize only that the selfobject, experienced subjectively as an extension of the self, provides those functions necessary for the development of the healthy, vigorous self, in contrast with the configurational, differentiated qual-

---

[1] In his last work, Kohut (1984) elevated the twinship (alter ego) selfobject to a place defining a third pole of the self.

ities of the libidinal object. Stolorow (1986) distinguished these qualities as alternating, figure-ground dimensions of the object. It should be
noted that the distinction between selfobject and libidinal object forms
the basis for the thesis of separate developmental lines between narcissism and object love.

With regard to the bipolar self, Kohut (1971) argued against
viewing the grandiose self as more primitive than the idealized
parental imago. He suggested that doing so reflected a prejudice that
assigns object love supremacy over narcissism. Rather, he stated, the
grandiose self and idealized parental imago represent parallel (rather
than linearly progressive) forms of narcissistic development. However, Kohut did imply that the idealizing selfobject transference – which
reflects a movement outward in an object-seeking direction – constitutes a developmental step beyond investments in the grandiose self.
For instance, "the therapeutic mobilization of the grandiose self may
thus arise either directly (*primary mirror transference*), or as a temporary
retreat from an idealizing transference (reactive remobilization of the
grandiose self)" (p. 133, italics added). Or, "an initial period of
idealization, followed by a secondary mirror transference, repeated a
sequence of events in his childhood (the brief attempt at idealization
which was followed by a *return* to the hypercathexis of the grandiose
self" (p. 140, italics added).

Despite Kohut's admonition against considering a linear, sequen-
tial development of selfobjects, he had implied earlier (through his use
of "retreat" and "return") a developmental progression of narcissism
from (1) investment in the grandiose self, to (2) movement outward,
in an object-seeking direction, toward investment in the idealized
parental imago, to (3) firming of the idealized parental imago and
its internalization (with the formation of psychic structure) through
idealization of the superego and resultant establishment of ideals
(for example, the ego ideal). I believe that this developmental sequence
is important in locating the place of shame in the context of self
psychology. Certainly, grandiosity/exhibitionism and idealization/
voyeurism do coexist in patients with self pathology and may, as
Kohut indicated, be jointly represented by primitive or more mature
forms. I suggest, however, that the developmental sequence just outlined represents an observable maturational tendency that allows us to
move beyond Kohut's explanation of shame as based solely on overwhelming grandiosity (to be elaborated later). Kohut's explanation,
moreover, implies an object-seeking (attachment) direction in the development of the self – a notion that potentially links his view of
narcissistic development with the quest for object ties. I suggest that the

idealized parental imago, as a developmentally more differentiated selfobject form than the mirroring selfobject, is created in part through projective identification of the grandiose (ideal) self into the external object. This view may provide yet another bridge between selfobject functions regarding self-cohesion and the self's developing participation in creating and connecting with its available supply of objects.

Kohut (1966) recognized early the relationship of shame to the frustration of the narcissistic self's exhibitionistic demands. Working within the framework of classical metapsychology at that time, he discussed shame in relationship to the ego ideal. He saw the ego ideal as "related to drive control," while the narcissistic self is the source of ambition, the wish "to be looked at and admired" (pp. 435–436). He went on to state, "Shame, on the other hand, arises when the ego is unable to provide a proper discharge for the exhibitionistic demands of the narcissistic self" (p. 441).

The shame-prone person is ambitious and success driven, responding to all failures (in the pursuit of moral perfection or external success) with shame. Thus, shame results when the ego is overwhelmed by the grandiosity of the narcissistic self, experienced, apparently, as failure. The ego ideal functions to protect the self from narcissistic vulnerability and shame by "controlling" the expression of exhibitionistic "drives."

Later, however, Kohut rejected the thesis of Piers (1953) and, as described in chapter 4, of Jacobson (1954, 1964,) Sandler et al. (1963), Bursten (1973), and Chasseguet-Smirgel (1985), among others, that shame is "a reaction of an ego that has failed to fulfill the (perhaps unrealistic) demands and expectations of a strong ego ideal" (Kohut, 1971, p. 181*n*). Rather, he stated again, the shame of narcissistic patients "is due to a flooding of the ego with unneutralized exhibitionism and not to a relative ego weakness vis-à-vis an overly strong system of ideals" (p. 181*n*).

Here Kohut was suggesting that the shame of such patients reflects the power and drive of their grandiose ambitions. Progress in the analysis of shame-prone patients is achieved through a shift in narcissistic investment from the grandiose self to the idealized parental imago and ultimately to the superego through its progressive idealization (p. 175). This shift occurs in the context of the analyst's acceptance and confirmation of the patient's grandiose self. In this manner, archaic grandiosity and "shame-provoking exhibitionism" become transformed into self-esteem and pleasure in success.

In 1972, Kohut mentioned the relationship of shame to exhibitionistic libido and defective body parts, suicide and disturbance in "libidinal cathexis" of the self, defect in the "omnipotent grandiose self," and the response of insatiable rage to narcissistic injuries. He stated:

> The most intense experiences of shame and the most violent forms of narcissistic rage arise in those individuals for whom a sense of absolute control in an archaic environment is indispensable because the maintenance of self-esteem – and indeed of the self – depends on the unconditional availability of the approving-mirroring functions of an admiring selfobject or on the ever-present opportunity for a merger with an idealized one [p. 386].

Here Kohut clearly related shame to narcissistic rage, to the suicides resulting from empty depression, and to the need for an unconditionally responsive selfobject. Thus, *selfobject failure* – to admire or to empathize – may also lead to shame as well as to unbridled grandiosity. However, Kohut's basic position with regard to the ego ideal remained unaltered: shame had to do with omnipotent grandiosity (and the uncontrollable/unresponsive selfobject) that threatens the integrity of the ego or the self. He (Kohut, 1971) related shame to what he called disavowed grandiosity and the "vertical split," not to failure and the ego ideal.

The Ego Ideal

Why did Kohut abandon the function of the ego ideal in controlling the exhibitionistic drive components and thus in preventing shame? Certainly, there was an evolution in Kohut's thinking away from the role of drives and drive derivatives, culminating in the abandonment of drives (Kohut, 1977). Thus, the need for the ego ideal as a drive-controlling structure became irrelevant after that time. But I think an earlier factor determined his movement away from the ego ideal; that is, the theoretical embedment of the ego ideal in a conceptualization of object relations (see Chasseguet-Smirgel, 1985.). In chapters 2 and 3, I attempted to show that the ego ideal represented the repository for internalized, idealized representations of parental objects (and their functions) in the establishment of individual identity and the self. Thus, the ego ideal represented the embodiment of the idealized object, the objective "beacon" toward which the ego aspired, the "rescue operation" for primary narcissism with resultant yearning for merger with that object. Kohut did not write about the ideal self, which we have considered to be the self-representation of the ideal (and which I shall discuss in terms of the self's grandiosity projected outward in creation of the idealized selfobject).

As Kohut delineated the separate lines of narcissistic and object development, he moved progressively away from the role of the configurational (that is, libidinal) object in favor of narcissism, the self, and the function of the selfobject. His approach assumed that object love had been granted too much emphasis in psychoanalytic theory. In fact, Kohut (1966) dismissed the contributions of object relations theory in psychoanalysis as lying "on the psychological surface that can easily be translated into behavioral terms," referring to these as "social psychology" (in Morrison, 1986b, p. 62). It is no surprise, therefore, that, with his rejection of object relations theory as superficial and embedded in a value system emphasizing object love and altruism over narcissistic phenomena, he would progressively dismiss the relationship of the ego ideal (and its connection to libidinal objects) to shame.

THE RESTORATION OF THE SELF

At this point a brief discussion of the evolution of Kohut's thinking may be helpful in preparing the groundwork for the application of self psychology to our study of shame. By 1977, Kohut, in his elucidation of self deficits, had abandoned the drive-conflict elements of Freud's structural theory. He posited at best a parallel development of conflictual/structural elements and of the self, with the self assuming a supraordinate position in relation to psychic structures. The major danger to the vulnerable self was "disintegration" (loss of cohesion), with "disintegration anxiety" signaling impending threat to cohesiveness. Kohut (1977) included within disintegration anxiety fears of "fragmentation, serious enfeeblement, or uncontrollable rage" (p. 138). And "the core of disintegration anxiety is the anticipation of the breakup of the self" (p. 104).

Kohut did not explicitly differentiate fragmentation from enfeeblement/depletion as elements in self disintegration. However, in differentiating castration anxiety from disintegration anxiety, he described the latter in terms of conflict between "the needs of a defective self vs. the avoidance of the mortification of being re-exposed to the narcissistic injuries of childhood" (p. 137). He stated that the narcissistic personality disorder "responds to the loss of the selfobject with simple enfeeblement, various regressions, and fragmentations" (p. 137). On the basis of the developmental schema proposed for the bipolar self, I suggest that fragmentation is the more archaic manifestation of self disintegration, reflecting primitive, prestructural failure of the mirroring selfobject to affirm and accept the self's grandiosity. By contrast,

I believe that depletion/enfeeblement anxiety represents failure of the idealized selfobject to satisfy the self's idealizing/merger needs for omnipotence and tension regulation. Depletion/enfeeblement anxiety reflects threatened absence of the early, longed-for configurational object – the idealized selfobject[2] – leading to feelings of emptiness, depression, and shame.

Kohut (1977) described fragmentation vividly as "the dread of the loss of his self – the fragmentation of and the estrangement from his body and mind in space, the breakup of the sense of his continuity in time" (p. 105). Tolpin (1978) acknowledged the distinction between fragmentation and depletion anxiety (that is, depression): "Thus the term [disintegration anxiety] refers not only to the fear of fragmentation of the self; it also refers to the fear of impending loss of its vitality and to the fear of psychological depletion" (p. 175).

Following our earlier consideration of the ego ideal and of the quest for worthiness and merger with the fantasied, idealized object, it is worth noting the similarity of this concept to that of Kohut's idealized selfobject. "Omnipotence," "merger," and "tension regulation" are all elements relevant as well to the ego ideal of Bursten (1973) and Chasseguet-Smirgel (1985). Kohut's emphasis is, of course, on the function rather than structure of the ideal. However, when seen as merger and reunion, rather than solely as an agent for drive control, as discussed by Kohut, the ego ideal closely resembles the idealized selfobject we are here examining.

Fragmentation is a primitive state reflecting the threat of psychosis. It is typical of the borderline conditions, which, Kohut claimed, are not amenable to psychoanalysis and which do not, usually, lead to shame.[3] Depletion anxiety implies the presence, I believe, of a more cohesive and developmentally differentiated self-state than is the case in fragmentation, with a greater capacity for structuralization and selfobject idealization. In general, the depleted self represents a response to the absence of the sought after, omnipotent, idealized selfobject and its accompanying internalized ideals,[4] with consequent empty depression.

---

[2]The idealized selfobject is, I suggest, the first approximation of a differentiated configurational object existing separately in the external world. It represents, in part, the creation of an object by the self through projective identification of the ideal self.

[3]See Fisher (1985), and O'Leary and Wright (1988) for a different viewpoint regarding borderline pathology and shame.

[4]This distinction between fragmentation and depletion cannot be rigidly maintained, since fragmentation and depletion concerns usually coexist in states of disintegration anxiety. But the developmental direction of these two conditions can be clinically observed and substantiated.

How do self-deficits (fragmentation and depletion) develop out of unmet exhibitionistic and idealizing selfobject needs? According to Kohut (1977), defects are manifested both in the early development of the psychological structure of the self and in secondary structures related to the primary defect – the so-called defensive and compensatory structures. A defensive structure covers over the self's primary defect, whereas the compensatory structure strives to make up for the defect. Thus, the compensatory structure attempts to counterbalance a weakness in one pole of the self (usually in the area of exhibitionism and ambitions) by increasing self-esteem through the pursuit of ideals. Pseudovitality in a narcissistic patient may be an attempt to hide "low self-esteem and depression – a deep sense of uncared-for worthlessness and rejection, an incessant hunger for response, a yearning for reassurance" (Kohut, 1977, p. 5).[5]

Kohut connected the primary structural defect in the nuclear self to genetic failure of the mother as a selfobject to mirror the child's healthy, age appropriate exhibitionism. Defects in the self's compensatory structures, on the other hand, frequently reflect failure of the father as selfobject to respond to the child's needs for idealizations. Consistent with the developmental sequence I have proposed, the first pole in self-formation (ambitions and the nuclear self) becomes established early; the second pole (ideals and compensatory structures), relatively later in development. This view of compensatory structures corresponds with my view of self-depletion as a developmentally later experience than fragmentation. Depletion, I suggest, reflects most prominently failures in compensatory structures of a self in the process of attaining tenuous cohesion, seeking to make up for its enfeeblement through merger with an idealized selfobject. In his discussion of the case of Mr. M, Kohut (1977) affirmed this view of a relationship between the "genetically later" failure of compensatory structures and "the father's selfobject function as an idealized image" (p. 7). The absence of ideals and goals as a result of failure of compensatory structures is, then, a major source of self-depletion.

From the perspective of self psychology, the process of psychoanalytic treatment involves either repair of the self's nuclear defect through repeated transmuting internalizations (utilizing connection with the mostly empathic analyst as a responsive selfobject) or through modification of compensatory structures by establishing more flexible

---

[5]This description by Kohut of a narcissistic personality disorder fits well with the psychodynamics of manic-depressive illness (as noted as well by Freud; see chapters 2 and 11).

and realistic ambitions, goals, and ideals. Modification of grandiose ambitions and/or the ideal of perfection may eventuate through identification with the accepting empathic selfobject/analyst, with important consequences for the palliation of shame.

Summary

According to Kohut, self pathology and disintegration anxiety reflect inadequacies in the structure of the parents' selves that have deprived the child of empathic mirroring or idealizing needs. On the basis of the developmental model presented earlier, I suggest that fragmentation signifies defects of the nuclear self resulting from insufficient mirroring and affirmation of age-appropriate exhibitionistic needs. Self-depletion, by contrast, represents problems with compensatory structures proceeding from deficiencies in the response to idealizing needs and to voyeuristic, object-oriented yearnings for merger with the selfobject's power and its tension-regulating functions. Reparation through psychoanalysis occurs when the analyst provides a context of empathic mirroring and allows for optimal idealization. Adequate nuclear self structure can be built anew, or adequate compensatory structure increased, through exploration and interpretation of the experienced empathic microfailures of the analyst, allowing for the transmuting internalization and structure building required to strengthen the patient's self.

THE ROLE OF SHAME IN THE RESTORATION OF THE SELF

Kohut (1977), in discussing the "guiltless despair of those who in late middle age discover that the basic patterns of their self as laid down in their nuclear ambitions and ideals have not been realized" (p. 238), spoke of a time

> of utter hopelessness for some, of utter lethargy, of that depression without guilt and self-directed aggression, which overtakes those who feel that they have failed and cannot remedy the failure in the time and with the energies still at their disposal. The suicides of this period are not the expression of a punitive superego, but a remedial act—the wish to wipe out the *unbearable sense of mortification and nameless shame* imposed by the ultimate *recognition of a failure* of all-encompassing magnitude [p. 241; italics added].

Kohut's reference here to "nameless shame" is one of the few references to shame in *The Restoration of the Self.* But throughout there is expression of feelings closely related to shame: mortification (p. 137, p. 224), disturbed self-acceptance (p. 94). and dejection (p. 97, p. 224). These allusions occur repeatedly in discussion of the self's "defeat" in the realization of its goals. For example:

> Theories of drives and defenses fail to do justice to the experiences that relate to the crucially important task of building and maintaining a cohesive nuclear self (with the correlated joy of achieving this goal and the correlated *nameless mortification* of not achieving it) and, secondarily, to the experiences that relate to the crucially important striving of the nuclear self, once it is laid down, to express its basic patterns (with the correlated triumph and *dejection* at having succeeded or failed in this end) [p. 224, italics added].

It is interesting that in these two passages, Kohut uses the word "nameless" to modify shame and mortification, as though the plaguing quality of shame were so painful as to defy articulation.

Although Kohut used the word shame explicitly only in the first quotation, the language of shame permeates his 1977 work in describing the experience of narcissism and the self. For instance, the feelings correlated with the defeat described in the second quotation can be conceptualized appropriately in terms of shame–the shame, mortification, dejection of the self at having failed to achieve its ambitions and ideals. The patient suffers from "disturbed self-acceptance" because he is ashamed at not having realized the "basic patterns" of the self. No other single word adequately captures the sense of self-evaluation and performance. Only "guilt" has the same self-referential quality, but clearly guilt is very different from the sense of self-defeat in failed pursuit of the self's goals. The idea of "nameless shame" suffuses Kohut's thinking, and this shame indeed involves more than overwhelming grandiosity.

Is the experience of shame possible for the patient with fragmentation anxiety (the more primitive narcissistic or borderline personality disorder) as well as for the patient with depletion anxiety (the less severe narcissistic personality disorder)? As indicated earlier, I believe that a certain level of self-cohesion is necessary in order for one to experience shame, whether in response to overwhelming grandiosity, unresponsive selfobjects, or failure to attain ideals. Kohut (1977) stated:

> I suggest that we first subdivide the disturbances of the self into two groups of vastly different significance; the *primary* and the *secondary* (or

reactive) disturbances. The latter constitute the acute and chronic reactions of a consolidated, firmly established self to the viscissitudes of the experiences of life, whether in childhood, adolescence, maturity, or senescence. The entire gamut of emotions reflecting the states of the self in victory and defeat belongs here, including the self's secondary reactions (rage, despondency, hope) to the restrictions imposed on it by the symptoms and inhibitions of the psychoneuroses and of the primary disorders of the self [p. 191].

I believe that shame deserves a prominent place in the list of the self's secondary reactions and that, as Kohut's language suggests – "acute and chronic reactions of a consolidated, firmly established self" – the experience of shame requires a certain degree of self-cohesion to register inadequate selfobject responsiveness, failure to attain a goal, rampant grandiosity, or disappointment in ideals or bodily functions. A self that is fragmenting does not have the energy or luxury to reflect on shame but rather is overwhelmed with panic and boundary diffusion.[6] Shame as a "secondary reaction" of the self may be a response to the failure of a compensatory self structure or even to the failures of the selfobject to respond to the idealizations of a healthy, cohesive self. A characteristic example of a compensatory structure offered by Kohut is the enhancement of self-esteem through the pursuit of ideals. Kohut's view appears to be too limited when he maintains that shame reflects only the breakthrough of unneutralized grandiosity and not failure to meet the goals and expectations of the ego ideal, or the more fluid and "experience-near" *shape of the ideal self*, as I prefer to view it. Using Kohut's language, I believe that shame can also be experienced because of failure in relationship to the idealized parental imago.

I suspect that Kohut rejected the connection between shame and the ego ideal because he viewed shame as a manifestation of narcissism and its vicissitudes, and the ego ideal as a metapsychological construct reflecting internalization of the libidinized object. Thus, Kohut rejected the ego ideal because of its relevance to control of the (now discarded) drives, as well as to object relations theory. Since the self's quest for merger with the idealized parental imago is clearly an aspect of narcissistic development, however, I suggest that shame over failure in the compensatory (or healthy) pursuit of ideals (as over any failure with regard to the idealized selfobject) is potentially as devastating as is the

---

[6]I have a similar problem with Spero's (1984) "weak self-boundary" explanation of shame from an object relations point of view.

shame from overwhelming grandiosity. In fact, failure of the parental selfobject to respond to the self's idealizing needs and quest for merger is a prominent source of shame vulnerability and a model for subsequent shame over the self's experience of its needs. Reflecting the developmental sequence from grandiosity to idealization, shame experienced in relation to the idealized parental imago tends to be less archaic and more differentiated than that experienced as a result of overwhelming grandiosity.[7]

Failure to attain an ideal or goal serves, then, as a major precipitant of shame, with the concomitant threat of rejection or abandonment by the "significant object" (Levin, 1967, 1971). Of course, the threat of abandonment may also reflect an earlier experience of failed mirroring of the self's healthy exhibitionistic strivings by the parental selfobject. Failure of the mirroring selfobject may then lead to a compensatory pursuit of ideals aimed at reversing the experience of selfobject disinterest and apathy. However, further failures in empathic responsiveness by the idealized selfobject to the self's quest for merger will, in turn, lead to a sense of emptiness, depletion, and despair.

What is the relationship between the idealized parental imago and the ideal self? In 1971, Kohut identified the idealized parental imago as a waystation in the evolution of the self from grandiosity to internalization of the idealizing function, leading to formation of psychic structure through idealization of the superego. By 1977, he had dispensed with structural theory altogether in explaining the development of the self. Some representation of the idealizing function must, however, be maintained in the narcissistic transformations that accompany the development of self-cohesion. I believe that as idealizing selfobject functions are relinquished during the establishment of a firmly cohesive self, they are internalized, but not necessarily in the form of an idealized superego. Rather, they become attached to the basically firm self in the process of attaining structuralization, and to its vigorous, esteemed, and valued qualities. This constellation of optimal, experience-near qualities and ideals forms the *ideal self*—the representation of the goal of perfection in the subjective experience of the self. The ideal self is thus an endpoint in the development of the cohesive and stable self—from grandiosity to idealization of the selfobject to final internalization of the "self as it aspires to be": cohesive, indepen-

---

[7]This perspective on the relationship of shame to failure with regard to the idealized selfobject represents a Kohutian counterpart to the view of failure in the worthiness of the self to attain merger with its ideal, discussed in chapter 4 and noted as the "malady of the ideal" by Chasseguet-Smirgel (1985).

dent, vigorous, and embodying values and ideals.[8]

It is again important to note that Kohut believed shame to be the result only of overwhelming, unmirrored grandiosity and selfobject unresponsiveness—a reflection of his emphasis on the self and self-selfobject matrix over its objects. In shifting attention to the ideal self and the ideal parental imago, I have proposed the role of "transmuting internalization" of functions from the idealized selfobject into the self. However, we have seen that the idealized selfobject does not represent a simple linear development. The self, in attaining cohesion (that is, in response to adequate mirroring and idealization), plays a part in the simultaneous creation of the idealized parental imago during the process of nurturing selfobject responsiveness. This process may occur, as I have noted elsewhere (Morrison, 1986a, 1987), through integration of empathically mirrored infantile grandiosity and perfection into the ideal self and its projective identification into the idealized selfobject. Thus, the relationship between the ideal self and the idealized selfobject may reflect an oscillation between reciprocal mechanisms of structuralization and projective identification, "borrowing" from, and creating, or "filling" the container.[9]

Earlier I indicated that depletion anxiety (absence of ideals) reflects a self-pathology less severe than fragmentation anxiety, is the result of failure of the more or less cohesive self, and can thus be a secondary reaction to failure of the compensated self to attain an ideal. Such ideals may even include the striving self's wish to gain the admiration or mirroring of a responsive selfobject. Shame, then, may also represent a secondary reaction to the failure of the self to obtain mirroring responsiveness of the selfobject, as is the case in overwhelming unmirrored grandiosity.[10] Rather, such grandiosity cannot be too overwhelming, as in states of fragmentation, since, as I have argued, the experience of shame requires a certain degree of self-cohesion. But whether it reflects the subjective experience of frustrated grandiose ambitions, failed attempts to compensate for unrealized ambitions, or unmet yearnings to attain ideals, shame is the hallmark

---

[8]Certainly, this viewpoint is similar to those of Schafer and Sandler et al. (chapter 2) with regard to the ideal self, but it emphasizes the attachment of ideal selfobject functions to the self, rather than internalization of the loving parental objects.

[9]This metaphor can readily be viewed as a representation, within the Kohutian framework, of an ego-psychological language for the "rescue operation" provided by the ego ideal for primary narcissism, as discussed in chapter 2.

[10]After all, grandiosity itself may at times represent failure and defect of the shape of the ideal self.

of the defeated self in a state of depletion, the self that has fallen short of its goals.

If shame reflects self-depletion rather than fragmentation, what is the relationship between shame and depression? I have already considered Kohut's view of the guiltless despair that results from the self's failure to realize its ambitions and ideals. This "guiltless despair" is characteristic of self-depletion in mid-life depression over failure to attain the goals of the nuclear self. In a discussion very closely related to Kohut's views, Bibring (1953) implied that depression results from the failure to attain ambitions and ideals. Although he did not explicitly discuss shame, Bibring came close to my conceptualization when he stated, ". . . the depression sets in whenever the fear of being inferior or defective seems to come true, whenever and in whatever way the person comes to feel that all effort was in vain, that he is definitely doomed to be a 'failure' " (p. 25). And, "In depression, the ego is shocked into passivity not because there is a conflict regarding the goals, but because of its incapacity to live up to the undisputed narcissistic aspirations" (p. 30).

Thus, both Kohut and Bibring suggest that there is a close relationship between shame and depression and that, for some patients, particularly those suffering from narcissistic personality disorders, the relationship of depression to the failure to attain ambitions and ideals may be most compelling. But, clearly, all people, including the relatively healthy (those with a firmly cohesive nuclear self), suffer at times from feelings of shame (especially, as Lewis, 1971, has noted, people who are relatively field dependent). Shame in healthy people can also be understood, from a self-psychological perspective, in terms of *micro*failures in meeting the aspirations of the relatively cohesive and differentiated ideal self. To put it another way, the ideal self is a construct relevant to self-cohesion (or neurotic character structure) as well as to more primitive, archaic self states. At issue here are the *intensity* and *magnitude* of the failure in the affirmation of ambitions and the development of attainable ideals. When viewed from the perspective of the self in the broader sense, it is clear that failures to attain aspirations of the ideal self need not necessarily reflect severe psychopathology.

PSYCHOTHERAPEUTIC TREATMENT OF SHAME

Though shame is frequently accompanied by depression, too often only the depression is treated in analytical psychotherapy (see chapters

7 and 8). Therapeutic attention to shame may also be missing in work with manifestations of narcissistic rage. In essence, narcissistic patients have difficulty in achieving even a modicum of self-acceptance and in believing that anyone else could possibly accept them, because of their sense of emptiness and failure to attain their own self-appointed, grandiose life tasks. This lack of acceptance by self and other is, I suggest, a central narcissistic quandary, related to the deeply felt shame of the narcissistic patient, and should be a target in their treatment.

Protracted empathic immersion in the feeling state of any patient, but particularly the narcissistic patient, as recommended by Kohut, will usually unveil deep and painful shame feelings. These may be difficult to detect because of the many defenses intended to cover over shame experiences, and the grandiosity, defects, failures, conflicts, and emptiness that engender them. But their discovery, examination, and working through by the patient, and the ultimate realization that therapist and patient alike can accept them, represent a major curative factor in every successful treatment. In achieving this goal, therapists should be helped and guided by recognition, through vicarious intro-spection, of their own personal failure to achieve goals and to realize ambitions and ideals, of personal grandiosity and failures. In short, therapists must be willing to face and acknowledge their own shame and the pain that accompanies it.

Many (for example, Curtis, 1984; Friedman, 1980; Stein, 1979) have suggested that the tenets of self psychology can be integrated within the theoretical framework of classical psychoanalytic theory. But our earlier review suggests that structural, drive-defense theory alone cannot fully encompass the importance of the affective experi-ence of shame, particularly for the narcissistic patient. In chapter 10, I shall explore the role of intrapsychic, oedipal conflict in generating shame. Here, I suggest that, unlike guilt, which can be well explained in terms of the conflicting vectors of traditional theory, shame as an affective experience can best be appreciated as a reflection of passive failure, defect, or depletion. Whereas guilt motivates the patient to confess, shame motivates one to conceal. For this reason, shame has been less richly considered in the psychoanalytic literature and less frequently dealt with in psychoanalytic therapy. For guilt, the antidote is *forgiveness*; for shame, it is the healing response of *acceptance* of the self, despite its weakness, defects, and failures. The selfobject/therapist must strive to facilitate self-acceptance through his own protracted empathic immersion in the patient's psychological depths. Modifica-tion of grandiose ambitions and the ideal of perfection may then eventuate through understanding, and through identification with the accepting, empathic therapist.

Further psychotherapeutic approaches to the treatment of shame will be considered in Section 2 of this book.

DISCUSSION

In this chapter, I have attempted to apply a self-psychological perspective to our theoretical understanding of shame and have suggested some therapeutic implications evolving from that perspective. Along the way, I have questioned some of Kohut's assumptions and have tried to broaden self-psychological theory through application of our view on shame.

Earlier, we considered shame in relation to the *ego ideal* and failure regarding the ideal, *primitive object relations*, and *narcissism*. Implicit in the assessment of these issues was the continuing limitation of classical theory to encompass fully and capture the dimensions of shame. Ultimately, we came to an understanding of shame in relation to failed aspirations and ideals, plaguing and unsatisfactory early object relationships, and narcissistic manifestations with shame at their core.

Kohut's approach to the understanding of narcissistic phenomena offers a supraordinate place for the self and a line of self (narcissistic) development separate from that of object love. Because shame is so centrally about the self and its narcissistic aspirations, we looked to self psychology to broaden our understanding of shame. Kohut's emphasis on empathic immersion in self-experience, and his elaboration of the selfobject function and the effect of selfobject failure in meeting the self's needs to attain cohesion and vigor, opened the way to a fuller appreciation of shame.

Adopting Kohut's vantage point, I have suggested that shame is a secondary reaction of the self, frequently a response to the failure of a self "compensatory structure." This translates to mean that shame reflects primarily the *depleted* self, having failed to receive responsiveness from the *idealized* selfobject. Such a self lacks realizable ideals and is burdened by excessive and unattainable ideals and goals. As Kohut wrote, shame is also a response to overwhelming grandiosity, but I believe that it reflects primarily a selfobject failure to meet the age-appropriate *needs* of the self, particularly those of the self striving to achieve vigor through attainment of its ideals. As a result of early, repetitive selfobject failure, particularly with regard to idealization, the self reexperiences shame in the presence of need itself. In other words, when one is unable to attain alone the ideal of power or self-soothing and looks instead to another (the idealized selfobject) to provide such functions, one frequently feels shame at the self's passivity, weakness, and need. This is particularly true because of American culture's high valuation of the ideal of independence and autonomy.[11] Shame occurs in the face of repeated selfobject failures to meet such needs, especially, but not exclusively, in the realm of ideals.

This framing of shame within the context of self-selfobject relatedness complicates our earlier discussion of shame as an internal, private experience. It introduces the inevitable need and quest for selfobject attunement and empathy – the selfobject function – to foster a subjective sense of well-being. The shame experience is likely to occur when the selfobject is unavailable or when a rupture in selfobject relatedness occurs, forcing us to face the shortcomings of a flawed self to meet its own perfectionistic expectations and ideals.

Stolorow and Lachmann (1984–85) have offered a useful conceptualization of the selfobject transference, from which to consider shame and selfobject failure. They suggest that the selfobject dimension of a human relationship is always required, functioning sometimes silently in the background when the "object relations" (configurational) dimension is paramount. Thus, there may be a moment-to-moment fluctuation in prominence between selfobject and object relational dimensions (in a figure-ground sense) within a given therapeutic session. I suggest that shame occurs during the periods of absences or rupture of the selfobject dimension, even when it has been operating silently in the background. A temporary rupture in the selfobject bond will invariably bring this dimension of relationship into figured, forefront focus; such a rupture leading to shame is reminiscent of Tomkins's (1962–63) perspective (chapter 4). I doubt that desire or wishes toward the configurational object (the classical "oedipal" or Stolorow and Lachmann's object relations dimensions) often generates shame.

Rupture in self-selfobject relatedness characteristically leads to impaired regulation of affect and tension, a sense of affect flooding, resulting in a momentary experience of disequilibrium and loss of self-cohesion (Socarides and Stolorow, 1984–85). This abrupt loss of harmony may generate shame (Tomkins, 1987) because of the renewed, desperate need for selfobject relatedness. Resolution of the

---

[11]See Kohut (1984), by contrast, for a discussion of the need for a matrix of mature selfobjects throughout life and the "myth" of complete independence.

self-selfobject impasse will often restore the sense of self-cohesion, homeostasis and self-acceptance, resulting in the abatement of shame.

We have seen that Kohut (interestingly, like Freud) dispensed with the notion of the ego ideal, its role in controlling the drives having become irrelevant as he minimized the place of drives and libidinal objects in relation to the self and because it too closely approached an object relations view of human development. I suggested, however, that the concept of an ideal self comes closer to the self-psychological viewpoint, allowing for failure with regard to the shape of the ideal self as an explanatory context for shame in relation to the ideal. In addition, projective identification of the ideal self, based on structuralization of initial grandiosity and perfection, allows for the self's participation in the creation of the idealized parental imago (the idealized selfobject).

Emending Kohut's theory, I have suggested a sequence by which the need for the idealized selfobject tends to dominate later in development than does the need for mirroring. Thus, the lack of adequate mirroring leads, customarily, to fragmentation, primary self-pathology, and the lack of self-cohesion; the need for the idealized parental imago arises later, and selfobject failure with regard to idealization results in secondary depletion and enfeeblement of the more or less cohesive self. The relationship of depletion anxiety to depression and shame was considered.

In conclusion, I want to emphasize that while distinctions between the mirroring and idealized selfobject functions cannot be made too sharply, the *need* for the selfobject itself leads to shame as well as to rage and despair, especially when the environment continually fails to provide the selfobject's satisfying functions. We have, however, noted that this selfobject need and hunger may itself come to represent a falling short of the imposed ideal of self-sufficiency.

PART II

CLINICAL APPLICATIONS

6

The Case of Mr. Dowland

With this chapter, we move from our theoretical consideration of shame to its clinical applications. We will consider the case of Mr. Dowland, a man whose treatment illustrates many of the issues that arise in the psychotherapy of shame. The way that shame pervades Mr. Dowland's life is not unusual. His case does, however, typify how I work therapeutically with shame.

Mr. Dowland, a well-dressed man in his early 40s, was a successful administrator of a local arts program when he first came for treatment, having recently relocated from another city where he had done similar work. He viewed his current move as a "step upward" in his career, although he missed the excitement of his former home and his homosexual lover, who still lived there. His homosexual yearnings and indiscriminate activities, despite a committed attachment to his lover, had worried him, especially provoking concern that his homosexuality might be discovered by co-workers, or that he might be physically harmed by the dangerous environment in which he had placed himself before the move. An acquaintance had recently been accosted while "cruising" and had been severely beaten by a group of local toughs, and the attack had frightened the patient. In addition, he was feeling depressed and was worried that he would not be able to meet the demands of his new job. He expressed no interest in changing his homosexual orientation but wondered about his wish to form new homosexual contacts and his lack of satisfaction with his stable relationship. He had undertaken psychotherapy previously, when he had made strides in assuming professional responsibility and in achieving self-esteem at work. In addition to dealing with vocational issues, he had worked on the oedipal components of his homosexuality, self-esteem, and his relationship with his male lover.

His parents had divorced when he was seven years old, an only child, and he had grown up with his mother. His parents had married late in life, but both were still living. Mr. Dowland, however, maintained only limited contact with them. He had always felt strange, unmanly, and insecure compared with his playmates. He especially felt "freakish" in the eyes of his father, who, he felt, always wanted him to be different from what he was. He recalled his father's wanting to play baseball with him – an activity that the patient disliked and that emphasized his own sense of incompetence and difference from his father and peers. He remembered an incident when his father had taken him to visit relatives and had told him to walk tall and not to wave his hands around. After introducing his son to his relatives, his father had looked at him with scorn, turned away, and moved into another room. Both parents had eventually remarried, and he believed that his stepfather felt the same contempt for him as had his father.

He attended a local college, dated women, and had meaningful sexual relationships with several women before acknowledging to himself his homosexual preference. He remembered feeling exhilarated and amazed that women could be attracted to him, despite his feeling of freakishness. In the meantime, he was becoming an accomplished musician and went on to graduate school, selecting arts administration for a career. Further differentiating himself from his parents, he developed a keen and committed set of aesthetic values and ideals.

As he began treatment with me, he was very shy, embarrassed, and reluctant to describe his current lifestyle and feelings. He was acutely aware of shifts in my attention and was concerned that I would be scornful of his homosexual preference and fantasies. Early in treatment, he described pleasure and gratification from previous episodes of "cruising" when a handsome man would choose to spend time with him and seemed satisfied and excited at the patient's appearance and sexual performance. "It is as if those contacts would momentarily make me feel good about myself, as if I were really desirable and attractive, worthwhile," he said. He also described a dream, in which "a big, tough man – you know, with a striped shirt and handlebar moustache—kicked sand at me and beat me up. I felt so puny." I commented on the "Charles Atlas, and 98-lb. weakling" quality of the dream, and, while mindful of the reversal of his aggressive and hostile impulses (turning active into passive) implicit in his own role in the dream, I picked up on the shame and humiliation manifest in the dream's images: "It seems to symbolize how much you felt the weak, contemptible 'sissy' around your father and stepfather."

Similarly, I underscored Mr. Dowland's pleasure and temporary restoration of self-esteem during his satisfactory, though transitory, homosexual contacts. Then I commented on the deep sense of self-hatred and shame that must have dominated his feelings about himself for him to have so needed, and to have felt so gratified by, these fleeting contacts: "For a brief period, you could forget that you felt that you were so freakish, so unlovable and unattractive." The patient responded, "That's right! I felt all right, attractive, if someone so attractive himself could want to be with me. For that time, I felt important, on top of the world."

I had acknowledged Mr. Dowland's deep sense of shame and self-loathing and the restorative quality of his anonymous homosexual activity. By so doing, I had attempted to convey my *acceptance* of these feelings—that they could be identified, named, and examined by both of us. In turn, he felt grateful and understood and told me that his shame, which had been so much a part of his inner life, had not been much discussed in his previous therapeutic work. Thus we had the basis for an energetic therapeutic bond and commitment to work on his negative feelings about himself and initiated, as well, an idealizing transference that carried Mr. Dowland into the early stages of his treatment.

Consistent with my acknowledgment of Mr. Dowland's shame sensitivity, subtle variations in the transference and keen attunement to shifts in my attention formed the cornerstone of his treatment. He moved easily between feelings of gratitude, hurt, and annoyance toward me, to memories of related childhood experiences with his parents. For instance, at one point he felt that I was being critical of his ambivalence toward his lover, and he associated to memories of criticism from his mother about his insensitivity toward her and his friends. Similarly, he frequently expressed the belief that I secretly wanted him to give up his homosexual commitment, which brought up a desire to please me and to submit to my imagined heterosexual designs on him. This feeling was reminiscent of his perception of his father's wish for him to be a "real man," and evoked transference feelings that we examined extensively. At other times, when he felt

deeply understood by me, his gratitude led to an outpouring of relieved
affection and tears, "Like when [his girlfriend] had appreciated my love
of Beethoven. It was unlike anything I had experienced before."

As Mr. Dowland continued to work on his shame and low self-
esteem, he began to feel progressively surer and more positive about
himself. Whereas, he had spoken in a soft, hesitant voice at the
beginning of therapy, averting his eyes, his voice began to gain in
self-assurance, and he presented himself more assertively. He expressed
delight that he seemed acceptable to me, and I proceeded to examine
the basis of his feelings of unacceptability. While he seemed to derive
strength from this assumption of acceptability, I spoke with him about
the childhood sources of his self-doubts and "freakish" self-image. On
one occasion, he faced me and declared, with genuine excitement, "I'm
all right! I'm really all right." We also considered the phallic-oedipal and
castration implications of his shame, (his puniness, his lack of power
compared with his father), but they were not a major theme at this
early stage of therapy.

As Mr. Dowland's shame feelings receded in the context of an
accepting, idealizing transference, so did his fantasies of anonymous
homosexual contacts and the intensity of his need for constant affirmation of his attractiveness. At the same time, with his growing
self-confidence, swelling grandiosity began to emerge in his work
relationships as well as in the transference. He expressed growing
dissatisfaction with the agency for which he worked, considering it to
be "small-time" and perhaps unworthy of his abilities. On the other
hand, he expressed rage and fury at being overlooked by the agency
director, who, he felt, had ignored his suggestions for resolving a
particularly challenging problem. He felt superior to the "petty hacks"
who were his bosses at the agency, confirming his view that "this city
is provincial." Alternately, he felt insignificant and "small" – rekindling
his sense of himself as small and shameful in the eyes of his father and
in relationship to his "powerful" boss.

He also longed to be my "special" patient, to be considered by me
as significant and important. At one point, I commented on this
"fantasy of being special to me," and Mr. Dowland took umbrage at
the use of the term "fantasy." He revealed that, at this stage of his life
(several years into therapy), he found it difficult to accept the idea that
his specialness might be just a fantasy, and much therapeutic work

centered on his rage and difficulty in contemplating giving up this
grandiose expectation. At the same time, there was a growing competitiveness with me, alternating with much genuine affection. The
idealizations began to diminish as he noted my "mistakes" in interpre

tations, "sloppiness" in dress, and my tendency toward "paunchiness." (Mr. Dowland himself was lean and was usually tastefully and impeccably dressed). He would now frequently attempt to beat me to the right interpretation but then would recognize his own competitiveness and would occasionally beg forgiveness. We examined his discomfort over competitive feelings toward me, as he related this to his father's scorn and withdrawal when he expressed any competition. Thus, these competitive themes could now be interpreted in terms of their genetic oedipal roots, with extensive examination of feelings of superiority toward, and anger at, his father for the way he had been treated as a boy. This work led, eventually, to a modicum of forgiveness and acceptance of his father and of his limitations, as well as to exploration of the feelings of disillusionment that began to enter the transference.

With work on his competitiveness and grandiosity, one other theme emerged, which related to Mr. Dowland's deep sense of shame. As he experienced less shame about himself, and as he allowed himself to experience moments of superiority and competitiveness toward powerful rivals, feelings of contempt began to emerge for these figures. His boss became, at times, a "pompous, silly fool" who was incompetent and ignorant. Perhaps his therapist was not so terrific after all — "Why, even without medical school, I could have made a better connection than that." These occasional outbursts alternated with concerns about his own competence and creative talent. At such times, I attempted to uncover Mr. Dowland's own shame and feelings of inadequacy and to indicate how these were then attributed to his "rivals" in his contemptuous dismissal of them as he attempted to rid himself of shame (see chapters 7 and 8).

In the later stages of therapy, as Mr. Dowland felt progressively empowered and "all right," an awareness of subtly emerging heterosexual feelings came to light. The genetic roots of his homosexuality in his attachment to, and identification with, an intrusive, critical mother were explored, as were his anger and hurt toward his distant, scornful father. However, from the perspective of our interest in shame, I want to emphasize his continued expectation that I would have preferred for him a heterosexual object choice, and his own resultant wish to "please" me. In addition, some of the social advantages of heterosexuality — feelings that "real" men prefer women and the growing yearning to experience parenthood — emerged. Along with these thoughts of relationships with women came guilt feelings toward his male lover. These were considered in the context of his growing self-acceptance and the resolution of his shame and grandiosity, I noted, "It seems that, as you feel more all right about yourself, more self-confident and less ashamed, you need less the affirmation of being desirable to a handsome man. With that come feelings that you might want to be with a woman and that this might be preferable to you. Of course, we know that this change would create complications for you."

Mr. Dowland greeted his heterosexual feelings with some curiosity, as well as with considerable anxiety, as he moved back and forth between wishes to explore the possibility of heterosexual relations and to leave "well enough alone" and end treatment with the gains he had made. At this point, he received an appealing professional offer in another city and decided to accept it. After considerable work on his decision to leave and, hence, to terminate, he left with the recognition that he might in fact be fleeing the tension of rethinking his homosexuality, but with the commitment as well to continue to explore his feelings on his own and to seek further psychotherapy if necessary. In the meantime, he appreciated the changes in his feelings, stressing his newly found self-confidence and self-acceptance and expressing fondness for, and gratitude toward, me for the work we had done together.

DISCUSSION

Diagnostically, Mr. Dowland fits well into the category of narcissistic personality disorder, with neurotic traits and defenses (obsessive-compulsive defenses; histrionic characteristics) and few qualities suggesting borderline or more primitive narcissistic (craving, or strongly paranoid) pathology. While he was clearly capable of meaningful and sustained friendships, it is significant that his libidinal object orientation was homosexual. Whether or not one considers this preference itself to represent psychopathology, we can here consider the nature of his homosexual attachments in the light of his shame sensitivity. His object relationships were quite good; he suffered no self-other boundary diffusion. From an object relations perspective, on the other hand, he did seem to have internalized negative, hostile, part-object representations.

From our theoretical framework about shame, Mr. Dowland and his treatment may be understood in terms of his creation, and the consequent nature of, his particular ego ideal and the evolving shape of his ideal self. If his history is to be taken literally—as I believe, in outline, it should be—he seems to have introjected hostile part-objects of a humiliating, shame- provoking father and a controlling, critical mother. Thus, from early childhood he found himself "wanting" in terms of the internalized ideals provided by his parents and their values. He felt himself lacking, deficient, inferior, with regard to the "shape of self" expected by them, particularly his father. I believe that Mr. Dowland's basic ego "firmness," his core self-cohesion, reflected the fact that he had received basically adequate mothering as an infant. These distinctions will be elaborated later.

Thus, from a structural point of view, Mr. Dowland's ego was firm, yet his superego reflected great shame sensitivity. His early concerns were primarily about the adequacy of his ideal self, the gap between his "real self" and his ego ideal, rather than about transgressions against others.[1] From this perspective, I believe that Mr. Dowland's experience reflected essentially a negative oedipal orientation in which his primary goal was to establish, and search for, an idealized, accepting paternal ego ideal, from whom he could gain sustenance and self-affirmation. At times, he attempted to deal with shame through the grandiosity that emerged following primary therapeutic attention to his low self-esteem and feelings of worthlessness. Since his father had rejected or disappointed his idealizing needs, he continually searched for an idealizable father in his bosses, homosexual partners, and male therapists. Gradual disillusionment with these figures in the course of therapy constituted a significant element of treatment.

It is worth reiterating that Mr. Dowland's personality demonstrated few of the primitive, archaic elements suggested by Jacobson (1964) in her description of the shame-prone personality, although his self-esteem and the quality of his object relations, did reflect the wide narcissistic fluctuations indicated by Reich (1960). Mr. Dowland's work was essentially competent and creative; his work relationships and friendships suffered the normal, expectable oscillations of a productive member of society; and his self was basically firm and cohesive. It was in the more microscopic elements of his object relationships, and within the transference, that his profound narcissistic needs and vulnerability to shame emerged.

How did Mr. Dowland's susceptibility to narcissism and shame, and his deeply rooted sense of freakishness, develop? It seems likely that there was, for one thing, a constitutional "lack of fit" between his basic nature and the expectations of his father. His natural longings for

---

[1]Not that guilt was absent. He clearly had much hostility toward his parents, manifest in transference anger, his rejection of women, and elements of his homosexual orientation. This anger, as well as libidinal feelings toward his mother, generated guilt and a partial passive retreat from oedipal issues and guilt to homosexuality and secondary, reactive shame (see chapter 4 and Levin, 1967, 1971, 1982) but this was not the fundamental dynamic of Mr. Dowland's shame.

affirmation from his father were not met. From his mother came greater acceptance, but also intrusiveness and control which alienated him from her as well. In addition, his parents had early marital conflicts leading to separation – a breach that Mr. Dowland desperately sought to prevent. He recalled longing to intervene, to prevent the breakup of his parents' marriage; success, he had hoped, would be achieved through exertion of his endless power. Failure to accomplish this reconciliation must only have added to his shame.

Mr. Dowland remained with his mother, thus achieving a spurious oedipal victory, given his fear of her intrusiveness and his negative oedipal longings (which, of course, led not only to guilt, but to shame over ultimate oedipal failure and insignificance). He recalled, also, that his father had blamed him for his loyalty to his mother. The father's withdrawing from the patient had made subsequent contact infrequent and difficult. Thus, the narcissistic injury and vulnerability of the father was passed on to the son – an equation made by Kohut (1977; see chapter 5). In this way, the patient came to feel even less acceptable to his father; he viewed himself as his father's betrayer, with consequent guilt and further experiences of shame.

Examination of Mr. Dowland's development, then, makes understandable his extreme shame sensitivity and its interrelationship with his narcissism. It is not surprising that these themes were played out in his earlier, fleeting homosexual encounters, offering momentary release from his deep-seated shame through affirmation of his attractiveness and of his underlying grandiosity. Because I seemed to understand and accept these feelings, and interpreted much of Mr. Dowland's experience in relation to them, he felt understood and grateful, developing an idealizing (selfobject) transference and a commitment to work further on these feelings.

Vicissitudes within the transference formed the basis for much of the subsequent therapeutic work. Interpretation of his external, social experiences and his relationship with his lover in terms of early memories of his parents were inferred from these vicissitudes. As his shame feelings became understandable and more acceptable to him, Mr. Dowland moved on to other manifestations of his narcissism – his grandiosity, his rage, his defensive contempt for me and for others – and ultimately to some work on his homosexuality and to the "bothersome" possibility of heterosexual attachments. He was able to integrate his disappointments in me, to accept my imperfections and – through identification, his own – and thus to allow for the possibility of mortal limitations. From our perspective on narcissism and the ego ideal, his treatment can be viewed as a loosening of ego ideal mandates or a strengthening of its loving and accepting functions. I think that this treatment essentially *was* work on the ego ideal, or on a more flexible sense of the shape of the ideal self. Of course, other elements were also crucial in this man's treatment – oedipal conflict, libidinal investments, guilt, other self needs – but shame sensitivity and other narcissistic manifestations were truly at the center of his psychopathology.

Clearly, a self-psychological approach informed this psychotherapy. In fact, the patient's work concluded before full resolution of his homosexual attachments and complete integration of object-libidinal elements could be accomplished. Thus, many would consider Mr. Dowland's an incomplete course of psychotherapy. Alternatively, self psychologists might suggest that this was a "good enough" outcome, with a strengthening of compensatory self-structure, even though without full attention to Mr. Dowland's object choices and the developmental line leading inexorably to object love.

I have underplayed the role of self psychology in this consideration of Mr. Dowland's treatment, so as to illustrate that earlier and alternative theoretical approaches can allow for implicit attention to shame, particularly with regard to narcissism and the ego ideal. But let us now turn to an integration of Mr. Dowland's case from a self-psychological point of view, to see what that perspective might add.

MR. DOWLAND RECONSIDERED

Mr. Dowland's homosexuality was seen to be a central factor in his character structure. As his shame and grandiosity were altered through the course of psychotherapy, an opening presented itself toward heterosexual object choice, reflecting improvement in his self-esteem. As he felt genuinely better about himself, his need for self-affirmation accompanying his homosexual activities and fantasies diminished. From a self-psychological perspective, it seems likely that Mr. Dowland's homosexual contacts served as fleeting mirroring selfobjects, affirming his self-worth and providing self-cohesion through reflected grandiose strivings and exhibitionistic yearnings. As his therapist, I accepted the legitimacy of these transitory homosexual mirroring experiences. I explored and provided understanding in the treatment, which enabled him gradually to relinquish them.

Mr. Dowland gradually incorporated the mirroring experience provided by me as therapist/selfobject and formed what Kohut (1971) called transmuting internalizations and beginning structuralization of a sense of self-acceptability. During this phase of treatment, I felt unacknowledged and undifferentiated by him, generating (expectable) countertransference experiences in which I felt ignored and irrelevant as a delineated object. I was able to understand, manage, and accept these feelings without confronting him or demanding to be considered otherwise. Progressively, Mr. Dowland moved from a need for absolute mirroring to a second stage, in which his needs for an idealized selfobject came to the foreground. As I indicated in chapter 5, I believe that the movement from predominantly mirroring to predominantly idealizing selfobject transferences marks an important developmental step in the structuralization (cohesion) of the self, as well as in working through the patient's shame and humiliation. As Mr. Dowland felt acceptable to the therapist/selfobject, the disintegrating/ depleting shame abated, and he was able to progress to idealization. As the therapist provides exclusively mirroring functions in the first stage of treatment, he begins to assume **configurational** dimensions in the second, when, however, the idealizing function still predominates. Idealization builds on the successful attainment of adequate mirroring although, as we have seen in chapter 5, both tend to coexist.

It should be noted that the yearning for acceptability, a product of shame over self-attributed failure and defects, itself may generate shame. I have suggested (chapter 5) that shame may result from needs and yearnings that are in conflict with the culturally imposed ideals of self-sufficiency, autonomy, and independence, and thus may reflect an internal sense of deviance from such an ideal. This response to need is a source of shame different from that of the overwhelming grandiosity described by Kohut (1971) and, from a classical psychoanalytic viewpoint, represents intrapsychic conflict emanating from **within** psychic structures (that is, conflicts of ideals and needs within the ego, or "conflicts of divergence" [Kris, 1985]).

Genetically, Mr. Dowland's psychopathology can be understood to derive from the failure of his childhood environmental surround to provide adequately empathic selfobject functions. Yet the strength of his intellectual and occupational achievements, as well as the integrity of his friendships, must be explained. Apparently, as an infant he received sufficient maternal mirroring and empathy to establish a basically cohesive self. His difficulties seemed to arise as he expressed himself in a style different from his parents' expectations, as he leaned toward artistic expression and veered away from a traditionally masculine lifestyle. It seems that he got into major trouble in traversing the second pole of the bipolar self – idealization with regard to his father. This narcissistically vulnerable man was impatient and rejecting of his son's personality and his strong attachment to him, generating in the son deep shame and humiliation. These feelings added to a sense of complete rejection and powerlessness when his parents divorced. His father felt similarly abandoned and rejected by the son, retaliating by cutting off contact with him. Mr. Dowland felt at fault for this alienation, somehow responsible for not keeping his parents' marriage together, thus compounding his own sense of inferiority and shame. As a reflection of these deeply felt empathic failures, particularly on the part of his father, Mr. Dowland continued to develop considerable narcissistic vulnerability and shame sensitivity.

As the mirroring selfobject transference became established in therapy and Mr. Dowland became confident of my ability to accept and understand him, he moved toward an idealizing selfobject transference. Here I am suggesting that one form of idealized selfobject is built upon and emerges from the satisfaction of needs for attunement by the mirroring selfobject. He then described me in glowing terms – a master at my trade. But progressively, as well, he became sensitive to my lapses in attention and my imprecise interpretations, my empathic failures. When he felt that I neglected to pay full attention to him – failed, that is, as an optimally mirroring selfobject – he experienced shame and the resulting defenses of rage and contempt (see chapters 7 and 8). Thus, the idealized selfobject revealed flaws and shortcomings, failures in providing the reliably and dependably soothing, perfectly attuned idealizable functions the patient yearned for. Such failures left him vulnerable to shame as he recognized his wishes for merger with, and his disappointment in, my perfection. His shame was then projected into *me*, as he responded to me with contempt and disdain (chapters 7 and 8). Yet my "failures" and lack of attunement, which could be discussed and resolved in therapy, were small enough for him to maintain essential elements of his idealization and begin to incorporate into his own repertoire (through transmuting internalizations) the soothing and accepting functions that previously only *I* was able to provide.

Interestingly, as he gradually incorporated and accepted a view of me as similarly flawed – was able to acknowledge his disappointment in my limited perfection – he became more tolerant of his own imperfections, which led to further abatement of his shame. As the idealizing elements of his selfobject transference lessened, he became more accepting of me as I assumed more human and configurational qualities. The selfobject transference took on more of a *twinship* (alter ego) nature (Kohut, 1984) in which Mr. Dowland could better acknowledge our human similarities. At this point, for example, he and I conversed occasionally about our shared interest in music. It was during this period of treatment also that Mr. Dowland experienced enough self-esteem to begin to question his homosexual orientation and to entertain the possibility of heterosexual object love. Although he left therapy before working on this possibility, he did some effective work on his relationship with his homosexual lover.

From this self-psychological perspective on Mr. Dowland's treatment, the major interpretive focus occurred *within* the selfobject transference relationship. Through elaboration of his shame and humiliation, and interpretation of the selfobject failures that generated them (attention lags, assumptions about my condemnation of his homosexuality), his attention could be drawn to the early experiences with his parents that had first elicited shame. The selfobject relationship provided the functions for integrating these experiences into his self-structure and thus for progressive self-stabilization. I was initially important to him only insofar as I functioned as part of, or was under the control of, his self. Only later, through gradual and tolerable disillusionments, did I begin to take on configurational shared human qualities in interaction with him.

7

Some Shame-Related
Phenomena

I suggested earlier that several related feelings often reflect shame experiences, for example embarrassment, remorse, mortification, apathy, and lowered self-esteem. However, because of the intensity of its pain, shame, in the clinical encounter, may be concealed and hidden from oneself or the therapist. In this chapter, I will consider the special relationship that obtains between shame and several other phenomena that may conceal underlying shame, but that reflect shame's power to motivate behavior, shape feelings, and influence the nature of human interaction and relationships. These include *anger/rage, contempt, envy,* and *depression.* Finally, I will examine *humiliation,* a special form of shame that specifically reflects its interpersonal context. These same phenomena are considered in chapter 8 as *defenses* against shame; they may also *precipitate* shame in certain circumstances.

ANGER/RAGE

Elsewhere (Morrison, 1984b) I have suggested that shame bears a specific causal relationship to rage and to narcissistic vulnerability when considered from the perspective of self psychology: "Kohut

101

seems to view shame and rage in a complementary way, the former as a response to the self overwhelmed by unmirrored grandiosity (1971), the latter as a reaction to the self's lack of absolute control over an archaic environment (1972)" (p. 87). In chapter 5 of the present work, I suggested that shame is an affect central to "Tragic Man," the narcissistic personality of self-depletion, suffering the empty depression of unmirrored ambitions and unrealized ideals.

With regard to narcissistic rage, I believe that the self's "lack of absolute control over an archaic environment" usually reflects a lack of responsiveness of the selfobject environment to the self's needs, demands, and longings, causing the impression of lack of control. It is that failure of selfobject responsiveness which generates the rage response and releases a feeling of overwhelming, demanding grandiosity, often leading to shame. I suggested earlier (see chapter 4) that shame may result as well from a falling short of the desired shape of the ideal self. From any of these sources (grandiosity, unresponsiveness of the selfobject, or failure of the ideal self), the resulting shame may be intolerable and must be expunged through concealment, disavowal, or projection.

One commonly used means of expunging shame is through a massive expression of rage aimed at the "offending" object (either the unresponsive selfobject who fails to mirror or to accept idealization, the rejecting object of attachment, or the "uncooperating" environment).[1] In addition to expunging shame (reflecting a feeling of helplessness), the rage response also fosters an illusion of power and activity, thus seeming to reverse into activity the sense of passivity and helplessness that itself generates shame. Shame, then, may lead to rage in response to a felt unmet need from the selfobject environment—that is, an awareness of the self's passivity and helplessness to bring about environmental responsiveness and attunement to its own needs and wishes. Kohut (1972) argued that the self's lack of control over its environment was enough to explain rage in the narcissistically vulnerable person. I suggest that this viewpoint overlooks an important intermediate step, often rapidly wiped out of consciousness (or even "bypassed" as expressed by Lewis [1971]) in which the person observes his own internal experience of shame as his need/wish/demand is ignored, as he notes his own feeling of passivity and insignificance, his unmasked sense of unacceptable grandiosity or failure. Within this

---

[1]This rage response to shame has also been noted by Wurmser (1981), among others.

perspective, then, many examples of narcissistic rage reflect an attempt to rid the self of the experience of searing shame.

Clinical Vignettes

Mrs. Bingham

Mrs. Bingham, a petite, competent advertising executive in analysis to work on her low self-esteem and its impact on her work and her intimate relationships, began an hour by describing an incident that had just occurred. While she was driving to the hour and anticipating that she would barely arrive on time, a taxi driver was moving slowly in front of her. She could neither pass him nor influence him to drive more quickly. She began to lean on the horn, and, when finally she was able to pull up next to him, she "yelled obscenities at him, and finally gave him the finger! I was really out of control."

As she examined her response, she wondered first whether she had in fact been angry at me. When this possibility seemed to go nowhere, she acknowledged her fury that the taxi driver had been ignoring her needs and treating her as insignificant. From Kohut's (1972) perspective, her rage was a response to lack of control over the taxi driver; she wanted to "obliterate" him because of his noncompliance.

Treatment might have consisted of clarifying this feeling, accepting her frustration, and waiting for the ultimate analytic transformation of her narcissistic strivings and rage into appropriate assertiveness and aggression. However, her rageful response became clearer when I asked her about her use of the term "insignificant." Associations followed about her own "puniness," her "weak femininity," her observation that the taxi driver had been a "big, burly, stupid man." She, by contrast, had felt passive and helpless—a theme that had been discussed many times before—and she had felt "embarrassed and humiliated" (shame equivalents) by her own weakness and insignificance to him. Elaboration of her own shame feelings followed.

This vignette illustrates the place of (sometimes sudden) shame in eliciting many rage responses and the potential utility of analyzing the underlying shame in gaining a fuller understanding of rage. As with many of the other shame-related responses considered in this chapter, analysis of rage in treatment often stops at the manifest level, without further sensitivity to the underlying shame. I suggest that an exploration of the place of shame in many rage reactions can lead to a richer, more complete understanding of such trigger responses.

Ms. Leitman

The following example (see Morrison, 1984a), reveals the shame that frequently underlies transference rage. Mrs. Leitman had encountered me, with my wife and another couple whom she knew professionally, at a public performance. In her next analytic hour, she ranted and raged at me for "daring" to ignore her by spending my time with other people, especially those who, it emerged, had slighted her on another occasion. I hadn't attended solely to her; others in my life had commanded my attention. Clearly, my lack of attention illustrated her lack of control over her selfobject environment—an adequate explanation of the rage response as described by Kohut (1972). But as we continued to explore her response, it emerged that she had felt "invisible," "insignificant" to me, of no importance, and therefore vulnerable to humiliation and shame. This incident left her feeling "mortified" and worthless. She was confronted with her own feeling of insignificance, as well as her own need for constant confirmation of her importance by me, her analyst. This need, as well as her own sense of irrelevance, had filled her with shame, a feeling she had desperately sought to eliminate. Rage for Ms. Leitman was a reflexive way to rid herself of overwhelming shame.

Several points emerge from this example. First of all, shame was a pervasive internal experience for this narcissistically vulnerable young woman. On several occasions, she noted that "humiliation is the most painful feeling of all for me to bear" (see chapter 4). Second, since the transformation of shame into rage was a frequent occurrence for this patient, it was relatively simple to work back therapeutically from the rage to the underlying shame. It would have been technically incomplete to stay only with the rage, looking, for instance, at a sense of entitlement to undivided attention from her analyst or even at the feeling of lack of control over her environment—without penetrating to her response of humiliation. Yet, that final step—of working back to underlying shame—is frequently overlooked in the treatment of rage. Finally, Ms. Leitman's shame was due *both* to the experience of her analyst's "inattentiveness" to her wish for exclusive attention and to her recognition of her own omnipotent need for that attention. The shame of narcissistically vulnerable patients is considered further in chapter 9.

CONTEMPT

Like rage, contempt frequently functions as a mechanism for ridding the self of unbearable shame, in this case by projecting the shame out of the self into another person. In a sense, contempt is a more structured attempt than rage to deal with shame; here shame takes form in the other person, with content similar to that which, consciously or unconsciously, has been experienced subjectively as shame. Contempt, then, may reflect the subjective disavowal of one's personal shame experience and its reappearance in feelings toward another person. Contempt requires a greater delineation of the object than does rage and so moves from selfobject *function* toward clarity of object *delineation*. The person toward whom one feels contempt usually displays qualities that resemble the disavowed shameful feelings and constructs experienced in the self. With the importance of the *configurational* elements of the object, I believe that contempt is a bridging concept like idealization, that enables the delineated (that is, *libidinal*) object representation to begin to become differentiated from the selfobject function.

Contempt, then, can be thought of as the *projective identification* of shame, a conceptualization that derives more clearly from an object relations approach than from a self-psychological perspective (see chapters 3 and 5). Elsewhere, I (Morrison, 1986b) defined projective identification as a process essentially similar to that detailed by Ogden (1979). I suggested that it represents

> a defense against an unwanted aspect of the self [e.g., shame]; a communication to the recipient of what the unconscious fantasy feels like; a form of object relationship and interaction with a differentiated "other" who serves as a container of the projection; and a vehicle for psychological change, through identification with the manner in which the recipient processes the projected material [Morrison, 1986b, p. 59].

Ogden (1979) delineated three phases of projective identification, including

> a fantasy of ridding oneself of an aspect of the self and . . . the entry of that part into another person in a way that controls the other person from within; . . . the interpersonal interaction that supports the fantasy of inhabiting and controlling another person; [and] the "psychological processing" of the projection by the recipient, and the re-internalization of the modified projection by the projector [p. 360].

When viewed from the perspective of projective identification, then, contempt is seen as an attempt to rid the self of shame. Shame is disavowed subjectively and relocated in another person, who must exhibit shameful traits similar to those of the projector. The object must, in turn, accept and take ownership of the projected shame, thus serving what Bion (1959) termed the *container* function. The next stage then entails an interaction between the subject and object, frequently centering on the projected shaming introject or shameful affect: the subject projects his shame "into" the object (the container), treats the object with contempt and haughty disdain, and thus distances himself from his own shame, while continuing to interact with it through the interpersonal relationship with the object. This stage represents the identification element of the equation. Finally, the object accepts the projection, contains it to greater or lesser degree, and must deal with, and alter, the shame (that is, "metabolize" the projection).

Clearly, this view of shame and contempt moves, developmentally, beyond an emphasis on selfobject function toward a perception of a more clearly delineated, configurational object, albeit an object distorted and determined by the projected shame. With this emphasis on perception of an object based on a projection, the object might be considered to be *created*, in part, by the subject (see Klein 1946). Thus, interaction with another person based on a view of him as contemptible, as container of the subject's own shame, suggests the fantasied creation of the perceived other to meet the internal needs of the subject to rid himself of shame.[2]

Clinical Vignette

Let us return to the case of Mr. Dowland to illustrate clinically the relationship of shame to contempt through projective identification. In addition to his individual clinical work (as summarized in chapter 6), Mr. Dowland participated in a therapy group I led. Another member of the group was a scientific researcher named Fred, who was in the midst of a painful marital separation when he entered the group and suffered as well from low self-esteem and inhibition of anger and assertiveness. Mr. Dowland was extremely angry and troubled by Fred. He looked on him with scorn and seldom passed up an opportunity to brush him aside during group interaction. In individual therapy, he readily acknowledged his contempt for Fred, but in the group he tended to hide his feelings about him.

One evening in group Fred was struggling to express his discomfort and self-doubts about dating a certain woman, as well as his lingering guilt and sadness toward his estranged wife. The group listened attentively, but, while other members were sympathetic and attempted to be helpful, Mr. Dowland scowled. Finally, as Fred con-

---

[2]In a similar way, selfobject idealization suggests beginning delineation and creation of an external object through projective identification of grandiosity or of the *ideal self* (see chapter 5).

tinued softly, Mr. Dowland blurted out, "God, Fred, you're such a wimp!" Fred reddened and turned angrily toward him, asking what he meant. Instead of responding, Mr. Dowland flicked his hand disdainfully, turned from Fred, and changed the subject to something of greater personal importance to himself. The group expressed surprise and attempted to question Mr. Dowland about his feelings toward Fred, but he continued to expand upon his own issue.

In his next individual therapy session, Mr. Dowland acknowledged his lack of respect for, and irritation toward, Fred. He related these feelings to a lack of admiration for the director at work. I asked him to explore these feelings and to associate to his use of the word wimp in the group. After a pause and further elaboration of his disdain for Fred, Mr. Dowland associated to his own feelings about himself as a child–passive, ineffective, and feminine. "I can't stand that guy's weakness; I guess it reminds me too much of the way I felt as a kid, or sometimes even now. He comes too close to the way I can't speak up at board meetings, how I have to sit on my own anger." Further examination of his response revealed his own shame and humiliation over his feelings of passivity. He recognized that, in the group, he was showing the same contempt for Fred that he believed his father had felt toward him as a child (identification with the aggressor/humiliator; see Nathanson, 1987). Subsequently, it became clear that Mr. Dowland could not let go of a close, hostile bond of contempt with Fred in the group. He found it difficult to modify his disdainful view of the other man, despite many efforts by members of the group to alter Mr. Dowland's viewpoint.

This vignette illustrates, I believe, the kind of relationship that frequently exists between shame and contempt as played out through the projective identification of shame by the subject into a willing, compliant individual/container. In addition, the bond between the two persons is often strengthened through identification with the aggressor, as the projector assumes the role of persecutor, emulating an earlier humiliating childhood figure. In this way, the projector maintains contact with his own familiar (now externalized) shame and has the opportunity to learn about it, to observe how it is processed by the object/container, and, it is hoped, to reinternalize and rework it through the therapeutic process.

ENVY

Since Klein (1957) wrote about envy, many authors (particularly of the British school) have expounded on this emotion. As noted by Greenberg and Mitchell (1983), Klein viewed envy as a malignant form of hatred toward the good object—as a need to control and destroy, to render it powerless. Thus, envy undoes splitting (which preserves the good object), increases anxiety and terror, and destroys hope. This view of envy has been used to explain the negative therapeutic reaction, in which difficult patients negate and refute all attempts by the therapist to be helpful or useful. In these cases, the possibility of help from a loving, competent, good other is obliterated, in part because of shame anxiety (the anticipation of shame) resulting from the power and ability residing in another person.

Several authors have noted the role of envy in psychotherapy. For example, in writing about the "other" breast, Boris (1986) suggested that we metaphorically empower the breast with strength and plentitude, longing to possess and control its supplies but despairing of ever being able to do so. We imagine stripping the breast of its powers and fantasize another breast, one that possesses everything the first lacks, thus protecting against the "bullying desireability of the first" (p. 51). Sohn (1985) wrote that envy leads to identification (through projective identification) with the powerful object, which becomes a possession under the control of the self. Sohn concluded that, by becoming its own powerful object, the subject controls and denies envy (as well as dependence, need, and illness).

Based as they are on a Kleinian perspective, these notions of envy emphasize the relationship of the self to a plentiful, uncontrollable, and intolerable source of power, with a consequent need to deny or protect against that object's importance. According to Sohn, this protection, initiated by envy (which itself must be denied), is intrinsic to narcissistic organization, reflecting what Modell (1975) called "the illusion of self-sufficiency." However, by emphasizing envy, these Kleinian views apparently presume the self's meagerness in comparison with the power of the envied other: if the enviable object is omniscient and omnipotent, the self must be viewed as (relatively) weak, defective, inferior, and failing by comparison.

Envy, then, is brought within our perspective on shame. For envy of the powerful object to flourish, that object must be compared with the shame-ridden, incompetent self. In addition, exploration of envy advocated by Boris (1986) and Sohn (1985) can be facilitated through comparable therapeutic investigation of the patient's underlying sense of shame. Even where shame may not seem a prominent experience of a given patient, it is implicitly involved when envy of another occurs.

Boris (1986) contrasted envy with greed, which wants everything and hence is essentially insatiable. Envy, according to Boris, protects against greed by rendering the object useless through the fantasied creation of the "other" breast. I suggest that envy also serves as a *protection* against the experience of shame, at least with respect to another object. The subject's attention shifts from the self's shame to the object's power and thus displaces preoccupation from the meager state of the self to the powerful state of the object. In addition, insofar as envy undermines the importance of the object, it may also lead to reduction in shame with regard to the formerly omnipotent other. I believe that in these ways envy bears a relationship to shame and is closely intertwined with it clinically: envy represents yet another means – along with anger/rage, and contempt – for the self to deal with and abjure its shame.

Clinical Vignette

Dr. Santos, a psychologist with a doctoral degree in education, was exploring with me the possibility of entering psychoanalysis. Dr. Santos's envy of my medical degree had long been implicit in his treatment, but, as the possibility of analysis was explored, it came to the center of the work. Dr. Santos said that I thought I was "so great" for having gone to medical school: I could prescribe drugs, treat patients in hospitals, and, of course, had been able to become a psychoanalyst and could command higher fees. He launched into a vituperative attack on analysts, who were so smug and who "lorded it over" the psychologists in the setting in which he worked. He went on to suggest that I looked down on the psychological testing that Dr. Santos did as part of his job. "When was the last time that you ordered testing for one of your analytic patients?" His anger grew as he expanded on the power of psychiatrists/analysts that accrued simply from their degree, not from any "intrinsic clinical superiority."

After a tacit acceptance that there might indeed be inequities in the system, I invited Dr. Santos to express more fully his anger at not having the power he believed inherent in the role of psychiatrist. He was able to clarify his envy, as he spelled out many of the professional rights that he felt were denied to him but were available to medical psychoanalysts. Before moving to the shame and humiliation that Dr. Santos felt about not possessing these perceived rights, I pointed out that he was in fact preserving for himself the power and right to render me impotent to provide that service which he so envied – psychoanalysis. After Dr. Santos acknowledged this fact, he was able to move on to his own shame at not having gone to medical school to become a psychiatrist. He had been afraid to undertake the basic sciences necessary to prepare for, and to undertake, medical studies. In fact, he had not even been admitted to a "proper" graduate program in psychology, but had had to "settle" for the Ed.D. program, which he considered inferior. He felt himself to be inferior, defective, a failure for not achieving these accomplishments. Subsequent work, deriving from Dr. Santos's envy of my status as a psychoanalyst, disclosed many facets of his own shame.

Thus, the enormity of his envy – and his self-defeating blocking of my ability to provide the analysis for which he yearned – was fueled by his own shame and humiliation at his own perceived lack of accomplishment. Therapeutic work on the underlying shame, with its relevant elements of oedipal and body inferiority, led to an easing of his self-critical attacks and, with this, a greater understanding of the source and power of his envy. This sequence is not atypical – moving through envy to deep-seated shame and, following adequate elaboration of the shame elements, back to a clearer understanding and resolution of feelings of envy (see Wurmser, 1981). Such an approach allows for exploration of what the patient desires "more of" for himself by clarifying what is envied in the idealized, omnipotent other.

The role of shame is too often ignored therapeutically as a major component in generating envy. If one explores exclusively drive-related elements of untamed aggression in the treatment of envy, these self-inflicted shame experiences will usually be bypassed, to the detriment of a more complete and useful therapeutic exploration. Such incomplete exploration, noted as well in work on anger/rage and contempt, may reflect too exclusive attention to object relational or drive-related elements without adequate understanding of the relevant and accompanying feelings of low self-esteem and shame. Avoidance of shame may also represent the therapist's collusion to ignore his or her own feelings of inferiority and failure with regard, for instance, to professional accomplishments and status – envy of one's colleagues.

DEPRESSION

Coyne (1986) has noted that psychodynamic, intrapsychic views of depression can be subdivided into an *energic* model (libido, drives, fixation, and repression) and an *information* model (the ego's awareness of a discrepancy between aspirations and potential for attainment). The former is described in Freud's and Abraham's papers (Abraham and Freud, 1965), the latter by Bibring (1953) and discussed by Rapaport (1967). Kohut's (1977) view of depression was very similar to that of Bibring, and, while Freud's (1917) theory of melancholia reflected an object-libidinal orientation, that of Kohut and Bibring essentially speaks to the relationship of depression to narcissism and the self. I shall try to demonstrate that our description of the phenomenology of shame parallels Bibring's and Kohut's perspective of depression's relationship to the self and narcissism. As it is in other emotional manifestations, underlying shame is frequently bypassed in the psychotherapy of depression (the "guiltless despair" described by Kohut).

In Freud's (1917) object-libidinal scheme, hatred and oral aggression toward the object—external or internalized—was seen as the source of depression. Abraham (1911) emphasized that hatred toward the object is projected outward, so that the object becomes the source of anger directed at the self. This self-hatred, then, becomes rationalized as reflecting badness and inferiority. Freud (1917) added that aggression toward the significant object is elicited by loss of that object (through death, separation, or the like). Such loss engenders anger; the object then is restored through internalization into the ego, and oral aggression is turned upon the self, leading to depression. Thus, in his theory of melancholia, Freud emphasized the role of *object* loss and internalization in generating depression.

By contrast, Bibring (1953) viewed depression as reflecting a developmentally early and central feeling of *helplessness*, which, in addition to causing ego inhibition (depletion) and lowered self-esteem, predisposes the vulnerable adult to depression. Such helplessness may indeed be a response to object loss, but, rather than emphasizing aggression turned on the abandoning internalized object, Bibring cited resultant blows to self-esteem, leading to feelings of "being weak, inferior, or a failure" (p. 23). Bibring noted that this sense of helplessness must reflect the continued importance of maintaining specific narcissistic aspirations; "It is exactly from the tension between these highly charged narcissistic aspirations on the one hand, and the ego's acute awareness of its (real and imaginary) helplessness and incapacity to live up to them on the other hand, that depression results" (pp. 24–25). Bibring went on to define these narcissistic aspirations as "1) the wish to be worthy, to be loved, to be appreciated, not to be inferior or unworthy; 2) the wish to be strong, superior, great, secure, not to be weak and insecure; and 3) the wish to be good, to be loving, not to be aggressive, hateful and destructive" (p. 24). Further, he indicated that depression "stems primarily from tension within the ego itself, from an inner-[intra-] systemic 'conflict.' Thus depression can be defined as the emotional correlate of a partial or complete collapse of the self-esteem of the ego, since it feels unable to live up to its aspirations . . . [which] are strongly maintained" (pp. 25–26).

Although he did not explicate the role of shame in this perspective on depression, Bibring approximated the conceptualizations of the present study when he stated that "the depression sets in whenever the fear of being inferior or defective seems to come true, whenever and in whatever way the person comes to feel that all effort was in vain, that he is definitely doomed to be a 'failure' " (p. 25). Again, Bibring noted: "In depression, the ego is shocked into passivity not because there is a conflict regarding the goals, but because of its incapacity to live up to the undisputed narcissistic aspirations" (p. 30).[3]

Bibring's view of depression is similar to that of Kohut (1977). We recall Kohut's use of the phrase "guiltless despair," which reflects depression and results from the self's failure to realize its ambitions and ideals. He proposed the relationship of self-depletion to the depression of middle life over failure to attain the goals of the nuclear self. Thus, there are some patients (for example, those suffering from narcissistic disorders) for whom the relationship of depression to failure in attaining narcissistic ambitions and ideals may be most compelling.

How does Bibring's (and Kohut's) viewpoint on depression relate to the current investigation of shame? I have already suggested (see chapter 5) that Kohut's language, including the descriptions of depression just noted, is essentially a language of shame. I also believe that the same holds true for Bibring's language. His very emphasis on helplessness is a view of the self perceived as weak and unworthy, self-experiences that clearly generate shame. Blows to self-esteem, which result in feelings of weakness, inferiority, and failure, also lead to shame, as noted earlier. Similarly, feelings of unworthiness, insecurity, defect, passivity, and hatefulness are causes of shame. In accord with Bibring's view of depression, I have noted (see chapter 5) that shame also usually reflects an intrasystemic conflict.

The whole matter of loss of self-esteem and its relation to shame deserves consideration. In his discussion of Bibring, Rapaport (1967) defined self-esteem in terms of the potential loss of object. Self-esteem thus served as a signal, an ego function, rather than as reflecting the ego's relation to the superego. Rapaport quoted Fenichel (1945) in

---

[3]Rapaport (1967) equated Bibring's use of helplessness with a "persisting state of loss of object," with fluctuations of self-esteem serving as a signal – analogous to signal anxiety – anticipating that helplessness. I suggest, however, that object loss, though important, is secondary to helplessness as a source of depression in Bibring's formulation.

relating loss of self-esteem to loss of supplies, specifically the loss of love or the need for "narcissistic supplies of affection" (p. 41).

In their introduction to a collection of papers on self-esteem in children, Mack and Ablon (1983) noted that self-esteem may represent "a subjective product of the relationship between ego and ego ideal" (p. 22) or, later, "the changing relationship between representations of an ideal and a current self" (p. 23). This delineation is reminiscent of the discussion of shame and the ego ideal offered previously (chapters 2 and 3). However, although Mack and Ablon did discuss shame as a complex emotion associated with low self-esteem, they did not include shame among those specific emotions which accompany low self-esteem: "pain, anguish, doubt, sadness, emptiness, and inertia . . . (p. 24). In fact, in their volume on self-esteem in childhood, there were strikingly few indexed references to shame.

I regard shame as a central ingredient to the experience of low self-esteem. While low self-esteem represents a broader set of affective and cognitive experiences than does shame, shame is prominent amongst those feelings of low self-esteem. It is probably appropriate, therefore, to consider that the low self-esteem (as well as the helplessness) so central to Bibring's view of depression may be built upon a bedrock of shame.

What, then, is the relationship of shame to depression? First of all, I find myself in agreement with Bibring and Kohut that many, if not most, instances of depression reflect helplessness, shattered self-esteem, and ego (or self-) depletion. Even in those cases where depression clearly reflects loss of object or its love, or aggression turned against the internalized object, the intrapsychic meaning of this hostility is that the self is unworthy or inferior.[4]

I indicated earlier that many of the attributes associated with depression are the very same qualities and feelings that generate shame and low self-esteem. In addition, the "searing" quality noted frequently in descriptions of the shame experience appears to reflect a sense of helplessness to alter the compromised state of the self. Thus, I believe that helplessness as well is part of both shame and depression.

My view, then, is that shame is an important ingredient – in fact, frequently a necessary stimulus – to depression. Frequently, embedded in depression are deep feelings of shame. The relationship of shame to depression provides another example in which a given painful emotion includes shame as a prominent element. This relationship can be

---

[4]This factor was noted by Fenichel (1945), as well as by those authors who described the failure of the ideal self in relation to the omnipotent, idealized parental object.

conceptualized as one emotion (for example, depression) interacting with, or being caused by another (for example, shame). The complete, and successful, psychotherapy of that first feeling – in this case, depression – is best achieved by seeking, uncovering, and working through the causes of the second – shame. This, of course, is the same clinical sequence I have recommended for work on the complex emotions of rage, contempt, and envy.

Clinical Vignettes

Cristophe

A graduate student, the patient was feeling deep despair about himself, his abilities, and his attractiveness when he presented for treatment. In fact, he entered treatment because of frightening desires to commit suicide. He was a tall, attractive, rather sinister-looking young man, who initially expressed grave doubts about therapy, fearing that he would become overly dependent. He felt that he should be able to sort out his problems on his own without the help of anyone. He contrasted his own discomfort with his father's self-determined independence. His father had been an immigrant who had left his homeland because of World War II, had come to this country as a young man, and had risen to professional and financial heights as a corporate lawyer on his own, without assistance from anyone. Similarly, his older sister had, in the patient's view, achieved academic success on her own, without need for psychotherapy or pressure from their parents.

Cristophe viewed himself as a failure – a mediocre student, without conviction about the graduate program in which he was enrolled and unable to work toward achieving the perfectionistic goals he had set for himself. He felt that he drank too heavily, but was unable to curtail his alcohol intake because he depended on it to blot out his despair and his bleak moods. His suicidal feelings emanated from his belief that he was helpless to alter the mediocre course of his life. Overall, he suffered from a characterological depression that seemed to reach back to a painful, insecure childhood.

In the course of several years of therapy, Cristophe developed an intense, ambivalent, intimate relationship with me. All the while, he was contemptuous of his own need for help. Anger alternated with gratitude and idealization toward me; he viewed me at times as being too distant, at others as tuned in to the sources of his depression and despair. Therapeutic work on his painful feelings inevitably reverted to his low self-esteem and self-hatred. As a child, he had felt inferior, a "poor little rich kid" compared with the neighbors, to whom he constantly gave gifts in order to buy their friendship. He recalled being considered "weird" at camp, the butt of constant, cruel pranks because he was "different." These experiences emerged as central to the continued exploration of his depression.

Cristophe's feelings of failure and inferiority seemed to have originated in his comparison of himself with his father and his eight-year-older sister. Throughout his life, the comparison was fixed—his actual self and his accomplishments against his vision of his father's expectations of him and his image of his sister's achievements. As a child, he idolized his father and his status and felt tormented by the belief that he could never live up to his father's expectations. This theme continued to plague him throughout his adolescent and young adult years, and he would sob heart-wrenchingly in treatment as he continually returned to memories and images of failure. Certainly, oedipal competition and anger also played a role in his treatment, but the negative self-images and low self-esteem seemed most directly related to his depression and feeling of inferiority.

Exploration of Cristophe's shame played a central role in his therapy, for it related to his pervasive depression and his feelings of incompetence, inferiority, negative self-comparisons with his father and sister. With this focus, progressively wider openings presented themselves in the clouds of doom that hung over his life. The periods when he did not feel suicidal became longer. He finally left graduate school and got a job where he performed progressively well. He also developed a gratifying relationship with a woman. When this relationship ended, there was a temporary return of despair, self-doubt, and feelings of humiliation, but these were resolved with time and a new sense of self-worth and acceptance emerged. Gradually, his successes in work and love began to take hold, and his sense of despair and life-long depression began to lift.

The course of Cristophe's treatment indicates the relationship of his low self-esteem and sense of helplessness (his shame) to his depression, as suggested by the theoretical perspectives of Bibring (1953) and Kohut (1971). In all likelihood, had the treatment focused instead on his innate aggression and hostility turned upon himself and his internalized objects, the therapy would have been incomplete, Cristophe would have felt misunderstood, and his depression would have remained relatively unchanged.

Ms. Kohl

A depressed mental health professional in her mid-40s, Ms. Kohl was referred to me for consultation. She had long suffered from depression, low self-esteem, and social isolation and had been in treatment over many years with several prominent psychotherapists and psychoanalysts. In consultation, she said that her life had no meaning, that she felt "stuck" and afraid to meet people, and had few friends. She also acknowledged that she was in a relationship with another woman, but did not think of herself as homosexual. She felt that she loved her partner but was embarrassed to be with her lover in public.

Ms. Kohl described her mother as overbearing and intrusive, while her father was aloof, hardworking, and usually absent from the home. Her brother, several years younger than she, was retarded and lived at home. As a child and in college, Ms. Kohl had had few friends; she made some close friendships only during graduate school. At that time she developed a relationship with a man with whom she lived for several years, but whom she described in terms of his physical ugliness. Even though he was talented and loving, she emphasized his facial tic, which had made it difficult and painful for her to accept him. He ultimately had moved to another city, and she had decided not to accompany him. Ms. Kohl felt lonely and isolated after she finished graduate studies, until she became involved with her current companion. She had sought intermittent treatment for her lifelong depression.

When I asked her to describe how she had come to understand her depression, she emphasized her anger at her mother, disappointment in her father, and self-consciousness when she was with other people. I inquired about Ms. Kohl's self-consciousness (another potentially shame-related feeling), and she spoke of feeling different, stiff, with nothing interesting to talk about. I had an impression of deep shame permeating her self-experience and wondered, "I get the feeling that you feel embarrassed about yourself, feel that you have to hide your feelings, thoughts, from others."[5] At this, she sat forward and peered intently at me, her voice gaining animation as she catalogued the series of humiliations that had characterized her life. She had always felt defective and strange, starting with her familial identification with her retarded brother. "I never felt comfortable bringing

---

[5]While I could have picked up on her anger at her mother's intrusiveness or her father's aloofness, I felt that her self-consciousness seemed most immediate and accessible and had probably been less explored in her previous therapy.

friends to the house—then they would know about my brother, the skeleton in my closet." Ms. Kohl talked about how embarrassed she had been at her mother's brashness, causing her to dissociate herself from her family in social situations. She had felt "weird" about being scholarly and not easily sociable or athletic during high school. Later, in public with her boyfriend, she had felt self-conscious about his ugliness and his tic. Currently, she is worried that her colleagues will find out about her female companion and will conclude that she is homosexual. "I guess more than anything," she said, "I wish I could feel—no, *be*— normal. You know, just average."

I commented that it seemed as though this feeling of not being normal was constantly with her, that, as part of her feelings of inferiority, she seemed to bear a heavy mantle of depression. She readily acknowledged that her experience of depression related to her sense of strangeness. We continued to discuss the relationship of her depression to feeling ashamed and humiliated about who she was, and we talked of her need to hide in order to keep these feelings secret. This concealment reflected Ms. Kohl's conviction that she was unlikeable and that there was no possibility for human discourse, a feeling that, in turn, intensified her depression. At the end of the consultation, she said that I had gathered an accurate impression of her depression and that, although she remained skeptical about being able to change, this line of inquiry had been interesting and possibly helpful.

I have presented these two examples to indicate my view of the relationship of shame to depression. I am not suggesting that shame is the only source of depression or that anger and aggression turned on the self and its introjects do not play a significant role as well in the generation of depression. Rather, since the latter relationship has been clearly delineated in classical psychoanalytic writings, I have emphasized (with Bibring, 1953) the relationship of shame, low self-esteem, and helplessness to depression, a connection that has been less frequently elaborated. Further, it is my conviction that shame and its related feelings are basic to the self-experience of many depressed patients and that these feelings often accompany the symptomatic depression. As with the emotions considered earlier in this chapter, thorough working through of shame-related depressions must penetrate beneath despair to the related problems of shame and self-esteem.

HUMILIATION

Humiliation differs from the other emotions described in this chapter in that it directly represents the experience of shame. However, it merits space here as a reflection of that special form of shame experienced in an *interpersonal* context, thus differentiated from the inner shame of the self perceiving its own inadequacy, inferiority, or defect—alone, or in relation to selfobject failure. Humiliation requires the external presence of a humiliator, a highly cathected object (a "significant other") who imposes shame on the self (Morrison, 1984a). The humiliator must be important to the self—frequently a parent—evoking an identification with the aggressor/humiliator, thus generating a form of masochism in many narcissistic personalities (Rothstein, 1984). Though originating in experiences with an actual object, humiliation may be perpetuated through internalization and representation of a "persecuting introject." However, that introject must retain identifiable configurational qualities as it continues the process of tormenting the self. Also, humiliation may occur through the mere presence of a significant observing other, who witnesses as *audience* the flawed self in its extreme discomfort.

Just as humiliation requires the presence of a shamer—past or present, active or observing, external or internalized—so too does it represent shame of high intensity. Social shame of less intensity is more appropriately described as *embarrassment*. Thus, the dynamics of humiliation and embarrassment are similar; they differ primarily in the intensity of the experience. Miller (1985) has suggested that embarrassment also reflects the breakthrough of disavowed libidinal wishes. Mr. Dowland's (see chapter 6) recollection of his father's tormenting him for the way he threw a baseball is a good example of humiliation, as is Ms. Bingham's (see section on Anger/Rage) feeling of smallness in the presence of the taxi driver who ignored her pleas for him to drive more quickly so she could get to her analytic hour. Other patients, recognizing the outbreak of sexual desire within the transference, which they assume to be unreciprocated, are apt to feel embarrassment. Many patients consider humiliation to be the most painful feeling that they have experienced, attesting to the searing intensity of that emotion.

According to this formulation, then, humiliation represents the intense, social manifestation of shame and requires the presence of an active or observing humiliator. Humiliation frequently serves as the activator of the other emotions described in this chapter.

SUMMARY

The emotions of anger/rage, contempt, envy, and depression each bear an intimate relationship to shame. As I have tried to demonstrate, each may be generated or triggered by shame, which frequently underlies the more readily manifest emotion. Anger/rage, contempt, and envy may represent an attempt to deal with, and to extrude, the intolerable shame through various available defenses (for example, projection, projective identification, reversal, disavowal, denial). These defensive maneuvers demonstrate the frequent intolerability of shame and humiliation and the fact that shame itself is so often hidden and concealed by the patient. In fact, each of these emotions, insofar as it serves a defensive function, tends to keep the subjective sense of shame hidden from consciousness. Alternatively, these emotions may on occasion themselves generate a response of shame (see Miller, 1985). I have argued that the complete therapeutic understanding of these emotions should involve penetration to the shame experience. This therapeutic approach will be illustrated in subsequent clinical chapters.

Depression relates to shame in a slightly different way, which might best be described as functioning in parallel with shame. By discussing the contributions of Bibring and Kohut, I attempted to show that the same qualities—helplessness, inferiority, low self-esteem, failure—may each generate shame or depression. Again, because depression is so observable whereas shame so frequently remains hidden, this relationship has not been emphasized, and the elements of shame frequently have remained unexplored. I have suggested that humiliation represents a direct shame manifestation, in its intense, interpersonal form.

In concluding this chapter, I emphasize that I am not suggesting that shame alone underlies these complex emotions or that shame always plays an activating role in their generation. Rather, I am underscoring the role that shame frequently plays in the expression of other complex emotions, a role too often overlooked in therapeutic investigation. Also, shame may play a role in generation of such other phenomena as ridicule, defiance, and boredom (Wurmser, 1981). However, unlike each of these manifest phenomena, shame characteristically remains underground. As Schecter (1979) has remarked, "There is no problem so great as the shame of it" (p. 377).

8

Shame and Defense

In previous chapters, I considered the pain that accompanies shame, a pain that leads to the concealment and hiding of shame sources and experience. In chapter 7, I discussed several shame-related manifestations and presented some relevant clinical examples. I will now attempt to reframe these manifestations—rage, contempt, envy, and depression—as defenses against shame. This formulation in terms of defense carries with it certain implications for treatment, as well as a perspective on resistance, defense, and defense analysis consistent with a traditional view of the defenses. This traditional perspective may be disputed or augmented, as Kohut (1984) has ably done. The self-psychological view of defenses will be considered at the end of this chapter. First, since we have seen that shame induces concealment, an exploration of the shame-related phenomena in terms of defense offers a useful clinical approach to their understanding and management. In addition, shame itself may present as a defense against other affects (see, for example, Morrison, 1984a). I have indicated previously (chapters 1 and 2) that Freud (1905) himself viewed shame as a reaction formation against exhibitionism. These factors will also be considered in this chapter.

DEFENSES AGAINST SHAME

Other authors (for example, Kaufman, 1985; Wurmser, 1981) have noted the defenses mobilized against shame. Lewis (1971) wrote of "by-passed shame," which she related to the patient's lack of awareness of the affective component of shame, including the frequent experience of guilt in shame's place. Bursten (1973) emphasized the narcissist's continued search to rid the self of shame in order to resolve his perpetual sense of vulnerability. These formulations all suggest the importance of defense mechanisms created to protect the self against shame. Psychoanalytic theory has traditionally viewed defenses as directed primarily against drive-derived manifestations of intrapsychic conflict (for example, A. Freud, 1936), although she also included painful affects as motives for defense. (A rich psychoanalytic exploration of defense may be found in the Supplement [1983]). Because of earlier reluctance to consider the self, and shame, from a psychoanalytic perspective, defenses against shame have seldom been considered. The unconscious model of drive/affect-defense was regarded as the sole source of intrapsychic conflict (Kris, 1985). As I have attempted to show, shame and the defenses against it do not lend themselves well to a traditional conflict framework but suggest, rather, a group of conflicts that Kris has called "divergent" conflicts. As noted, Kohut (1984) offered an alternative view of defense, which I will consider later in relation to shame.

From another perspective, defense may be considered a metaphor for personal attempts to control, achieve distance from, and deal with painful experiences of shame and humiliation. As we consider these attempts within paradigms of defense, we must keep in mind the potential goals of managing and regulating dysphoric affects. This view will introduce the idea of shame as interacting in a complementary way with the related phenomena/defenses, sometimes as figure, sometimes as background—that is, with rage or envy as a response to underlying shame, or, occasionally, the opposite. We shall see later that the tenacity of the defensive functions may reflect the specific nature or pervasiveness of shame with regard to particular symptoms or character structure. I shall try to show that these defenses/phenomena often are attempts to regulate unconscious or disavowed shame (see Socarides and Stolorow, 1984–85, for a discussion of affect regulation). I believe that a conceptualization of the phenomena to be discussed in terms of defenses and defensiveness against shame offers a useful clinical approach to treatment.

Since the specific defenses against shame relate to a model of defense mechanisms, it becomes useful to examine this particular framework. Vaillant (1977) has offered an adaptational, hierarchical perspective on defenses that will serve this task and that relates to the self-psychological perspective to be considered. According to Vaillant, there are four levels of defenses (which he calls Adaptive Mechanisms), from Level I (the Psychotic Mechanisms) to Level IV (the Mature Mechanisms). His *adaptational* perspective on defenses seems less judgmental than some other traditional viewpoints and moves closer to that of Kohut (1984) to be considered. I suggested earlier that psychotic patients, preoccupied as they are with self-fragmentation, seldom have the luxury of attempting to deal with shame. There is one important exception to this suggestion in Vaillant's Level I, which includes the use of primitive denial. Although Vaillant believed that this psychotic mechanism relates only to external reality, I suggest that it may involve as well the denial of primary affect states. Thus, as I hope to demonstrate in chapter 11, denial of shame is a primary mechanism of mania, representing as it does the most severe form of underlying narcissistic vulnerability.

Level II includes Vaillant's *Immature Mechanisms, such as fantasy, projection, hypochondriasis, passive-aggressive behavior* (as in masochism and turning against the self), and acting out. Each of these may relate to the affect of shame. Fantasy may indeed include the narcissistic grandiosty that can overwhelm the ego in Kohut's (1971) vertical split and that he considered to be the principal cause of shame. Projection was described by Bursten (1973) as the means of expelling shame from the self. I will elaborate my suggestion that projective identification, a mechanism not described by Vaillant, is the means by which the self relocates its shame into another person through the emotion of *contempt*. Also, through projective identification of the ideal self, the emerging self begins to create (as well as respond to) the idealized selfobject, which I have indicated (chapter 5) as the bridging construct on the way to delineation of the libidinal object, with its distinct configurational qualities.

Hypochondriasis may be an attempt to deal with shame through withdrawal of attention from the outside world and its objects into the self and its experienced defects and inferiority, which must be protected and covered. Passive-aggressive behavior, as reflected in masochism and turning against the self, may sometimes represent punishment of the self for its shameful inadequacies and failures, as well as for guilty actions. Finally, acting out behavior not infrequently represents the third step in the guilt–shame cycle of Piers (1953) whereby the self responds to its intolerable, shameful, reactive passivity by actively lashing out against the environment.

Vaillant's Level III, the *Adaptive (Neurotic) Mechanisms*, includes Intellectualization (isolation, obsessive behavior, undoing, and rationalization); Repression; and Dissociation (neurotic denial). By and large, these mechanisms relate to neurotic shame, or reactive, secondary shame (less intense shame than that of pervasive narcissistic vulnerability) as described by Levin (1971; see also chapters 4 and 10). Among the Intellectualizing mechanisms, isolation represents the affect of shame as split off from the sense of self-defect and infirmity that might be expected to generate it; this mechanism is similar to the by-passed shame described by Lewis (1971). Obsessive behavior may represent attempts to master and overcome shame and shame anxiety (Levin, 1971) through perfectionism and slavish attempts to attain the ideal self, just as on other occasions it represents attempts to overcome guilt. Undoing, at times, is aimed at repairing the shameful states that generate despair, for example, turning passive into active, striving to make up for "organ inferiority" through sexual conquest, and so on. Rationalization may attempt to justify and alter those failures and feelings of inferiority which lead to shame.

Repression involves the forcing into unconsciousness awareness not only of guilt and anxiety, but also shame, humiliation, and embarrassment. It also represents another source of by-passed shame. Reaction Formation may, like acting out, be an attempt to deal with the reactive shame of the guilt–shame cycle, particularly by turning reactive passivity and dependency as a response to primary aggression into fierce independence and assertiveness. More directly, clinging dependency and meekness leading to shame may itself be a reaction formation against "killing" anger and hatred, or against exhibitionism, as first suggested by Freud (1905), with shame serving as the defense. Shame itself also generates at times a reaction formation into grandiosity and superiority.

Displacement of shame relates especially to humiliation, where the source of shaming, frequently one person (for example, a parent) may be relocated in another (the boss). In psychotherapy, displaced feelings of shame are frequently experienced in the transference, with the source of humiliation being experienced as the therapist. Dissociation, or neurotic denial, may be manifest as a lack of conscious awareness of shame as an affect and of the sense of inferiority and defect that generates it. Neurotic denial is, I believe, analogous to Kohut's (1971) concept of disavowal, by which shame is shut off from consciousness through the vertical split.

Level IV mechanisms, the *Mature Mechanisms* common in healthy adults, include sublimation, altruism, suppression, anticipation, and humor and do not lend themselves so easily to a framework for shame. One might argue, however, that the anticipation of shame (shame anxiety) can be suppressed in order to enable one to take certain risks. This suppression might occur when, for instance, a business executive makes a decision that could lead to great success, but might also result in a major failure. Similarly, a healthy perspective on the decision-making process might allow such an executive to express humor about past or potential failures.

The partial failure of defense (repression or denial) by which unconscious affects and drive representations, including the experience of prohibited sexual yearnings or anger, begin to break through into consciousness frequently results in embarrassment. These feelings certainly may lead to guilt and to rerepression, but, when the person is concerned that lust or fury may be observed by someone else, he–or more frequently she–experiences the flush of embarrassment (see Miller, 1985).

The Specific Shame Mechanisms

Vaillant's (1977) hierarchical adaptational model of the traditional defense mechanisms has provided an opportunity for us to consider shame's potential relationship to defense. In the previous chapter, I delineated several responses to shame that I view as frequent manifestations of the shame experience. I shall now consider these from the perspective of defenses against shame.

Anger/Rage: I suggested earlier that shame, feeling so intolerable that it frequently must be expunged, is often the underpinning of narcissistic rage. The self may thus attempt to purge shame through attacks on objects, living or inanimate, that may momentarily be seen as shame's source. A related view (that is, Kohut, 1972) is that shame may result from selfobject failure and that narcissistic rage is then turned upon the selfobject for "causing" the shame experience. One of the most frequent sources of the shame–rage relationship is the subjective experience of *need,* about which the self experiences a sense of intense humiliation, either through recognition that the *other* may be scornfully aware of the self's requirement for sustenance or through a perceived selfobject failure to meet the need (for instance, for support, love, comfort, affirmation). In either case, the self-experience is one of being pathetic, ridiculous, or insignificant–all shame counterparts.

Shame with regard to perceived need is often expressed by

patients as "shoulds" and "should nots." A good example is Cristophe (chapter 7), who frequently expressed distress about his "need" for therapy. On one occasion, following a brief interruption in treatment, Cristophe stated that he had very much missed coming for his sessions, that he had been depressed and lonely and had deeply felt his need for contact with me. He then launched into a tirade against therapy, proclaiming that he *should not need* treatment so badly, that I had made him feel dependent, and that his need made him feel weak and pathetic. He contrasted his own state of dependency/need with that of his father, who had hidden out on his own during World War II, had emigrated to this country, and had made a success of himself without assistance from anybody (least of all, a psychotherapist!). I acknowledged Cristophe's anger at me and suggested that his feeling of being pathetic meant that he felt humiliated for needing to come for treatment; we then began to explore the childhood roots of Cristophe's feeling of shame and "weirdness" around his needs.

Thus, shame may be a response to need, with the defense of anger aimed at the needed object for making the individual feel insignificant, dependent, and unworthy. A similar sequence may occur when a patient condemns himself or herself for feelings of *desire*. Ms. Bingham (chapter 7) entered into a stage of triangular (oedipal) wishes toward me, which were manifest in displaced desires for a sexual relationship with another man. As the transferential meaning of these feelings became evident to her, she stated that she felt humiliated and insignificant, because the therapeutic relationship "isn't real; you have your wife and family, and you don't give any indication that you desire me. These feelings [of desire toward me] are make-believe." She then elaborated her feelings of being insignificant to me, that her desire was not in the slightest reciprocated, and that I would mock her for it. This state made her feel pathetic, and she then expressed rage at me for making, or allowing, her to feel this way. As we continued to explore her feelings, she realized that she felt angry, humiliated, and helpless because of her unreciprocated wishes, which had clear reverberations with unacknowledged childhood desire for her father and envy of her mother.

No doubt such feelings of desire can elicit traditional oedipal guilt, generating repression and what Kris (1985) has called "conflicts of convergence." I am suggesting here, however, that desire unreciprocated may lead as well to feelings of vulnerability, pathos, and weakness, causing the shame and humiliation described by Ms. Bingham and generating retaliatory rage toward the unresponsive therapist/object. I believe that this leads to an either-or dilemma for the patient with respect to desire for, or withdrawal from, the object – an example of Kris's (1985) conflict of divergence. In addition, as noted earlier (chapter 7), rage creates the illusion of turning passive into active and is itself another means of reversing the source of shame.

The defense mechanisms involved in this process of turning shame into rage include particularly (projection) by which the source of shame is changed from inner failure and defect to external callousness. It's not my failure, desire, or need, but your scorn or lack of reciprocal concern, that makes me feel this way. Also, through dissociation, or neurotic denial, the dysphoric affect itself is disavowed or ignored and is changed from shame to anger and rage. (This sequence is an example as well of turning one feeling into its opposite, or, specifically, of turning passive into active.) In healthy people, these mechanisms act transiently, as the rage is felt only for a short time and the underlying shame and vulnerability become amenable to therapeutic intervention and interpretation. When rage is experienced within the transference, leverage is potentially available for interpretation and working through of the underlying sources of shame. This was the case with Ms. Bingham (chapter 7). In more primitive personalities, the rage response

tends to be more tenacious, and it is more difficult to work back to underlying, defended shame (which itself is pervasive and tends to include apologies and self-accusations about even existing in the world). Annie Reich (1960) has described such conditions, as has Kernberg (1975), although Kernberg ascribed rage to an internally generated source.

Contempt and Envy: As noted in the previous chapter, I view contempt as a frequent manifestation of the projective identification of shame into another object-as-container. I discussed the function of this defense mechanism in detail at that time and identify it here only as belonging to the present category of shame-related defenses. Several other matters about projective identification, however, deserve elaboration at this time. As I have noted elsewhere (Morrison, 1986b), projective identification serves, in addition to its role as an adaptive mechanism, as means to an interpersonal relationship and as a form of communication (that is, the countertransferential awareness by the therapist of the patient's disavowed or idealizing affect/introject). Projective identification takes its place as a cornerpiece of the British Object Relations School and as such is not readily translatable into a traditional or self-psychological perspective. However, I believe that its explanatory power is so great, particularly with regard to shame, that it deserves consideration in the present context (see Grotstein, 1981; see also chapter 7, this volume).

As a vehicle for a continuing relationship with an object, the projective identification of shame into another person as contempt forms an interpersonal bond that firmly cements that relationship. Mr. Dowland's relationship to Fred in the therapy group (chapter 7) is an example of this use of projective identification to bring about a tenacious relationship; it maintained Mr. Dowland's contact with his own projected affect (his shame). Such a relationship, scornful and distasteful though it is, has considerable durability, as illustrated by the difficulty of the group members to intervene in Mr. Dowland's continued scornful attacks on Fred.

As an example of the communication of shame (as contempt) within the transference, I will describe Jacob, a student at a local university. He had participated in previous psychotherapy and was continually comparing me unfavorably with his previous therapist. He was having difficulty in school, feeling perpetually overwhelmed and isolated. In psychotherapy, he accused me of being too "laid back," by which he meant inactive and unassertive. He wanted evidence that I really cared about him and his feelings, that I understood his feeling of aloneness. Despite my many efforts to indicate my interest and to interpret the sources of his feelings, Jacob continued to accuse me of lack of interest and verbal precision, conveying his sense of superiority and haughty disdain. I began to feel helpless and inept in my efforts and noticed a countertransferential sense of failure and clumsiness in my work with Jacob. I recognized that these internal feelings most likely reflected Jacob's own feelings of incompetence about himself in school and with his classmates, and I shared this observation with him. I also questioned whether the contempt that Jacob was expressing toward me might reflect similar underlying feelings about himself. At this point, Jacob became quite lively, stating that this was exactly the way he felt most of the time and that he finally felt quite understood. We then proceeded to explore Jacob's own feelings of ineptness, failure, and isolation, and the shame that underlay them.

Certainly this example of contempt might be explained solely as affect communication rather than as projective identification (as recommended by some clinicians), but I felt that Jacob **wanted** me to suffer the pangs of ineptitude as he did. This wish, I believe, was motivated not only by the expectation that I would empathically understand his distress, but also by the fantasy that he could rid himself of his inferiority feelings by making me suffer in his place. This impression could be discussed, unpunitively, in terms of Jacob's wish to be rid of his shame. We returned productively on several occasions to his fantasy of relocating his feelings in me, a fantasy that Jacob readily acknowledged.

I have discussed envy as a state, related to contempt, that attempts in part to deal with underlying shame by expressing hatred for the power of the other in relation to the self. Envy also diverts attention from the meager state of the self by focusing on the despised strength of the other. The case of Dr. Santos (chapter 7) illustrates this process. In essence, when the power of someone else is central to one's attention, that power implies an assumption of defect and relative inferiority of the self—hence, potential shame. Emphasis on another's strength can serve as a marker of those idealized qualities toward which the self strives. This sequence may also occur through projection of the self's grandiosity and omnipotence onto another. The hatred of the envied other occurs through a projective mechanism similar to that described for anger and rage, only instead of blame for causing the self's shame, envy emphasizes the relative power differential between the defective self and the omnipotent other. Also, displacement occurs in envy, from the state of the self to the plentiful condition of the other.

Depression: Traditionally, depression has been viewed as a primary emotion, an experience and symptom that needs no further reduction. This is the case in Freud's view of melancholia, in which the affect itself reflects ambivalent anger turned against the abandoning, lost object maintained as an introject within the self. I have contrasted this view with that of Bibring (1953), in which depression is the result of helplessness and low self-esteem, where the self is viewed as being unable to alter its powerless state of inferiority and failure or to live up to its unattainable aspirations. In chapter 7, I compared this view of depression to that of Kohut (1971) and suggested that shame is a response to feelings of depletion, powerlessness, and failure.

It is relevant in this section to consider whether Bibring's (and Kohut's) view of depression (guiltless despair) may in fact represent a defense against shame. I believe that, when so viewed, depression may indeed function as a defense. The shame, and object-related humiliation, which reflect specific feelings of failure, inferiority, and helplessness (those conditions described by Bibring) frequently are so painful and intolerable that they must be covered over, concealed, by another feeling, even one so unpleasant as depression. While depression and shame are, under these circumstances, closely related experiences that frequently interact, depression at times is a defense. It may be experienced as a generalized, nonspecific self-experience, hiding the more explicit and loathesome qualities of self-defect that generate underlying shame. Thus, depression may reflect disavowal, and even repression, of shame or displacement from the one affect to the other. Whether or not depression is viewed as a defense against shame may seem semantic, but I think the treatment implications of this perspective are important, as noted earlier, in mandating work toward underlying shame in relevant states of depression (see Christophe, chapter 7).

Shame as a Defense

Miller (1985) has presented a perspective opposite to the one I have suggested on the relationship of shame to anger; she viewed shame principally as the defense against underlying anger. While she noted that sometimes anger may stand against shame, most of her cases were in the opposite direction. Anger seemed the more intolerable affect, and shame (about the experience of anger, about the self as a hostile and aggressive agent) seemed to be the more acceptable experience, thus standing as a defense. For instance, manifest shame was frequently described by Miller's subjects, and only on more thorough questioning did underlying anger, or themes of hostility, emerge.

It is difficult to explain Miller's findings, for, in most of my own psychoanalytic and psychotherapeutic practice, anger and rage seem to emerge more directly and frequently than the underlying shame that so often generates it. Certainly, the clinician sees instances of shame in response to, or as a cover for, underlying hostility, but this sequence seems less frequent to me than the reverse. Perhaps this difference reflects the subjects whom Miller interviewed, volunteers from a university population paid to talk about their shame experiences. Thus, the task was to focus on shame, and, in this context, shame might well have been more readily accessible to these subjects than was their rage. Since Miller had advertised for paid volunteers to discuss shame, perhaps she collected a sample more aware of, and sensitive to, shame than is the average population of clinical patients.

Another possibility lies in the nature of Miller's interviews themselves. Her study was to be a phenomenological assessment of shame, in which the subjects' conscious awareness of shame was to be discussed. Thus, these people may have been less conscious or aware of their rage and anger. Also, since the subjects did not know the interviewer and were seen only for several interviews, they might have been on compliant, good behavior; because they were being paid for their time, they may have been less inclined toward anger! Perhaps, as well, there was something soothing and nonthreatening about Miller's manner during the interviews that kept latent anger under wraps.

Whatever the explanation for this difference between Miller's and my own observations about the relationship of shame to anger, it is noteworthy that she viewed shame principally as a cover for underlying anger and thus regarded shame as a defense. I would conclude that, at least in certain circumstances, shame can serve as the *defense* against anger (or, for that matter, against contempt or depression) rather than the opposite, depending on the specific nature of individual vulnerability.

Certainly, Miller's conclusion parallels Freud's (1905) view of the defensive function of shame (chapter 2). As I have discussed, Freud saw shame (along with morality and disgust) as a *reaction formation* against the scopophilic/exhibitionistic drives and thus as sources of resistance against sexual experiences. Later, Freud (1914) stated that repression occurs when libidinal instincts conflict with cultural and ethical ideals as determined by the self-respect of the ego. Such conflicts of self-respect reflect, I believe, feelings of inferiority and failure in relation to ideals, that is, shame. Thus, in Freud's view shame may also mobilize these defensive manifestations (reaction-formation, resistance, and repression) against libidinal forces, which would otherwise cause diminished self-respect. The ego ideal was the structure against which the ego (or self) measured its success in attaining self-respect and thus was the ultimate source of shame and subsequent repression.

Thus, Freud also viewed shame – generated by the ego ideal as a cause of (stimulus to) repression – as both a direct affective experience and a self-reproach, which led in turn to hiding and concealment. Clearly, shame itself also can generate, as well as function as, a defense – in this case, repression and defensive withdrawal to protect the flawed self from discovery. This aspect of shame in Freud's writing (e.g., as a stimulus to defense) has been little appreciated in the classical assumptions about shame.

Kohut's View of Defense

Kohut (1984) put forth an alternative view of defense that bears consideration in relation to shame. His view more closely approximates Vaillant's (1977) view of the Adaptive Mechanisms. Vaillant wrote, "I am really writing about adaptive styles rather than 'mental mechanisms' " (p. 10).

Kohut stated, "My personal preference is to speak of the 'defensiveness' of patients – and to think of their defensive attitudes as adaptive and psychologically valuable – and not of their 'resistances' " (p. 114).

Thus, for Kohut, defense motivation is viewed in terms of the current state of the self and as an attempt to save those aspects of the nuclear self which have been maintained despite developmental insufficiencies from selfobject unresponsiveness. In one case example,

Kohut described a particular patient's turning of passive into active (feeling shamed and embarrassed into active shaming), as a means of preserving the hope of attaining a vigorous, cohesive self. For this patient such a sequence represents, in Kohut's terminology, an attempt to establish compensatory and defensive self-structures through identification with a potentially idealizable, vigorous father. In this context, Kohut discussed "narcissistic rage" as an attempt to address, and to safeguard the self against, selfobject failure to provide functions facilitating self-growth and development and to protect against harmful attack and intrusion (pp. 137–140).

In reinterpreting the voyeurism-exhibitionism theme delineated in the patient just mentioned—that theme so central to Freud's (1905) view of the defensive (reaction-formation) view of shame—Kohut noted that whenever the patient's thwarted need for self-enhancing mirroring appeared, he felt intense shame and embarrassment. However, he preserved his self-cohesion by turning passive into active—by exposing the selfobject or its surrogates to humiliation and ridicule.[1] In Kohut's view, then, defensive functions serve primarily to perform protective and assertive acts aimed at the establishment and augmentation of self-cohesion. For this patient, an *idealizing selfobject transference* provided for self-stabilization through the development of what Kohut called "compensatory structures" (that is, the generation of ideals). Traditional resistances are viewed by Kohut as "healthy psychic activities [safeguarding] the self for future growth" (p. 148). So too was intellectualizing for this patient viewed as a self-preserving strength developed to maintain the intactness of his personality.

I believe that Kohut's formulation of defense, and its relationship to our understanding of shame, represents a useful conceptualization complementary to the traditional conflict model. As Shane (1985) stated, the motive for defense is the principle of *self-preservation*; that is, the goal of a defense is primarily to maintain the integrity of the self, with only secondary emphasis on what is defended against (that is, dysphoric affects like shame). Tolpin (1985) wrote that defensiveness maintains self-organization and prevents deterioration by overwhelming affects and experiences or wishes that would lead to repeated injuries and selfobject failures.

Kohut's position can be considered in the clinical examples of defense reviewed in this (and in the previous) chapter. For example, in

---

[1]This sequence will be seen to resemble my view of turning passive shame into active contempt for the other through projective identification. It also underscores the previously noted relationship between need and shame.

the case of Ms. Bingham's *rage* at the taxi driver, who she felt was
preventing her from arriving at her analytic session and in whose eyes
she felt insignificant and ashamed, Kohut might have considered her
behavior as an attempt to preserve her core self-identity against dispar-
agement by a devaluing selfobject. Similarly, Mr. Dowland's *contempt*
for Fred in the therapy group may be viewed as an effort to hold on to
his fragile self-esteem through projective identification and extrusion of
his negative self-concept and shame into another person. The continued bond provided in the therapy group between Mr. Dowland and
Fred allowed Mr. Dowland to maintain self-esteem and cohesion by
relocating his shame into another and thus keep alive those self-
elements which he valued.[2] Through interpretation of the function of
his contempt, both in the group and in individual therapy, Mr. Dowland came to learn the self-sustaining use to which he was putting his
disdain for others.

Likewise, Dr. Santos's *envy* of his physician/analyst's power and
status may be viewed as an attempt to preserve for himself the
self-regard and integrity of his own ambitions and skills, qualities that
presumably had not been adequately supported and acknowledged by
his parents. Once his therapist understood and explained this function
of his envy, the self-defeating elements of his stance (maintaining his
own power by rejecting analysis and thus minimizing the therapist's
importance to him) could be interpreted and worked through.[3]

In my earlier discussion of depression (chapter 7), I emphasized
the similarity between the views of Bibring and Kohut, where the state
of helplessness, shattered self-esteem, failure, and inferiority (Bibring,
1953) is analogous to the guiltless despair and lack of self-vigor elaborated by Kohut (1977). From Kohut's perspective, such patients have
failed to defend against, or compensate for, the self's lack of vigor or
esteem in any meaningful way and thus feel undefended, frequently
becoming suicidal. I would emphasize here that many suicides, particularly those in middle to later life, reflect the failure of defense against
the self's sense of failure or shame (see chapter 12). Thus, shame and
humiliation frequently underlie those depressions not directly related

---

[2]It may also be that the patient needed to maintain some (distanced) contact with his projected
shame because it had long been such a familiar aspect of his self-experience and thus played a part
in his sense of self-stability and aliveness.

[3]It should be noted that Kohut's approach to understanding defenses, though universalized and
metaphorical, avoids the frequent dilemma in classical defense analysis in which interpretations
of resistance seem critical and self-deflating (i.e., humiliating).

to object loss; the psychotic defense of mania may be a desperate attempt to cover such shame and depression (see chapter 11).

The example of Cristophe (chapter 7) illustrates the relation of depression and deep despair to a sense of shame and worthlessness resulting, in this case, from Cristophe's comparison of himself with his successful and unempathic father. As long as Cristophe felt totally empty and a failure, there was no vestige of vigor and wholeness available for implementation of Kohut's kind of defensiveness. As a result, initially Cristophe felt profoundly suicidal. I could find no basis to question his underlying despair. Therapeutic leverage had to come from investigation of the sources of his deep sense of shame through my active and accepting intervention; I offered an alternative to his image of an uninterested and preoccupied father. Building on my understanding of, and questioning about, his shame-filled self-assumptions, Cristophe was able to enjoy, first moments, and then longer periods, of improved self-esteem and happiness. These periods often had the denying quality of reaction-formations, but they provided some attenuation of self-criticism, which eventually enabled Cristophe to develop a sense of self-esteem and expanding pockets of vigor. Thus, he was gradually able to compensate for his degraded sense of self and to evolve a beginning self-structure where previously there had been little.

Is Kohut's perspective on defensive structure antithetical to the defense mechanisms just elaborated, or can defense mechanisms and defensiveness complement each other? I suggest the latter, as these qualities represent different aspects of the patient, enmeshed in the shifting forces of valued and despised attributes. As originally conceived by Anna Freud and other analysts, the defense mechanisms form a hierarchy of means to counteract drives, drive derivatives, and painful affects (including, as I have tried to show, shame). They most frequently appear as resistance against investigation and treatment. Kohut (1984) moved the function of defenses away from drives and resistance and toward the progressive evolution of life designs which aim to preserve areas of vigor and self-cohesion. These two perspectives can be seen as differing aspects of the whole self, and each can be emphasized in treatment–now one, now the other–as it is empathically discovered to predominate for the patient at a given time. Vaillant's (1977) conceptualization of Adaptive Mechanisms is a useful bridge between these two views of defense. From either vantage point, shame plays a central role in the elaboration, or restitutive construction, of the defensive process.

9

Shame and
Narcissistic Pathology

[handwritten: pri primary, internal → narcissistic
secondary. external → neurotic]*

In the first section of this book, we considered the relevance to shame of the concepts of the ego ideal, the ideal self, primitive object relations, and narcissism. We then examined narcissism from several different perspectives, particularly with regard to *failure* and resultant narcissistic *vulnerability*. Finally, we looked at the contributions of Kohut and self psychology to see what they might offer to our understanding of shame. In this Clinical Section, I have so far presented the case of Mr. Dowland, to suggest how I work therapeutically with shame, and then have indicated several specific clinical phenomena that I believe frequently relate to shame, often as defenses against it. I believe that successful treatment necessitates reaching beneath these phenomena to the underlying shame when it exists as a fundamental motivating affect. In this chapter, using other clinical examples, I shall consider again shame as a dominant painful affect of patients suffering from narcissistic vulnerability. Later, in chapter 10, I shall try to show that shame presents differently in neurotic patients, for whom it tends to be more circumscribed than it is for narcissistically vulnerable patients, for whom the manifestations of shame are more pervasive.

Levin (1967, 1971) discussed primary and internal shame, with primary shame being based on an intrapsychic view of the self as

134

fundamentally flawed and defective, and internal shame being the ego's or superego's harshly judgmental view of the self (for example, with regard to failure and the mandates of the ego ideal). These conditions of primary and internal shame fundamentally represent states of narcissistic vulnerability. Levin also described conditions of secondary, external shame. Secondary shame relates to reactive retreat from intrapsychic conflict and drives (where shame functions as a defense); and external shame reflects failure to attain the conditions of a reality-derived goal (frequently in the presence of a social shamer or a viewing audience). These shame states are usually manifestations of neurotic or character problems (Morrison, 1984a, see chapter 10).

THE CASE OF MS. STEIN

Ms. Stein was first seen by me in therapy when she was a student at a local college. She was extremely diffident, speaking in a barely audible voice as she described her great pain and self-doubts with regard to her studies. She had difficulty concentrating – both in her school work and during therapy sessions – and presented her concerns tentatively, obviously trying to hide her distress from me. She talked of her family relationships, emphasizing that she and her mother served as each other's confidante but that her mother seemed always preoccupied with her own work as a mathematician. The patient frequently wanted contact with her mother but usually felt that she was being intrusive when she tried to talk and that her mother was "suffering" her presence until she could return to her own work. Ms. Stein (who preferred to be called by her first name, Lily) described her father as a tempestuous, insecure man who constantly put his own needs ahead of those of his family. Lily's mother had reached her limits in the marital relationship shortly before Lily entered college, and Lily had helplessly witnessed an acrimonious separation and divorce. She was not close to her sister or brother; the middle child, she felt that she was the child closest to each of her parents.

Lily quickly developed a positive idealizing transference to me. She felt that she could easily share her self-doubts with me. She worked on her hurt and anger at her parents over their unavailability or unwillingness to meet her needs, and on her obsessional self-doubts about studying, writing papers, and taking exams. I listened with interest as Lily expressed these concerns, relating her self-doubts to insecurity about being able to gain her parents' attention and approval. "Perhaps if you were perfect in your schoolwork," I said, "they might value you and give you the kind of interest you want." I suggested that she must also be angry at her parents because of their preoccupations, but Lily strongly denied being angry, except at me, for making such a suggestion. Her idealization within the transference lessened over time, but she continued to feel trusting and helped in therapy. Although she occasionally felt and expressed anger at me for my "mistaken" views, Lily did not move into the transferential disillusionment that might have been expected from a woman with such low self-esteem and with her vulnerability to inattentiveness from significant selfobjects. She progressively felt better and more self-confident in college, with several satisfactory, though fleeting, heterosexual relationships. Her relationship with her mother improved somewhat during this time. However, she refused to consider the transferential implications of her feelings toward her parents and boyfriends, choosing instead to terminate treatment after considerable symptomatic relief rather than investigate deeper layers of her self-doubt and feelings within the therapeutic relationship.

When, after an interlude, Lily wanted to resume treatment, I did not have time to work with her and referred her to a colleague. For several years subsequently, my contact with her was limited as she graduated from college, went to graduate school in two universities in different parts of the country, and undertook several rounds of psychotherapy with different therapists. She would contact me periodically on visits home or by phone, updating me on the course of her life, requesting referrals to new therapists in different cities, or just to "touch base." Several times she emphasized how much she cared for, and felt understood by, me. She spoke also of her physical attraction to, and love for, me.

This was the background against which Lily contacted me many years after having first entered treatment. She asked that I see her again in therapy when she returned to the Boston area to teach and finish her dissertation. I agreed to do so, and we resumed intensive treatment several months later.

On meeting Lily again, I was struck by how much more confident she seemed. She dressed more carefully, slouched much less in the chair, and spoke more directly and audibly, though, by no means, forcefully.[1] As she filled in details of the intervening years, my impression was that she had benefited from her subsequent treatment experiences and from her movement from adolescence into womanhood.

---

[1]Slouching posture, inaudible speech, and averted gaze are hallmarks of narcissistic (primary, internal) shame, reflecting subjective apology about the self's very existence.

She, however, felt she had not progressed far enough. She said that her time in graduate school had been excruciating—she had become "crazy with self-doubts" as she had prepared a lecture for her department. Her most recent therapist had not understood or believed her panic about her work, and Lily had found her to be cold and unapproachable. Lily's work on her dissertation was not progressing, and she remained immobilized with self-criticism about her writing ability. She wanted me to understand and accept the reality of her self-doubts and insecurity.

During the intervening years, I had become attuned to, and interested in, the devastating pain of narcissism and its vicissitudes. I focused now on Lily's self-doubts, her wishes that her previous therapist had been more available, more accepting of her. "It seems that you felt you couldn't bring your needs to her, that if you became too needy, you feared that she would push you away." I equated this response of her woman therapist with Lily's experience of her mother's impatient self-preoccupation when Lily would turn to her for support. Lily sat forward and became quite animated as she agreed, indicating that she had always felt that her needs had been overpowering and had caused people to move away. I silently recognized Lily's fear that I also would not be able to accept her needs or the reality of her experiences, that I too would not want to hear of them and would push her away.

Thus began the second round of treatment with Lily, as I indicated my understanding of her fears of expressing need and her conviction that she was flawed and unacceptable because of her neediness, causing the important people in her life to withdraw. Either she had to hide her needs or again face the inevitable disappointments and rage that their expression engendered. In addition, she readily agreed that her needs—for contact, support—made her feel inferior, ashamed, and humiliated because of people's failure to accept or meet them. Because of some evanescent idealization/alliance, her hope had persisted that I might be able to tolerate her "demands" and memories, and help her understand and correct her self-doubts and despair. She also hoped to alter her work inhibitions and to be able to progress with her dissertation.

During this first phase of the new treatment, I attempted, principally, to understand Lily's feelings of neediness and self-doubt, to reflect back this understanding, but in no way to challenge her self-perception. Frequently, the glaring contrasts between her manifest talents and abilities and the way she viewed herself made it hard for me to accept her internally consistent, negating, and shameful self-image as well as the validity of her painful recollections. However, each time

I attempted to question her vision of herself as flawed and to impose my view of her strengths, she became hurt or angry, claiming I was doubting her experience; "You are just wrong." I felt cornered; there seemed to be no way to interpret or share my view of Lily or my interpretation of her predicaments. I felt frustrated and unacknowledged.

This, then, was to be an essential element of Lily's treatment: to accept and believe as real and significant her own feelings about her experience, her psychic reality; to pay attention to those instances, in which I appeared to have failed to appreciate or agree with her perception. Thus, the fairly frequent instances of incongruity between my impression of Lily's apparent accomplishments and her own perception of failure led to her sense of not being understood or believed when I questioned her viewpoint. Similarly, major breaches in the therapeutic relationship occurred when I attempted to interpret my sense of Lily's underlying hostility or anger toward me, as suggested by various of her comments or actions. Finally, as might be expected, Lily was extremely sensitive and perceptive about shifts in my attention, and much effort in treatment involved exploration of her reactions to her perceived variations of my moment-to-moment interest in her.

For Lily, then, her feelings and experience had been undervalued and unattended by her parents because of their own narcissistic needs and vulnerabilities. Of primary importance to her was a sense of my interest in, and empathic acceptance of and attunement to, her stated, conscious feelings and perceptions of her own experience. She frequently felt misunderstood or "accused," and much of the therapeutic work consisted of detailed exploration of these moments. It will become clear that one important element in establishment of trust, and of "repair" of the inevitable ruptures engendered through empathic selfobject failure, was my willingness to explore, reveal, and in some cases reconsider my own feelings during these incidents of failed communication. Finally, I hope to demonstrate that at the core of Lily's self-experience was a deep sense of defect and inferiority, leading to a primary and pervasive feeling of internal shame.

An indication of Lily's deeply entrenched shame was the striking style of her self-presentation to the world. While she was currently somewhat more assertive than she had been as an undergraduate, she still seemed to pull back, retreat into herself as she sat with me. At the end of each session, she backed timidly toward the door, awkwardly saying goodbye as she looked down. In our sessions, her voice was soft and hesitant, especially when she was talking about feelings or matters of particular importance to her. It was as though in every gesture she was apologizing for her very being (see footnote 1). Lily seemed determined to hide every external manifestation of her inner feelings, thoughts, or flaws. When I first commented on her apparent wish to conceal herself, Lily readily agreed. "It's as if you're ashamed of something deeply personal about yourself, and the more you can recede from sight, the better." Comments of this nature, especially those identifying her shameful feelings, seemed very useful and on target for Lily, as she communicated her sense of being understood.

At the same time, the defensive, conflictual nature of Lily's apologetic style seemed readily apparent, and sometimes quite palpable. For example, I would attempt to identify the hostile feelings behind her soft voice, suggesting that her withdrawal, and even occasionally her shame, were attempts to hide anger and assertiveness about one matter or another. Such interpretations, however, invariably led not only to angry denial and attack, but to deep despair. Lily would insist that I did not understand, or even believe, how bad she felt about herself. She felt that I, like her mother, was saying that what she felt was not really the case, but was something else – she was really feeling fine, strong, or angry. It became clear that interpretation of anything other than matters relating to Lily's manifest distress, shame, and feeling of failure felt to her like a betrayal, a reflection of my agenda rather than her own, a failure of empathic appreciation of her experience. Such interpretation of conflict, and of the secondary, reactive nature of some of Lily's shame and self-doubt, would have to await belief and improvement in, and understanding of the source of, her distressed self-image and her concern about others' ability to tolerate her needs.

With regard to the therapeutic technique for dealing with the self-doubt and narcissistic vulnerability demonstrated by Lily, I cannot overemphasize the importance of initially staying with the patient's explicit experience and identifying only those elements which readily relate to that experience. For Lily, this meant identifying, and taking as important, her expression of deep self-doubt and criticism and respecting equally her accurate experience of my failure to follow her lead on these matters. Genetic acceptance, interpretation and reconstruction of relevant parental or environmental failures are important and useful at these times.

For example, Lily frequently expressed doubt about her writing ability, as she described her experiences in graduate school and her fears about anticipated difficulties in approaching her dissertation. I often was struck by the apparent contrast between these doubts and interpretations of events and what I had inferred about her writing successes and feedback from other authors. When I attempted to "reality-test" her perceptions, however, Lily inevitably felt misunderstood, hurt, and despairing about the potential for therapeutic help. I concluded that, for the present, any attempts at challenging her view of herself and surviving her angry attacks were not useful and would lead, instead, to withdrawal, a break in the therapeutic bond, and lack of trust. Rather, these inevitable failures in selfobject attunement could be usefully addressed when I could identify the moments of disagreement between us and correctly surmise that she was feeling upset and misunderstood by me. She would then usually counter with a jab, like "Yes, you don't seem to believe me when I say that there's a real problem with my writing." I might at such times attempt to learn more of her experiences with instructors and acknowledge her distress at my previous intervention:

> It sounds like it felt as though I was following my own lead, not yours. Like your mother did, when she would automatically reassure you that school was going just fine. Also, it's clear that writing isn't just some neutral activity for you. That your mother has had difficulty making her own mark in theoretical math, and it would create problems for you to succeed in writing while she has had trouble in her career.

Lily was able to reestablish contact with me following such acknowledgment and identification of breaches in communication, and also to make use of interpretations that connected with her experience.

She began appearing at sessions with a notebook, paper, or torn envelope on which she had made extensive notes during the time since the last session. She would rivet her eyes on this paper, turning it over and over to decipher every last notation. At first, I encouraged Lily to explore her current thoughts without relying on her notes. She retorted by emphasizing the thought and effort that had gone into the creation of the notes the previous evening; she wanted to make use of her notes, not to forget the points she had written down. It became clear that a power struggle was unnecessary and would simply leave Lily feeling misunderstood once more, "bested" by her therapist and, as a result, humiliated and shamed. In addition, as the written word was not neutral in the rest of Lily's life, neither was it trivial in therapy. This was the area around her work in which she wanted help, and it was important for me to acknowledge her writings. Therefore, I accepted her use of the notes.

Another example of Lily's sensitivity to misinterpretation, and the shame that frequently accompanied it, related to feelings regarding her apartment. She had lived for several years in an apparently appealing apartment that she had been able to rent at reasonable cost. Her great fear, however, was that her colleagues would envy her space and criticize her for paying more in rent than a graduate student was entitled to spend. In fact, this became such an obsessional fear that Lily would go to great lengths to prevent friends from seeing the building in which she lived, let alone her apartment. When prodded about this, Lily said that she thought it was "too good" for her, that people would criticize and attack her for living too well. Further exploration led to shame and humiliation at the thought of being exposed for living in luxury while others had mere student apartments.

This shame at being exposed was similar to that which Lily felt at the thought of her writings being read. Like her apartment, her writings would reveal her self-defects. However, while shame about her writing symbolized her body shame and inferiority, as revealed in therapy, the apartment shame represented her concerns about hubris and pride. Lily's apartment shame recalls Kohut's (1971) observation about the disavowal of shame-generating grandiosity and exhibitionism as delineated in his concept of the vertical split. Similarly, Lily's shame over her apartment might also be seen, with Freud (1905), as a reaction formation against her wish to exhibit, or her own wish to look (voyeurism). However, any attempt to interpret her shame as being itself defensive against underlying wishes was felt as unempathic and insensitive.

For instance, during one session she described, in great detail, the problems and tribulations that she had experienced while packing her possessions for the movers and moving the landlord's furniture back to its original position. I made two errors in empathic attunement, reflecting imposition of my *own* sense of reality. At one point, I wondered whether one of Lily's friends might not have been willing to help out (and thus allowing them to see her apartment). Second, I commented that it was fortunate that the moving ordeal only happened infrequently. Lily, tearful and angry, replied, "You don't seem to take what I was going through seriously. You were minimizing it, like it was trivial and insignificant." Initially surprised, I had to contain an impulse to object, to point out that I had only been trying to be helpful and supportive.

This, then, seems to be the major point: therapeutic attempts to ease Lily's distress through observations based on *my* perception of reality were the very ones that appeared to be so unfeeling and dismissive of her own experience. Further discussion of her experiences about my observations revealed that she had felt shamed and humiliated by me: "It felt like you didn't believe what I was saying, that I shouldn't have found it so hard to move. It made me feel embarrassed, like there was no need for my reaction." I acknowledged her experience of having been humiliated by me, as I recognized silently that my "helpful" comments had in fact made her feel helpless and misunderstood. Any interpretation in terms, for instance, of so-called masochistic attachment to suffering would have been incorrect in the context of Lily's experience and would have been felt only as an accusation and a negation of experienced distress.

Reflections

The issues raised in the treatment of Lily underscore her great sensitivity to faulty therapeutic attunement, leaving her feeling ashamed, humiliated, and despairing about the possibility of ever being attended to or understood. I am suggesting that this experience of not being understood indicates the fundamental need of such patients to establish empathic connection and that this focus, along with explorations around the experience of empathic failure, is the initial, primary task of treatment. For these patients, manifestations of their narcissistic vulnerability, and their resultant shame sensitivity, are elicited by the sometimes subtle shifts in attunement of their important selfobjects. These shifts and misses, then, must become the major interest of therapeutic work for long periods of the treatment, particularly as experienced in the transference.

This focus clearly derives from the contributions of Kohut, with emphases on attending to and *understanding* empathic failure, the importance of the selfobject function of empathic attunement, and the inevitable evolution of the more archaic, mirroring, and idealizing selfobject transferences. While narcissistically vulnerable patients like Lily may demonstrate as well conflictual and defensive manifestations (for example, passive, shame defenses against hostility and anger; grandiosity and entitlement hidden behind self-effacing obsequiousness), these are not the problems that are most usefully available for interpretation. As Lily once put it, "You want to talk about my anger and hidden criticism of you, but that's not what I'm here for. Damn it, I can't even put myself together, I can't do my work. And that's what I need to talk about to feel whole."

Ultimately, then, the immediate focus of therapy became empathic appreciation and the *mirroring* of her pervasive sense of unworthiness and shame as a reflection of unresponsive parental selfobjects, the resultant paucity of selfobject availability for providing under-

standing and empathic resonance, and interpretations of these experienced parental failures as sources of shame and fragmentation. Interpretations of intrapsychic, oedipal conflicts are indeed important, but
they require patience and sensitive timing before they can be therapeutically useful; otherwise, they may seem like yet further accusations or
irrelevancies.

THE CASE OF CRISTOPHE

Cristophe was discussed in chapters 7 and 8 to illustrate the underpin-
nings of shame in a man with a characterological depression based on
low self-esteem. His depression was seen to reflect continued idolization of his elderly, remote, very successful father, and his belief that he
was, by comparison, insignificant and inept. This configuration is an
example of Chasseguet-Smirgel's (1985) articulation of the ego ideal
and her suggestion of the resultant malady of the ideal (chapter 4).
Thus, Cristophe tormented himself for his self-defined failures and
flaws and consulted me after being frightened by suicidal urges. He
entered intensive psychotherapy in an attempt to alter and resolve his
deep despair and suicidal thoughts.

While Cristophe and Lily certainly share many dynamics of
narcissistically impaired patients, their self-doubts and related shame
are somewhat different. Lily was particularly sensitive to the current
repetition of failed selfobject mirroring and attunement, and therapeutic attention to such moments, particularly within the transference,
proved therapeutically most useful. Cristophe, on the other hand, was
preoccupied with his own sense of inferiority and flawed self, as played
out in his idealization of, and negative self-comparison with, a successful father and older sister—themes that were repeated in the transference. The therapeutic implications of this distinction will be considered in the presentation of moments from Cristophe's treatment.

During much of the early phase of treatment, I encouraged
Cristophe to express his despair, shame, and self-loathing, to speak of
himself, his childhood experiences, and the inevitable comparisons to
his parents (see chapter 8). At first, he recounted primarily idealizations
of his father, who had come to the United States as an immigrant
escaping the Nazis, had worked his way through college and graduate
school, and had attained an important position in a large corporation.
Cristophe remembered, wistfully, Saturday morning walks with his
father and presents his father had bought him on those occasions,
presents that had come to signify his father's love. However, Cristophe

recalled also that his parents had gone out on weekend evenings, leaving him in the care of different housekeepers. Despite living in a large, well-appointed house, he remembered spending most of his time in front of the TV in the housekeeper's quarters. He would use the house's swimming pool to buy friendship with the local children, but he recalled being teased and tormented for being different. He sobbed inconsolably as he remembered names hurled at him that played on his last name and implied difference, fatness, or homosexuality.

With these recollections, then, came great pain and wrenching despair as he uncovered ambivalence, anger, and disillusionment toward his formerly idealized father, and experiences of abandonment by both parents. However, his focus remained on what it was about himself that had caused these painful assaults and injustices. Thus, symptomatically he remained depressed rather than entitled, for example, which might have been anticipated along with his sense of specialness. His self-loathing took the form of doubts about his intellectual ability and competence, doubts that reflected his painful comparisons with his father and sister. With these doubts came deep shame and humiliation over his less than perfect performance in school and his difficulty in immediately obtaining a high-status job.

Therapy focused on the pain of his memories and current feelings about himself; the familial, childhood sources of this pain; and the various means that he used to avoid it (alcohol, repression, sexual conquest). In Cristophe's case, reality-testing—in the form of reminding him of his current stature compared to childhood, his academic successes, and, ultimately, his competence and satisfaction in a job he had obtained for himself—served well in furthering the treatment. These reminders tended to counter attacks by a harsh, punitive superego over lapses from the ego ideal and offered a more accepting, internalizable voice to counter his parental representations. Cristophe explicitly utilized the words from therapy to confront his punitive self-criticism, with progressive easing of his shame-based attacks on himself.

This reality-testing brings up the nature of Cristophe's transference. Clearly, therapy had become very important to him, as he began to soften his harsh self-image and to feel increasingly more self-accepting.[2] However, in the inevitable complexity of his transference, he reexperienced with me, his therapist, all aspects of his feelings toward his father, including idealization, anger, disillusionment, and

---

[2]Interestingly, the notion of self-acceptance was very helpful, as he explicitly utilized it to counter his brutal self-attacks.

the sense of his own inadequacy. He repeated with me his feeling of being inadequate as a patient, just as he had felt intellectually inadequate compared with his father and sister. He sometimes felt contempt toward me for being a feeling type, rather than a doer like his father, here emphasizing differences between us (see case of Mr. Jackson, chapter 10). Cristophe's contempt toward me and others largely reflected projective identification of his own shame into the other (see chapters 7 and 8) and his potential for maintaining contact with that aspect of himself through interaction with me-as-therapist. His shame and self-contempt were represented by his need for therapy in the first place: "If I were strong and self-reliant, I wouldn't need to be coming here all the time, I wouldn't need to hang on to your words in order to feel better about myself. Christ, my father never saw a therapist in his life."

So, for Cristophe, the very act of coming to therapy became a crutch with which he could beat himself for his dependency, further attesting to his faults and imperfection. His dependency on me was another source of shame. Thus, he *idealized* me for the selfobject functions of power, understanding, and merging acceptance I provided; *hated* me for his experience of my superiority and aloof self-containment, represented in his paternal transference; *scorned* me for falling short of his paternal ideal; *blamed* me for inducing shameful dependence on therapy; and, ultimately, *loved* me for providing the context to reexperience and rework his painful feelings of despair and self-hatred. Each of these configurational and selfobject transference elements was considered in great detail during the course of Cristophe's treatment.

One day, for example, Cristophe came for his session and remained silent for the first few minutes, a not infrequent beginning. Finally, he looked up and admitted that he had been drinking the night before and had even had a drink before coming. He then excoriated himself for falling short of the ideal he had established – he was to have had no drinks for four days in a row. I commented both on the severity of his sobriety schedule and his harsh self-criticism for failing to stick to the regimen. I mentioned also the likelihood that through drinking he had attempted to hide some painful feeling, as he often had before. He agreed, but then blamed himself for the triviality of his problems: "I'm just a spoiled, wealthy brat, who can't take even the usual pressures of life." I pointed to the similarity between this self-criticism and his recollection of kids calling him a rich kid/sissy. He then described his feelings from the previous day.

At work, one of his supervisors had criticized the quality of a report into which he had put considerable effort. A friend then called from out of town, telling Cristophe that he would not be able to make a weekend visit they had recently planned. Finally, when he returned home, his current girlfriend had criticized his commitment to her, saying that his lovemaking had seemed abstract, not especially "centered." "Each of these things was small enough in and of itself," he said. "But together, I just couldn't handle them. They said 'You're a fuckup, man; a worthless asshole.' And then the old suicidal thoughts were there. God, I've sure come a long way!" With this, Cristophe burst into tears.

I invited his associations, and he began, almost ritualistically, to compare his productivity and abilities with those of his father, emphasizing his father's presumed disappointment in him. I wondered whether he thought that I would be disappointed in him as well—for drinking again, for making mistakes, and for not sustaining progress in therapy: "Like you won't please me if you don't do well here, if you feel suicidal again." He agreed and then began to cry again, pleading, "Why am I so goddamned hard on myself? It's so easy for me to slip into hating myself again." I commented that it seemed difficult for him to accept any imperfection or mistake because he assumed that his father/I would become critical and rejecting.

As his associations continued, he spoke of how harsh and critical his female supervisor seemed. He then talked of his girlfriend, whom he also felt to be critical: "Like my mother. When I was a kid, we'd get into these bad shouting matches, where I felt she was always telling me what to do. I couldn't stand that—I felt so small and helpless." This association brought him back to his supervisor and girlfriend, each eliciting similar feelings. With his girlfriend, however, it was as if he had no choice, although, in fact, he recognized that he did have choice. She was right, actually; he was not much attracted to her sexually. But he almost automatically faulted himself for his lack of sexual attentiveness. A spark of self-understanding and acceptance entered Cristophe's voice.

I then wondered in whom the self-critical voice was originating now: "Is it really your girlfriend, your boss, your father or mother now, or are these echoes from earlier voices? Isn't it your own self-criticism and disappointment, not mine, that cause you such grief, make you feel so ashamed?" He readily agreed, seemed to derive considerable relief, but then returned to a concern about how he would ever alter his self-hatred and whether he would always need the help of a therapist to feel better. I pointed out, again, how he turned even his therapy into a source of disgrace, but then indicated that he had in fact already come quite a distance in altering his view of himself. Setbacks certainly occurred, but he did seem better able to maintain some perspective on himself and on his improvement and was more accepting, less self-denigrating, than when he had entered treatment.

At other times, therapy focused on Cristophe's defenses against anger and aggression toward others, including his use of shame as a defense. On one occasion he had learned from his father of the symptomatic progression of a recent, moderately debilitating physical condition. He found himself worrying about his father and his mother's reaction to the illness, but then associated to his own weakness and awkwardness in sports as an adolescent. His thoughts then centered on his shame and embarrassment with classmates at the prep school he had attended. I commented, "It seems as though it's easier today for you to think about your own incapacities than your father's." He blushed and then continued tearfully to anticipate his father's gradual deterioration and weakness. I asked whether he might be feeling some disillusionment with his father: "This picture doesn't square with the image of a totally strong, capable, infallible idol, does it?" He acknowledged his concern about his father's deterioration and possible future weakness and frailty. "So then, maybe you'll become the strong one, and he, the weaker, don't you think?" I asked. This unleashed a torrent of associations including anger toward his father for his age and infirmity; then for being preoccupied with work and being inattentive when Cristophe was young; then for having "sent him away" to a prep school where he had suffered many indignities. His self-oriented shame then turned outward, into guilt for harboring such angry and aggressive feelings toward his father. Ultimately, I wondered whether he might even be feeling "some triumph over your father, as you move into success in your life and he declines from it in his. Some pleasure in his weakness, as well as disillusionment and sadness."

Thus, after quite some time in which Cristophe's shame and self-criticism had been uncovered, reviewed, accepted, and interpreted in terms of failure by childhood parental selfobjects to meet his needs for affirmation and idealization, it seemed relevant and timely to bring his attention to guilt over competitive, aggressive feelings toward his father. The oedipal constellation, which had indeed been present since the beginning of treatment, could effectively be brought to Cristophe's attention, but only after acceptance and thorough investigation of his flawed and shameful view of himself. He continued to work on, and accept, his aggressive, oedipal feelings toward his father, as well as on his shame-soaked self-image, with a gradual shift toward the former as treatment progressed.

Another aspect of Cristophe's treatment, and the relationship of shame to grandiosity and exhibitionism, needs to be mentioned. Although he characteristically presented his shameful self for examination and review, on occasion he displayed contempt and haughty disregard for someone in his life. For instance, he spoke with disdain about the social and academic background of a woman who had been hired as his equal at work. Clearly, envy and rivalry were involved in this picture, as well as externalization of his own shame. However, I noted a sense of genuine superiority in his description of her and commented on this. Cristophe responded with a proud description of the background of his father's family in Europe, in which he represented them as the Jewish intellectual aristocracy of the metropolitan city in which they had lived.

He elaborated on his family's background and cultural heritage and spoke with pride of his own affiliation with it. These reminiscences led to a discussion of his complex, ambivalent feelings about his own Jewishness, including much self-loathing, which seemed to alternate with the pride he was now acknowledging. His ambivalence seemed to parallel similar feelings in his father, who had gone to great lengths to distance himself from his Jewish, European heritage. Nonetheless, it was a surprise to Cristophe to realize his own pride and haughtiness and his inclination to disparage someone whom he viewed as socially inferior. These responses were not congruent with his political liberalism and active involvement in the movement for sexual equality. Thus, we were able to investigate further his reaction formations and other defenses, including obsequiousness and shame, against feelings of haughtiness and superiority, as well as those specifically against anger and shame. This theme emerged at other moments in Cristophe's treatment, especially with regard to manifestations of his entitlement.

DISCUSSION

These two vignettes are representative of two slightly different types of narcissistic difficulties. In each, I have attempted to show that shame plays a role as a central organizing affect. Lily, with her great sensitivity to lack of empathic attunement and shifts in attention away from her (inadequate mirroring) typifies a group of patients for whom such continuing, precise attention is the necessary ingredient for a sense of cohesiveness and well-being. Without it, these people feel fragmented, hopeless, and humiliated. Cristophe, on the other hand, is someone for whom a fundamental self-loathing and despair reflects a chronic state of low self-esteem and comparative, unmodulated idolization that is independent of momentary attunement and contact with others. Certainly these distinctions are not absolute; Lily also experienced fundamental shame and self-loathing, and Cristophe's depression could be eased temporarily by meaningful personal contact. However, Lily's present need for attunement, as contrasted with characterological despair over past insults and abandonments, seems relevant.

These differences reflect Kohut's (1977) distinction between the functions of *mirroring* and *idealizing* selfobjects and his elaboration of the concept of the bipolar self (see also Panel, 1981). The bipolar self represents the self's two poles—ambition and exhibitionistic strivings, on one hand, for which age-appropriate mirroring is the most relevant selfobject function; and, on the other, goals and ideals, which seek satisfaction through merger with, and idealization of, the powerful, soothing, and competent parental selfobject. Between these poles occurs what Kohut called a "tension arc" of skills and abilities that determine, I surmise, competence and achievement. From the perspective of the bipolar self, one is "pushed" by ambitions, and "pulled" by ideals. It seems to me that within that tension arc lies the self's potential for the experience of shame, which relates to failure and flaw in the attainment of ambitions and inferiority with respect to ideals. Ultimately, it is the recognition of failed skills and abilities, and the impossibility of their realization, that determines the shame experience.

How, then, do the concepts of mirroring and idealization, and the related concept of the bipolar self, help in understanding patients like Lily and Cristophe and in informing their treatment? Lily's need for mirroring, empathic attunement, and finely differentiated attention has been amply discussed: with these needs met, she feels contained and soothed; the needs unmet, she feels jangled, despairing, and hopeless. This need for empathic attunement dictates the importance of the therapist's here-and-now presence and attentiveness. I think it also reflects the relative blurring and haziness of the therapist's actual (configurational/libidinal) qualities. I have suggested elsewhere (Morrison, 1984b, 1987) that these elements of the mirroring selfobject tend to develop earlier, to be less differentiated, than those of the idealized selfobject, and relate usually to the maternal function (see also chapter 5).

On the other hand, Cristophe has been shown to have a profoundly self-punitive and shameful self-image, independent of moment-to-moment attunement from his object/environment. This self-experience seems to have evolved from early limitations in parental responsiveness, particularly on the part of his idealized father. Such apparent lack of paternal responsiveness to Cristophe's idealizing longings was interpreted by him as evidence for his own unworthiness and was a stimulus for his profound sense of shame. Treatment consisted less significantly of my precise and unfailingly attentive attunement than of my consistent presence over time and availability for idealization/identification. This function relates more frequently to the father, may develop later than the need for mirroring, and generally represents a more highly differentiated image of the configurational object (Morrison, 1986b, 1987; see also chapter 5). In fact, I have hypothesized that the idealized selfobject, with early identification and creation of a beginning outline for a differentiated object, may represent a bridge from earlier selfobject needs to internalizable, delineated objects.

This difference may also be considered from the perspective of *overstimulation* and *understimulation* (Kohut and Wolf, 1978). Lily, who yearned for perfect attunement, had been highly valued by both parents; in fact, she felt that she had played a significant role in mediating their fighting and ultimate separation. She felt that she had been the favored child, her mother's confidante and friend. Thus her family experience was of feeling overstimulated and burdened, with insufficient attention to the boundaries of her own needs, thoughts, and differentiated self. Cristophe, on the other hand, felt like the dopey sibling, frequently abandoned, left behind, or cast out. No one seemed to value or have enough time for him; his thirst for acceptance and interest from his idealized father went unmet. Cristophe, then, felt understimulated and alone; his shame was from despair over some personal defect that he believed must explain his loneliness and abandonment. This portrait is consistent with an earlier formulation (Morrison, 1984a) that shame relates to *depletion* of the previously delineated self. Cristophe's shame does not derive from boundary diffusion, but rather from isolation. Thus we see two different paths to the self-blame and criticism characteristic of the underside of narcissism.

The cases described here reflect differing manifestations of narcissism and shame resulting from deficiencies of separate selfobject functions. In Lily shame emanated primarily from the nonattainment of her needs for empathic attunement, interest, and attention. These needs reflected deficits in the **mirroring** function, made manifest by overstimulation and burden by her parental selfobjects, with their resultant failure to appreciate Lily's separateness and individuality. Cristophe's shame, on the other hand, resulted largely from failure in response to his need for merger with power/perfection by his idealized selfobject, his father, leaving him feeling depressed, isolated, and depleted. These narcissistic manifestations may indeed represent the overstimulated and understimulated personality disorders described by Kohut and Wolf (1978), or the resultant behavioral manifestations of mirror-hunger and idealization-hunger. Through these examples, I have attempted to show the central place of shame in narcissistic vulnerability.

In the next chapter, I turn to the external, reactive, and frequently defensive nature of shame in neurotic and healthier character conditions.

10

Shame and Neurotic (Differentiated Character) Conditions

There are those people for whom narcissistic, that is, self-problems may not be uppermost, or who have successfully worked them through in treatment. And yet, even these healthier people also experience shame, as we all do. For these patients, the shame experience is not so devastating, central, or fragmenting as it is for the narcissistically tormented patients just described. Shame exists for them, not as a negation of their whole self-experience, but rather in response to some specific failed objective or ideal. For them, shame tends to relate more to a behavioral goal of omission or commission or to a desire rather than to a need. It seems more contained and limited to that act or desire and is of less intensity or duration than in the case of narcissistic conditions. Narcissistic shame tends to be more *dyadic* with respect to need for one or another selfobject function; the shame in neurotic personalities more often represents familiar conflict involving triangulated, configurational objects. Neurotic shame may also represent a modulated response to the expression of need and selfobject failure, but more frequently it is, I believe, a *defensive* reaction against painful oedipal conflict and aggression (Morrison, 1984a).

For these patients, the guilt–shame cycle of Piers (1953) is most relevant, as shame frequently reflects passive withdrawal from sexual

152

or aggressive, guilt-inducing actions and fantasies. The following clinical examples illustrate these issues, including the differences between neurotic and narcissistic shame.

THE CASE OF MRS. BARLIN

A forty-year-old married woman with two children, Mrs. Barlin entered therapy because of feelings of guilt that she had not done an adequate job as a mother, and phobic fears that her youngest son would be attacked and criticized. We worked extensively on issues surrounding her mothering, including her resentment of and disdain for her nonacademically oriented son, whom she felt to be "cut from a different cloth" from her husband and herself. Related to this disdain, she expressed considerable external shame that her neighbors, and the school community at large, would think ill of her for her poor job of mothering. While guilt about buried anger toward her mother was an important issue in her treatment, I will focus here on the nature and course of her shame in therapy.

Mrs. Barlin's associations to her shame took her to feelings about her family. Her mother, raised in rural Greece, had come to this country as a young woman to marry Mrs. Barlin's father, who had emigrated several years earlier. The marriage had been arranged by the two families in Greece. Mrs. Barlin's father died when she was eight years old, and her mother insisted that she and her older siblings put him out of their minds. All photos and traces of their father were put away, and the children received a clear and explicit message that their father had been inferior. They should forget about him and get on with achievement and success in this country. Mrs. Barlin, who still remained very close to her elderly mother, had complied with this pressure and had pursued academic excellence. She had married a professor and was herself professionally successful.

In reviewing her feelings about her family, Mrs. Barlin readily acknowledged some shame about her parents' origins as foreigners and how important it had been for her to do well to erase this personal "blemish." While in graduate school she had married a man whose roots were in this country and who showed considerable intellectual promise. As we reviewed her marriage, she agreed that her husband "was supposed to please my mother and assure that things would go well for me here." Her associations moved between shame and anger at her son for his failure to achieve and her "obligations" to be successful to improve the status imposed by her father's humble origins. She gradually became aware of a connection between her shame over fantasied criticism toward her and her son from neighbors and the school community, and shame about her immigrant background.

I wondered whether she might, with this shame, also feel angry toward her son for making life difficult (there had been frequent struggles between Mrs. Barlin and her son over homework, use of the car, and the like), and toward her mother for having caused her to lead so constricted and controlled a life. It was difficult for her to experience anger, but we were able to uncover hidden fantasies and desires to lead a freer, more imaginative existence. Her associations became more readily available and included sexual dreams that contained transferential feelings toward me. In addition, she was able to acknowledge, at first irritation and then actual anger toward her son, husband, and mother for demands made on her.

We then talked about Mrs. Barlin's shame about her Greek origins, and specifically about her father. I commented on her apparent total lack of memories about him: "After all, you were eight years old when he died. Doesn't it seem strange that you don't remember a thing about him?" She agreed that it was strange, but there was nothing she could do about it–nothing would come to mind. She had tried to talk with her mother about him, but the old woman had only murmured a few generalities and then changed the subject. One older sibling had some vague recollections about their father's warmth. The mother had instilled shame in connection with any specific details or memories about Mrs. Barlin's father, and his image seemed to have slipped away.

Her sister's comments about her father's warmth led the patient to question the stereotyped image of him as a profligate nonachiever who stayed out late and drank with friends. Then, one day, she entered my office with great pleasure and excitement, sharing with me her joy at finding in an attic box a photograph of her father and herself. In it, she saw a happy little girl, beaming as she stood nestled against a handsome, roguish-looking man who was smiling contentedly down at his daughter. She described in great detail her father's contours from the photo–he seemed fairly short, and very dapper in a white suit, with a broad-brimmed panama hat. He had a large mustache, which appeared to be carefully waxed and twisted at the ends. He seemed to be most pleased and proud to be this close to his daughter–his eyes twinkled. Mrs. Barlin told of how happy she–then a girl of about seven or eight–had seemed in the photo to be snuggling close to him.

The discovery of this photograph, coupled with therapeutic progress in gaining access to Mrs. Barlin's feelings, led to a major shift in the course of treatment. She brought into treatment many more vivid feelings – of love, anger, personal goals for herself profession-ally – and she seemed better able to tolerate and reflect on these feelings. We considered how her shame had defended against, and substituted for, these more authentic feelings and had contained them and kept them out of awareness. I said, "Though it's very painful, it seems that shame may be a more acceptable feeling for you than the more intense ones like anger and love which we're getting to now." Mrs. Barlin agreed and continued to think with renewed vigor about her father.

While actual memories of her father remained limited, she was intrigued and energized at the realization that he had probably been loving and interested in her and that apparently she had been actively engaged with him throughout their time together. This realization felt like a great gift from therapy, and she was very grateful to, and to some degree idealizing of, me. Also, some of the excitement of her original paternal relationship was rekindled in the transference, as she had loving, exciting dreams and fantasies about me that we were able to connect with her newfound understanding about that relationship. Finally, work around her shame led to the realization that love and acceptance of her father felt like a betrayal of her mother and her mandate that Mrs. Barlin despise and forget about him. We explored her guilt about that maternal betrayal and arrived at implicit oedipal themes long buried in this "Greek tragedy."

Clearly, Mrs. Barlin's shame had defensively covered deeply hidden anger toward both her mother and her son, and forbidden oedipal longings toward a dead, forgotten father. For neurotic patients, as for the narcissistic patients described in the previous chapter, shame is frequently the presenting symptom or affect and must be taken seriously and dealt with before proceeding to underlying genetic fac-tors. For the narcissistic patients described earlier, shame is internal and primary, permeating all aspects of the self-experience. In Mrs. Barlin's case, shame may be seen both as a significant, primary element of her own self-view and her perspective on her family, and as a reaction formation against underlying oedipal and aggressive conflicts and the guilt that usually accompanies them. In this way, Piers's (1953) guilt–shame cycle is represented for Mrs. Barlin by a sequence in which wishes for her father, and anger at her mother, are repressed because of guilt, leaving instead a defensive passivity and feelings of personal and familial inferiority, which then cause shame. As the dynamics of this shame response are worked out, the sources of the underlying guilt come into focus, and the cycle can be untangled.

THE CASE OF MR. PROUT

An Irish-Catholic, married executive in his early 40s, Mr. Prout entered psychotherapy because of generalized dysphoria and dissatisfaction with his life. He expressed unhappiness in his marriage, feeling that things had become too routine: "All the excitement has gone out of the relationship; and out of everything else, for that matter." He was a neatly dressed, handsome man who related easily and with humor, seeming from the beginning to want to charm and engage me, his therapist. Always he began by asking how I was and then would make some complimentary observation or other about my clothing or office. When I inquired about the reasons for his interest in me, he seemed confused, as if to say, "Well, isn't that the way you're supposed to interact in the world?" Politeness and engaging charm seemed to be paramount to him.

He told me of his childhood and his family. His mother had been born in this country; her father, a successful contractor, had made quite a bit of money and had been a local politician of some renown, known for his good looks and rumored womanizing. Mr. Prout had grown up very close to, and adoring of, his mother, whom he described as warm and saintly. His father had been someone he admired, but always from afar; he found him distant and felt that he had never really known his father, who had frequently been absent from the home. His father's aloofness from the family, and supposed sexual affairs, had caused his mother great pain. As a child Mr. Prout had felt responsible for delighting his mother and easing her distress. His sense of responsibility also included caring for his sister, three years younger than he. When he was grown, he married an "appropriate" woman from his own background whom he loved very much but to whom he readily transferred the feelings of responsibility he had learned with his mother. Fairly quickly, the spark of sexual desire left his marriage and he acknowledged frequently feeling frustrated and attracted to other women. He abstained from extramarital affairs, however, saying that his father had been "a good model about what not to do in that department."

In therapy, he readily discussed his feelings of love and obligation for his mother and his anger at, as well as admiration for, his father. With relative ease, he talked about guilt and hatred for his father, noting enviously, "Why, they even named a small square uptown for him – wreath and everything!" He understood that beneath his purified and laundered love for his mother must lie sexual feelings, and that these had been repressed out of guilt and some kind of feared retaliation by his father.

I was struck by the ease with which he identified and spoke about guilt, and commented on this. He then spoke in great detail about his childhood experiences with religion and the Church. He had taken his Catholicism very seriously; he had gone regularly to Mass and had served for several years as an altar boy. He had identified with Jesus and long considered going into the priesthood, a plan that had greatly pleased his mother, who was devout. He also regularly had attended confession, and his memories of the confessional were stark and vivid. He had frequently felt guilty, especially over "impure" sexual wishes and images, and recalled regularly seeking forgiveness from the priest. "Come to think of it," he noted during one session, "that's what feels so familiar about this [the therapeutic] situation – you remind me of my priest in childhood, and this room is like the confessional." I expressed interest in this analogy. "Though larger and messier," he added with a laugh. I repeated "messier," and he associated to how reassuring the orderliness of Catholicism had once been to him, in contrast to the jumble of his current feelings.

He had done a lot of work on the relevance of his repressed oedipal longings to his relationship with his wife, as the lack of marital excitement reflected in part his wife's differences from his mother. He had also thought about his ambivalence toward his father and how these feelings had made it hard for him to decide how much like his father he wanted to be. Of course, he had recently deciphered transference feelings coming from childhood recollections of the priest during confession – part friend, part judge. From this expectation of judgment, however, I still had the feeling that Mr. Prout was hiding a secret, concealing some important piece of information from me. I determined to bring up this impression of a secret at the appropriate time and waited for the right moment to present itself.

The moment arrived on one occasion when Mr. Prout was recalling the confessional, as he spoke of hesitating to tell the priest certain things because they might make him "look so bad." I commented that I frequently seemed to remind him of his priest and wondered whether the same thing happened here: "Are there things – is there a secret – that you're keeping private here, that you don't want me to know about, because you're afraid it will make you look bad?" He seemed stunned by this question and fell silent for awhile. During a subsequent session, however, without alluding to my question about secrets, he said that there was something going on that he wanted to talk about. Haltingly, he described a whole secret life in which, several nights a week, he went into the red-light district of the city, picked up a prostitute, and proceeded to enact certain specified sexual rituals with her. Besides ordinary variations of sexual intercourse, these usually included what the patient called "golden showers," in which he would insist the woman urinate onto his face and into his mouth.

Allegedly, I was the first person whom he had ever told about these activities. Much of the subsequent therapy consisted in working on this secret, both to clarify his feelings about prostitutes and the meanings of their actions and to understand specifically his feelings about revealing his secret life. It came as no surprise that Mr. Prout felt a certain license to seek and express sexual feelings with prostitutes: "After all, they exist to satisfy a man's longings. You pay them, and you get what you want." This license he readily contrasted with oedipal sanctions against such activities with his wife-mother and his guilt over sexual yearnings for either of them. In addition, the prostitutes usually gave him the reassurance, for which he clearly yearned, about the large size of his penis and his proficiency as a lover. These yearnings related to his lifelong self-doubts and insecurities, and ultimately as well to competitive and castration concerns with regard to his father.

These dynamics, however, did not account for the satisfaction he derived from the "golden shower" or for Mr. Prout's concealment of his nocturnal activities. When I asked for associations to the pleasure of a woman urinating on his face, he immediately responded, "It's wonderfully humiliating." As we explored this, he depicted a scenario in which he created a secret context for humiliation, with no one else aware of his action except the already degraded prostitute, who "didn't really matter." Thus, in addition to the dynamics of this particular perversion—which included the desire to be humiliated and punished for his tabooed sexual fantasies and activities, as well as for aggressive feelings toward his father—lay the need to keep the activity deeply concealed from others. It was the golden shower that no one else must know about, the conscious wish for degradation that must remain secret. So, for Mr. Prout the very wish to be shamed became shameful and needed to be concealed, especially from his priest/psychotherapist. Thus we have an example in which humiliation, far from being painful, is the goal of the perverse behavior.

Mr. Prout represents a deeply neurotic character with masochistic tendencies, for whom shame elements are often difficult to tease apart from feelings of guilt. He seemed to feel guilty about sexual and oedipal yearnings, for which he found an acceptable outlet in his secret life with prostitutes. Particularly in the urination did he find multidetermined, perverse satisfaction of sexual yearnings as well as adequate punishment/degradation for his desires. From the prostitutes he also received affirmation of the integrity and superiority of his phallus, and reassurance about his masculinity and heterosexuality. (Homosexual concerns and wishes had emerged in relation to his desire for prostitutes and in the meaning of the golden shower.)

Shame played an important part in therapeutic work with Mr. Prout with regard to his perverse activities, his need to keep these secret, and his ultimate wish to be humiliated as a means of atoning for his feelings, especially guilt. His shame over these specific activities caused him to keep this life secret for a long time in treatment. Without therapeutic attention to his need to conceal and to maintain a secret, he might not have revealed his shame and the clandestine life that generated it. In addition, it was exploration of his shame feelings that led to disclosure of the meaning of the golden shower.

THE CASE OF MS. BINGHAM

Ms. Bingham, who was described in chapter 6 to illustrate shame and feelings of insignificance in relation to anger and rage, offers a good example as well of shame with regard to oedipal desire and guilt. As her analysis progressed, she had become more deeply engaged in transference feelings and sexual desire for me. She noted that since the analysis began, she had not been involved in any significant sexual relationships and occasionally would explode in anger against me over the futility of our relationship. "A lot of good this is doing me—wasting my time pining away for you, when you're so totally unavailable to me." Since my office was in my home, she occasionally encountered my wife and had developed a deep envy of, and antipathy toward, her. She observed with interest that her anger was toward the woman/ wife, rather than toward me/the man, whom she continued to protect. In spite of her frustration, however, she was greatly interested in and curious about the events and individuals in my family.

During one session in which Ms. Bingham was describing her longings for intimacy, and relating this to the absence of any sense of calm closeness with her father when she was a child, she recalled a dream. In it, she was having long, leisurely sex with a previous lover when her former husband entered the room and expressed displeasure at this situation. She was upset because she had yearned for the leisure time for this intimate encounter. Associations took her to early primal scene memories of occasions when she had slept in her parents' bedroom, perhaps witnessing their sexual encounters. Her own wishes for sexual intimacy were forbidden because they seemed to relate to unattainable, tabooed involvement with her father. She then thought about the meaning of "leisurely" and was reminded that she had been feeling internal pressure to terminate analysis before she became "overwhelmingly dependent" on me. She readily equated me/the analyst with her lover in the dream, as she had several times previously. (Associations to her former husband were plentiful but are not relevant to this discussion.) Then she realized with a shock that part of the sexual excitement in the dream had come from the fact that her lover had been "fucking me from behind!" leading directly to association of the location of my chair behind the couch.

These, then, were examples of fairly familiar oedipal transferential feelings in analysis as they appear, displaced, in dream material. What I want to emphasize, however, is the difficulty with which these thoughts and associations came and the length of time spent in work on resistances to them. For a time, Ms. Bingham said that she had no thoughts; nothing came to mind. She frequently said that she had no feelings at all toward me – she felt entirely neutral. Careful investigation usually revealed that beneath these blank periods of time lay thoughts and longings about me – sometimes as the preoedipal mother, sometimes for the mirroring selfobject function, and sometimes as the exciting, oedipal father.

For the purposes of this discussion, I want to illustrate the role that shame played in guarding from detection the sexual desire that made her feel vulnerable. Even in the dream just described, shame quickly entered in the following manner. Just as she recognized the meaning of her lover's entering from behind and its relation to the position of my chair, Ms. Bingham started to cry: "It's so intense; I want to talk and I can't. I hate crying in front of you – it feels so humiliating." I acknowledged her feelings of humiliation and wondered whether she feared that crying, speaking of her feelings, might give me too much power. She said yes, that what she really wanted from analysis was a feeling of intimacy – sexual and otherwise – but that this longing made her feel stupid, pathetic, since she knew that I would never reciprocate her feelings. I also noted how her shift to crying and feelings of humiliation deflected defensively away from feelings of desire.

Other examples further demonstrate how Ms. Bingham invoked shame in response to her sexual transference feelings. For instance, on one occasion when she was talking about conflicts over sexual feelings, she suddenly found herself feeling humiliated. When I inquired about this, she added that she felt unattractive and hence any sexual feelings would not be reciprocated. "So the danger," I wondered, "is that you'd be rejected if you expressed your feelings; I wouldn't respond to them, just like your father didn't when you were a little girl." She continued that she was always the initiator, that she had rarely felt pursued by a man. "Unless I do the pursuing, I go unnoticed; I feel insignificant. And it feels so miserable in here, because once again it feels like that's what I'm doing," she said. I added the implicit clause, "and it feels like I don't notice you anyhow." She then associated to her parents and her frequent feeling of having been abandoned and forgotten by them.

On another occasion, Ms. Bingham spoke of the intensity of her feelings and how much she hated experiencing them. "I feel humiliated, having these feelings toward you and knowing that they're not reciprocated. I should be ashamed; but I also feel exposed and vulnerable." I wondered why she should be ashamed and whether she feared that I would in some way laugh at her for her feelings. She replied that she was more concerned that I would not take her feelings seriously. She then recalled an incident just prior to the previous session when I had abruptly been called by my wife. "You should have protected me; if you really cared about me, that wouldn't have happened." She immediately covered this complaint with self-criticism about how "ridiculous, crazy" such a thought was and how alienating I would find it. She should conceal such thoughts, or I, like everyone else, would retreat from her intrusiveness, her craziness, and would ultimately reject her. Once again, her sexual desire for me, her longings for closeness, were experienced as pathetic and humiliating–they could only be considered a reason to feel shame.

Ms. Bingham exemplifies the interactive presence of shame with guilt in response to sexual desire in the transference, or the function of shame as a feeling about another feeling. To desire sexually exposes the vulnerable self to mockery, laughter, unresponsiveness, and, ultimately, rejection. The desired object may rebuff the self because of *erotic unworthiness*–such fears in part caused Ms. Bingham to hide her sexual feelings and to find their exposure so painfully humiliating. Concealment of sexual desire may also be seen in the shame attending anticipated selfobject failure to accept and respond to the self's wishes.

For Ms. Bingham it is somewhat difficult and arbitrary to separate guilt from shame feelings, although such a differentiation seems relevant and important, with implications for treatment. If anything, guilt about her oedipal (and preoedipal) wishes seemed first to arise and then be repressed, being replaced by manifest and palpable defensive shame and humiliation. Once again a guilt–shame cycle seems useful in conceptualizing and understanding the interaction of these two affects in this patient. For Ms. Bingham, shame and humiliation may serve as a defense against underlying guilt about her desire. But it is important also to recognize that this patient experiences shame principally in regard to her sexual wishes (rather than guilt), and, therefore, this emotion must be taken seriously and understood. At another point in her analysis, Ms. Bingham stated that "humiliation is the most painful feeling I have ever experienced."

Ms. Bingham had indicated that her major wish from analysis was for intimacy, a wish about which she felt both guilty and ashamed. She was convinced that this wish would be both mocked and not met—an example of perceived selfobject (empathic) failure, leading inevitably to shame. The analytic challenge, then, was to accept, work with, and help the patient understand the sources of her shame, leading then to an appreciation of the guilt feelings that had caused them. When this process is successful, and the patient begins to feel less humiliation and guilt over her desires, frustration of the wish for a so-called real, intimate relationship with the analyst generally will take its place as an acceptable trade-off for the newfound self-acceptance and authenticity.

DISCUSSION

The essential difference between shame in neurotic character disorders and in narcissistic conditions has to do with its intensity and its permeation of the entire self-experience. In patients with primarily neurotic character disorders, shame tends to be more specified and delineated in response to particular activities (Mr. Prout) or feelings (Mrs. Barlin, Ms. Bingham). It does not underlie the self's total subjective experience, as tends to be the case with patients whose primary difficulties are those of narcissistic vulnerability. For this latter group, shame seems to constitute their central negative affective experience, while for neurotic patients shame shares the spotlight with other painful feelings, principally guilt and anxiety. Also, the affects reflecting positive self-esteem are more frequently experienced by less severely impaired patients.

As seen in each of the patients discussed in this chapter, shame and guilt seem to go hand in hand, with greater complexity in differentiating one from the other than for narcissistic patients. The guilt–shame cycle is more relevant for these neurotic patients, and oedipal issues are more tangible. Similarly, configurational qualities of the libidinal object are clearer as the traditional transference unfolds, and it is less clear that archaic selfobject needs play so important a part. However, the experience of selfobject failure (or, as formulated classically, frustration of transferential libidinal desire) continues to play an important role as a precipitant of shame (Ms. Bingham). Here, shame may be masked by anger and rage. Alternatively, guilt over oedipal wishes toward the father and betrayal and anger toward the mother may be concealed behind shame as a defense (Mrs. Barlin).

I think that the importance of *secrets* as a manifestation of shame is demonstrated by these cases, although secrets may also be important for narcissistic patients. Secrets essentially represent the need to conceal and hide shameful experiences, feelings, or qualities, particularly when these lead to a fear of public ridicule. They may be consciously withheld from the observer (Mr. Prout) or maintained unconsciously (that is, repressed) against recognition by the self (Mrs. Barlin, Ms. Bingham). In my opinion, it is the public quality of shame – the presence of a shamer or of audience – that specifically defines the attributes of *humiliation*.

For the two women patients, shame reflected failure to attain the goal or ideal of complete self-sufficiency, without need or dependence and without desire. Should desire be triggered through treatment (as for intimacy with the analyst – Ms. Bingham; longings to reclaim memories of her father – Mrs. Barlin), shame is the automatic response, with a fear of humiliation by the analyst (Ms. Bingham) or by the mother (Mrs. Barlin). Thus, for these neurotic patients, *desire* must remain a repressed or disavowed secret, or they run the risk of facing shame and public degradation, in addition to guilt; for narcissistic patients, secrets that defend against shame relate more to selfobject *need*. It seems to me that narcissistic patients tend to take refuge in desire, as a defensive alternative/coverup against need. Neither shame nor guilt seems prominent in the expression of sexual desire by narcissistic patients.[1]

As described in relation to the three neurotic patients of this chapter, shame reflects the "breakthrough" of secrets maintained against self-recognition or public scrutiny. For Mrs. Barlin, this had to do with longings for closeness or reunion with her lost father; publicly she maintained a pretense of shame about his social status. Mr. Prout's secret related to his search for degradation through the golden shower, and to his concealment of erotic evenings with prostitutes. Ms. Bingham's shameful secret gradually emerged as her transferential desire for

---

[1]Kohut (1972) has described such expression of sexual and oedipal desire in these patients as defensive disintegration products of a fragmenting self.

the analyst intensified. As described by Levin (1971), these shame manifestations can be understood as secondary and external; I suggest that they also tend to be reactive and defensive against underlying, tabooed wishes (Morrison, 1984a). Thus, for these patients shame is closely related to guilt, and the guilt–shame cycle may be usefully invoked to understand and work with them.

One other important relationship of shame in neurotic patients remains to be demonstrated: shame as passive withdrawal from conflict involving aggression and castration fears. This relationship existed for Mr. Jackson, an unmarried executive in his late 20s whose analysis centered on his complex feelings toward a competent, strong, but aging father, and his right to lust for women who differed from his passive, somewhat aloof mother (Morrison, 1984a). A wide range of oedipal feelings came into play in work with Mr. Jackson and became clearly manifest in the transference. However, it was striking how central Mr. Jackson's experience of shame was in relation to his oedipal competition and assertive feelings. In dreams and many associations, he withdrew from competitive, aggressive, or assertive situations into passive failure and shame. His principal concern was usually about his shame, however, and it was only after I accepted and worked analytically with it that interpretation of genetic derivatives of hostility and fears of retaliatory castration became useful, both from memories and as they occurred in the transference.

This relationship was illustrated by an instance when Mr. Jackson was uncharacteristically late for an analytic session. He began by berating and heaping scorn on himself for being late and for the other ways in which he was an "inferior" patient. I wondered what this inferiority feeling was like for him, and he associated to other ways that he had "fucked up" at work. His associations then went to how he felt about being in analysis—analysis was a passive retreat for nerds who couldn't make it in the real world. Not only was he inferior for needing analysis, but I was a passive jerk for just sitting back and doing this for a living (an interesting similarity to Cristophe's feelings in the previous chapter). He then contrasted us both with his image of his assertive, successful father, and also with Teddy Roosevelt, about whom he was currently reading. I wondered whether his anger at me, and his wish to change his own image by skipping analysis, might have played a part in his being late for the session. He acknowledged this possibility, but then expressed concern that I might resent his derision of me and want to kick him out of analysis. We were then able to explore the competitive wishes and castration fears that lay behind his passive, shame-laden retreat: "It looks like it feels safer to feel ashamed than to be assertive or hostile, to win in competition." Examples of the relationship between shame and assertiveness were frequent for Mr. Jackson, as he worked on his fear of assertiveness and success as a major focus of his analysis.

This case represents, again, the neurotic activation of shame as a defense reaction against internal conflict, this time with regard to aggression and assertiveness and the resultant fear of castrating retaliation. Shame manifestations in neurotic patients are more circumscribed than for more narcissistic patients and tend to represent reactions to external failures of the ideal self (e.g., desire for an object who does not reciprocate, the quest for golden showers, passive retreat from competition at work).

As I have tried to illustrate in this chapter, the treatment of shame in neurotic patients is similar to that outlined previously for more narcissistically vulnerable patients. The first goal must be recognition and articulation of the shame experience and acceptance of its importance to the patient. This is so even if, as it did for the patients here described, shame may seem secondary to an underlying conflict. The therapeutic inclination frequently is to bypass shame and directly interpret the source, defense, or secret desire. This, I strongly believe, is an error—only after shame has been acknowledged, accepted, and understood can underlying causes and defensive meanings be usefully interpreted. After acceptance of, and work with, shame, the unconscious or disavowed secret desire or competitive assertiveness can be interpreted and explored, especially in work with healthier patients.

11

Shame and
Manic-Depressive Illness

This chapter focuses on the special affinity that exists between shame and manic-depressive illness, with its underlying strata of narcissistic vulnerability. (I touched on this relationship earlier, in chapter 2; see also Galatzer-Levy, 1988.) I will begin with the description of a clinical case, to show the essential role of shame and narcissistic vulnerability in generating this patient's manic episodes. It was, in fact, in work with this particular patient that my awareness of the clinical importance of shame first developed. I will then attempt to relate these findings to the classic description of manic-depressive illness enunciated by Cohen et al. (1954). Recent studies strongly suggest evidence of genetic and biochemical influences on manic-depressive affective disorder (Coyne, 1986), but it seems likely that genetic/biological factors alone are not enough to cause a major affective illness. Rather, some interaction of genetic, biochemical, and psychological factors is necessary. That assumption will inform the following assessment.

THE CASE OF ALLAN B.

Allan B. was a 36-year-old, married father of two children when I first met him, following his second episode of manic psychosis. He was the son of two artists, the eldest sibling of four sons and one daughter. He had an engaging, appealing manner, spoke easily, and, not insignificantly, related freely to me as another man of his own age. At first he described his childhood as having been pleasant and easy. He had done well in the parochial and public schools he had attended and had many acquaintances. However, his parents, who were of European background, were disdainful of their suburban environment and his neighborhood playmates. It was clear to him from early childhood that his parents expected him to be an artist like themselves, and his mother undertook to teach him drawing. One of his earliest memories was of a "mystical" summer when he was a favored pupil of an idealized woman painter who encouraged him in his artistic pursuits. During high school, he was the winner of a highly regarded artistic competition as judged by a renowned local painter – he described this as his lifetime "moment of glory."

Allan talked about his father in warm, affectionate tones as a loving and attentive, but very passive, man constantly under the domination of the patient's cold, authoritarian mother. His father took refuge in alcohol as he maintained friendships with acquaintances outside the family. He was a painter who had immigrated as a child to this country and had risen from poverty through his efforts and talents in art. He had become an expert colorist and was currently represented in several national collections. He and the patient frequently drank together, and the father would complain about, and express anger at, his wife. However, despite his father's unhappiness, there was never a move toward divorce. Allan frequently recalled with some bitterness that his father had never protected him from his mother's attacks.

He referred matter-of-factly to his mother as "the dragon lady." As his ideal description of childhood began to unravel, he described her as harsh, severe, and suspicious. He recalled that she had been verbally and physically abusive to him when he was a child. She punished him for misdeeds and intruded on his privacy. Her punitiveness was especially painful to him when she acted as his drawing instructor, in which role she was harsh and demanding. And dinners at home had always been particularly tense.

Despite Allan's manifest talents, his father (presumably doubting the level of his artistic talent) had advised him during high school that it would be difficult to make a living as a painter and urged him to study drafting in college. Allan attended a college that had strong fine arts and architectural departments, and, although he yearned to paint, he followed his father's advice. During college he met and fell in love with the woman he was to marry after graduation.

The couple returned to Boston, where Allan got a job as a draftsman in a local architecture firm, where he has remained, with one interruption, to the present. From the start, he disliked his work, feeling himself to be an underachieving functionary who deserved more out of life. Rather quickly he began to feel unhappy with his wife, who he felt did not appreciate or support him. He equated her with his mother; both he and his wife responded to the marital tensions by having several affairs. He felt entitled to the support and affection of other women since he had found his wife to be cold and unresponsive. Nonetheless, the couple had their first daughter shortly after marriage, and a second child several years later.

He had his first manic episode in his late 20s and was hospitalized briefly. He recovered quickly and resumed his unsatisfying work, returned to his marriage, but showed little interest in his children, and experienced great sensitivity to rejection. Several years later he had a second manic episode, during which he was quite grandiose, agitated, and fearfully paranoid about being attacked, especially by vengeful women. He was fired from his job, and was referred to me for psychotherapy. When I first met him, he was, despite his pleasant and charming façade, deeply depressed and despairing, fearing how he could possibly make a living. From the beginning, he was despondent about his failed ambitions.

I initially offered support and attempted to examine with him his symptoms and feelings. He was drinking heavily in an attempt to deal with his despair and continued to be phobic about eating with other people. He created ritualized and obsessional schedules around eating, sleeping, and drinking. We explored his anger at his mother for her harangues and his memories of battles with her around dinner and drafting exercises, as he recalled her expectations that he would excel at artistic expression. He felt that his mother had caused him to feel superior to his many friends and playmates.

In once-weekly therapy, he dutifully reviewed his past, his feelings and disappointments, and his anger at his wife, children, and former employers because of their lack of confidence in him. However, he doubted the potential usefulness of psychotherapy and seemed to be coming for treatment largely out of a bond with me. He related to me as someone who seemed to be successful, a man of his own age and educational class, who shared with him an interest in painting (which we had discussed on occasion). Thus, there was a mutual fondness between Allan and me, although he would experience sudden flashes of anger (over my "insensitivity" or incorrect interventions), which we then explored extensively. His rage centered particularly on the fact that he was being charged for his therapy and yet was expected to work in treatment and to help himself. He also was furious about his former job, at the ignominy of having been fired and not treated as special. As his depression continued, I prescribed antidepressant medication, and he saw some alleviation of symptoms.

A third manic episode, two years later, was ushered in by renewed interest in painting and frenzied artistic activity. I hospitalized him. He remained for three months, and lithium treatment helped him to manage his rampant grandiosity and paranoid delusions. During that hospitalization, his wife made an irrevocable decision to dissolve the marriage and moved from Boston with their children. Following this traumatic event, Allan became more deeply depressed, feeling alone, abandoned, and vulnerable. For the first time, it became apparent to me that Allan felt a deep sense of failure and an emerging sense of shame, which we began to explore.[1] At this time, however, he was rehired by his former employer but in a lower level job at which he continued to work during the next several decades. He was grateful for this demonstration of confidence but remained bored and depressed at work, as well as in his other activities.

As treatment continued, I attempted to maintain a supportive and friendly atmosphere in which we faced and discussed his loneliness, the challenges of work, but particularly his disappointments and shame at his personal, marital, and work failures. He began to describe his humiliation over working in an office and not reaching the artistic heights for which he had been groomed. We again focused on his drinking and fears about eating in public, but this time from the perspective of how these masked and related to his great sensitivity to shame and resultant despair. Because of financial difficulties, he stopped individual therapy for a while and joined a therapy group I was conducting. In this context, we examined his arrogant dismissal of other group members (as his mother had dismissed his playmates), and then considered this from the perspective of his underlying shame and projected self-criticism. During this phase, he moved from depression to feelings of emptiness and boredom, and he ultimately left the group to seek, for awhile, the excitement of a gestalt therapist, and then the ministrations of a hypnotist. He and I maintained intermittent contact during these "boredom" years, when he had several threatening

---

[1] As noted, it was with this patient, at this point in treatment, that I first began to consider the role of shame as a significant factor in psychological experience. I think that it was no coincidence that my observations about his shame were of someone whom I liked and with whom I identified because of the similarity in age, interests (i.e., art), and wishes for specialness in life.

"highs," though not a full-blown manic episode again. Interestingly, his manic phases always began with a renewed interest in painting, which he would do energetically and at all hours of the day or night. During our occasional meetings, we recognized that this phenomenon signaled the danger of impending mania. He began a relationship with Cecile, which has been intermittently ongoing until recently.

Several years later, he resumed regular treatment with me (as his finances then allowed) around conflicts with Cecile, with whom he was living, her children, his ex-wife over payments and visitation issues, and the emptiness he felt in his life and in his relationship with his own children. Allan again spoke of depression and low self-esteem. By this time my own interest in narcissism, self psychology, and shame had evolved – an interest, again, that had been stimulated in large part by my earlier work with this patient. I responded quite differently to him now, appreciating and examining his narcissistic vulnerability, feelings of failure, dashed hopes and expectations for him as artist, draftsman, husband, and father. We spoke together of his hurt at feeling rejected by his children and of his feeling unaccomplished and unappreciated at work. This was not the way his life was supposed to have evolved – he was born to be great and should be appreciated without having to work hard at painting, at relationships, or at work. That his life had not turned out this way had dashed his fragile self-esteem, and he had taken refuge in alcohol, in compulsive rituals, in social concealment, and in mania, all in an attempt to fill and repair his fragile self.

For the first time in treatment, Allan became animated and actively engaged as he explored his shame, remorse, and humiliation about the unexpected course of his life. We examined his acknowledged shame – that he was not a great painter; that his children did not respect or appreciate him; that Cecile accused him of failing his responsibilities in their shared household. For the first time he felt the usefulness of mutual understanding and of therapeutic work. He took hold of the concepts of narcissism (fragility of self, reactive grandiosity, the wish to be unique), entitlement, shame, expectations, and vulnerability. He worked with them, applying them to his boredom and outrage at work; to his relationship with Cecile, from whom he expected total acceptance and identity of interests; and, finally, to the vacillations within the transference. His shame was manifest in feelings that I would look down on him for his failures, envy of my presumed professional successes, contempt for my ordered and bourgeois lifestyle, and so on.

Following some intensive work on these issues, and after a

frightening gastrointestinal bleed resulting from aspirin and alcohol intake, he made some dramatic changes in his life. He sharply curtailed his drinking, joined Cecile and her family for meals (rather than eating in isolation, late at night), went to bed at the same time as Cecile, and awoke, rested, to go to work, on time and with greater vigor. He felt optimistic, began taking responsibility for his behavior and feelings, and engaged intellectually in the work of psychotherapy. Treatment finally made sense to him. He and I became partners at a work task; he felt accepted, and began to understand the source of his despair.

How I worked with Allan around his narcissism, shame, and low self-esteem is illustrated in a vignette that began with my comment, early in one session, about a mounting, unacknowledged bill. He had entered the office smiling and in a good mood, but with this comment his affect changed, and he became distant and matter-of-fact. He began reciting the details of a current work problem. He then said, "I had hoped to explore long-range issues–about shame, my wish to be treated as special. But since the bill is on *your* mind, I don't know what we can do." A long silence followed. My inquiry had indeed reflected a concern of my own, and thus represented the intrusion of my issues – from his perspective, a selfobject failure – so I pursued his affective response. "I gather that you feel angry, withdrawn, and hurt. Can we try to understand it?" He acknowledged his anger and disappointment, and then said that he had hoped to be special to me, that I would both understand his current financial difficulties and make allowance for it. "I guess that's my entitlement, that I should be treated specially. But you didn't, so what's the point in pursuing it?"

As he withdrew, I suggested that this moment between us reflected his difficulty, his sensitivity, his way of relating to, and moving away from, people when he had uncomfortable feelings. He agreed and then said that I had caught him in an area of his vulnerability and humiliation. He had attempted to hide his hurt and anger by silence. He associated to his precarious financial situation. "It's *unfair* that I should be poor and needy – I should be financially secure, and I wish it were so. I feel vulnerable, humiliated to feel so precarious, but I wish you would respect my need, not confront me with my poverty." I had let him down, disappointed him by calling his attention to the bill. I explored his feelings about this empathic failure on my part, and his underlying humiliation at not being financially secure, his wish to hide this by not thinking about the bill, and his anger at being so confronted by me. He worked on these feelings during the remainder of the session and arrived at some meaningful acceptance of the reasonableness of my inquiry.

During the next session, he said that he had been thinking a lot about his anger and humiliation over the matter of the bill. He had come to realize that I should have the money and should not have to worry about it. He reiterated his feeling of failure at not earning more and his lowered self-esteem about his financial situation. He then discussed work issues and his decision that he would ask for a more responsible position with a higher salary. In subsequent sessions, he explored his concern that he might be laid off at work but emphasized that he felt very different from the way he had 14 years earlier, when he had lost his job. "I'm doing my best to set up alternatives. I'm no longer feeling so empty, scared, or a failure. If I lose the job, I'll manage, I'll find something." He then talked about his concerns that things were not working out with Cecile. He could even imagine the unimaginable: "I might even be better off on my own, that *I* have doubts about *her*, not simply feeling inadequate because she might be bored with *me*. This work on being special—my fears, entitlement, shame—it's really made a difference."

 I think that the work noted by Allan *had* made a difference in his self-esteem and that our emphasis on his narcissistic vulnerability, his yearnings (and expectations) to be special, his underlying shame and its defensive manifestations in rage, haughty superiority, envy and contempt, had provided a meaningful frame for therapy where previously there had been none. I also believe that similar dynamics frequently underlie the psychopathology of manic-depressive psychosis, operating synchronously with genetic/biologic predispositions. This does not mean that Allan will never again suffer manic attacks, but I think he is less prone to do so.

THEORY OF MANIC-DEPRESSIVE ILLNESS

Not often does an individual study represent a whole class of thought about a given subject. One such study, associated with Frieda Fromm-Reichman, does offer a psychoanalytic perspective on the family dynamics of the manic-depressive patient. This landmark paper (Cohen et al., 1954) begins with a summary of contributions to a psychoanalytic understanding of manic-depressive illness, including a view of the manic attack as a defense against the realization of failure. The analyst is seen as an appendage to a greatly inflated ego (Dooley); the manic episode as a triumphant reunion between the ego and ego ideal, leading to expanded self-inflation (Freud); the manic phase as a denial of guilt (Rado); mania as a denial of narcissistic deprivation

(Deutsch); and the good internalized object as being threatened with destruction by the bad internalized object, leading, again, to guilt feelings (Klein).

Cohen et al. then described their observations about the family background and character structure of manic patients. The family was viewed as isolated and feeling inferior and different from others, with the patients assigned a central role in the family's quest for a higher social position. The patients were expected to conform to a high standard of good behavior—"It's not what you are, but what you do"—to gain parental approval. The mothers in these families were seen as intensely ambitious, concerned with the prestige of the family. They were the moral authority, but seen as cold, contemptuous, and blaming. The fathers in these families, on the other hand, were seen as weak, failures (frequently alacoholic), but lovable. In general, the patients loved their fathers and attempted to justify the father's standing within the family.

During early development, these patients had difficulty during the rapprochement subphase, as delineated by Mahler, Pine, and Bergman (1975), and felt the threat of abandonment for displeasing the mother by displaying independence, rebelliousness, and the like. Patients were often labeled "bad." During later development, they frequently excelled in creative activities but were burdened with great responsibility for the prestige of the family and were competitive with their siblings. Competition often threatened the loss of maternal love, and the patients had little time for interpersonal relatedness and consequently suffered great loneliness. They often were made to feel responsible for family failure and were especially sensitive to the envy and competition of others, having to hide the extent of their achievements.

As adults, these patients demonstrated social ease, but their relationships were stereotyped and superficial. While they had a few dependent relationships, they offered very little in return. They frequently had feelings of inferiority and great need and often feared abandonment by family or their few friends. They were anxious at the thought of being alone and often felt very empty. Manic attacks were often precipitated by loss of love and abandonment following an episode of depression and served to defend against recognition of their feeling of aloneness. Frequent suicidal episodes reflected failure in attempts at relatedness, leaving the patients feeling hopeless and helpless.

The authors' elaboration of the dynamics of mania bears a striking resemblance to the development and character pathology of my patient Allan. To be sure, following Freud, Rado, and Klein, they suggested a prevalence of guilt and strong superego manifestations, accompanied by severe and hypermoral standards. It seems to me, however, that an equally important, or perhaps greater, relationship exists for these patients between the ego ideal and shame. In describing the patients' lack of conviction in their own worth, and a concern with what other people will think of them, the authors are calling attention essentially to shame and narcissistic vulnerability. The rigid preconception of authoritarian expectations, which they strive to meet but can never attain, leads to a vulnerability to feelings of failure and shame. The authors suggest that guilt feelings function to regain the approval of significant objects. My view, which coincides with that of Lewis (1981), Chasseguet-Smirgel (1985), and Bursten (1973), is that shame, more than guilt, is for the manic patient a signal to attempt to restore lost affectional bonds and become worthy of fantasied reunion with the parental ideal.

In discussing the diagnosis of these patients, Cohen et al. describe a dependent, demanding, oral interpersonal relationship that ignores the real characteristics of the object, as the patient attempts to remake the bad mother into a good mother. The patients' need for love is always urgent, suggesting the threat of object loss, or abandonment. Their emptiness and envy lead to exploitation of others to fill in their depletion; they use the object to "patch up" their ego weakness. These descriptions reflect the need for selfobject mirroring, idealizability, and empathy in the quest for self-cohesion and esteem. These patients demonstrate profound narcissistic vulnerability and shame sensitivity, with a conviction of absolute unacceptability and unlovableness by the important other (the selfobject). Their emptiness also dramatizes narcissistic depletion, as described by Kohut (1971, 1977) in relation to disintegration anxiety.

The narcissistic vulnerability of manic-prone patients leads inevitably to difficulties in therapy. These difficulties have been addressed by Kohut (1971, 1977, 1984). Within the transference, patients like Allan develop an exploitative, demanding, clinging dependency that is impossible to satisfy. Interpersonal relations with the therapist are stereotypical. The therapist becomes not a person in his own right, but an object to be manipulated, a moral authority, a critical and rejecting judge. Such patients show little empathy for the therapist (as in the episode around the bill), reflecting conviction of their own unlovableness. These qualities represent these patients' overwhelming shame and their need for selfobject mirroring and idealization that bypass the real, configurational attributes of the therapist-as-object. I believe that

Kohut (1971) was right to encourage therapists working with these patients to manage their own feelings of personal "obliteration" and allow the full emergence of the patient's narcissistic needs. (This "obliteration" was exemplified by Allan's initial response to my mention of his overdue bill.) The therapist's countertransference awareness recognizes the importance of understanding and accepting the manic patient's demandingness and stereotypic responses within the transference.

Cohen et al., like Kohut, emphasize the importance of a nonverbal, empathic approach, which Kohut (1984) called the understanding phase of treatment. They stress that the therapist should not attempt to gratify the patient's "irrational demands," but rather should allow such needs to come into the open within the transference. This empathic approach includes acceptance and recognition of the therapist's importance to the patient. From Kohut's perspective, this approach includes interpretation of selfobject needs and wishes, including the experience of therapist/selfobject failures. I would add the importance of identifying the almost inevitable feeling of shame and humiliation when such patients expose their needs in therapy; I have already argued that identifying this shame is central to the empathic understanding of the patient's experience of the treatment situation.

THE RELATIONSHIP OF SHAME AND NARCISSISM TO MANIA

What, then, is missing from Cohen et al.'s brilliant and convincing contribution to the psychoanalytic understanding of manic-depressive disease? From our perspective on shame, I believe that their study pays insufficient attention to the role of narcissistic vulnerability and shame sensitivity in patients suffering from manic-depressive psychosis. Of course, their paper was written before the elucidation of narcissistic phenomena and shame upon which my view of mania is based.[2] I believe that Kohut's elaborations on narcissistic phenomena, and the introduction of the relationship of shame and humiliation to mania, complete Cohen et al.'s early attempt to understand the psychodynamics of manic-depressive disorder.

Mania can best be understood psychoanalytically as a specific state of weakness of the self and vulnerability to selfobject failure and

---

[2]Piers's (1953) paper, which really initiated exploration of the relationship of shame to narcissism, had only just been published.

loss, more than as an interaction between superego and guilt. It is a
state of narcissism and vulnerability to shame; of self-defect and failure;
of lack of internalized ideals and inability to meet overly demanding
expectations. As illustrated by Allan, the manic episode reflects shame
over the state of the whole self, particularly self-depletion, and fear of
abandonment and rejection (lack of self-*acceptability*). I suggest that
Cohen et al.'s paper can be reframed within a self-psychological perspective on narcissism, with the addition of *shame* as a central dysphoric
affect of such narcissistically vulnerable persons.

These patients reveal defensive grandiosity, which must be
brought into, and accepted within, the dialectic of narcissism. Specifically, like Allan, these patients have been groomed to feel special, to
serve as the instrument for attaining family prestige. They received
inconsistent maternal gratification, overindulgence regarding their
specialness alternating with punitive and rejecting responses to their
failures and "badness." Their mothers functioned as inconsistent selfobjects, failing to provide regulation, containment and mirroring of the
children's age-appropriate grandiosity and ambition. Their fathers
tended to be loving yet weak, causing failure and inadequacy in
attaining satisfaction of the patients' idealization needs and leading to
shame-producing identifications.

The attempts of these patients to meet their family's needs for
specialness and social status through their own grandiosity and exhibitionism lead to a sense of failure and reactive withdrawal, self-depletion with regard to ideals, passivity and avoidance of competition and
rejection, and concealed neediness, all ending with a sense of profound
shame and humiliation. The family's failure is the patient's failure.

The prototypical manic episode represents a defense against
depression over these experienced failures. However, our perspective
on shame vulnerability suggests a deeper set of feelings, which themselves oscillate with, or generate, the manifest depression and despair.
As noted earlier (chapters 7 and 8), I believe that *shame* most frequently
underlies the depression of narcissistic vulnerability. It reflects the
passive failure to attain ideals, uncontained grandiosity, and the conviction of a defective self. This viewpoint is similar to that of Bibring
(1953) who related depression to helplessness, failure, and decreased
self-esteem and a narcissistic supply of self-love; and to that of Kohut
(1977) who described "guiltless despair" and self-depletion. It is this
shame-based depression, then, which triggers the defensive manic
attack in constitutionally vulnerable patients, as well as many of the
suicides of middle and later life.

REVIEW

From a self-psychological perspective, the transferential relationship with manic patients like Allan is characterized by dependent demand-ingness, which frequently overlooks the real, object-embedded qualities of the therapist or the configurational elements from an earlier relationship. This is the selfobject transference, in which need for the sustaining, supportive function of the therapist takes precedence over awareness of fuller, configurational attributes. These patients use the therapist/selfobject to provide missing aspects of the self in the attempt to "patch up" self-defects. Owing to these defects, manic patients feel a fundamental shame and unlovableness, with an urgent quest to be loved and accepted. They may exploit others to fill in their sense of emptiness and depletion.

In treatment, these patients tend to ignore the fuller, human qualities of the therapist, instead demanding their "rights"; this tendency was previously thought of as narcissistic entitlement. However, such demands may also be viewed as manifestations of what Kohut called age-appropriate expectations for the selfobject functions that had been denied them earlier in life, in large part because of parental demands that the patient correct the wrongs illuminating their own narcissistic vulnerability. The "stereotyped interpersonal relationships" noted by Cohen et al. represent in part the need of these patients for generalized selfobject functions as manifest in external and transferential contacts. The flat, two-dimensional quality in the expression of these selfobject needs is apparent within the transference, just as the external relationships of these patients may be charming, but lifeless and superficial.

Cohen et al. emphasize the importance of a nonverbal, empathic technique in treating these patients. Their approach is consistent with the empathic attunement informed by a self-psychological approach in work with narcissistic patients. Self psychology emphasizes the significance of eliciting, and allowing to flourish, the unmet, age-appropriate selfobject needs within the transference, which should be accepted and understood, rather than criticized and suppressed. Interpretation will focus on articulation and a genetic understanding of the source of these needs. In addition, I suggest that the disdain and contempt that these patients impose on their therapists, as Allan did in the episode of the bill, can be understood as the projective identification of their shame.

Given the narcissistic vulnerability and shame sensitivity of these patients, therapeutic exploration will focus on selfobject needs within the transference, rather than on premature dynamic interpretations, which may be experienced as critical and accusatory. In place of refusing to meet the archaic demands of the manic-prone patient (for gratification, admiration, and idealization), therapeutic attempts should be made to understand the source of wishes and the feelings of shame, inadequacy, and failure they represent.

Cohen et al. made a major contribution to the psychoanalytic understanding of manic-depressive illness in their landmark work, just at a point when elaboration of the ego ideal, narcissism, and shame was beginning. Had our current perspective on these phenomena been available at that time, the authors no doubt would have integrated them into their study. However, without this perspective, their study remains incomplete.

12

Epilogue

I began this book with a review of some central issues about shame. Why has it taken so long for shame to become differentiated from guilt as a fundamental psychological phenomenon, a major source of human distress? Is shame a defense against other feelings, or is it itself a primary affect, an experience potentially as devastating as any other that we can know? From which psychoanalytic perspective can shame best be understood – classical, structure-drive theory, or a psychology of the self and its deficits? In other words, does shame represent a defensive, regressive flight from structural conflict, or does it accurately reflect subjective experience, a sense of a defective, failed, inferior, or depleted self? Must shame always be a response to an observing, or an actively shaming, other – a response of the public self to the presence of an audience or shamer; or does it sometimes reflect a private, silent recognition of personal failure, a nod to the fact that an important goal of the self alone has not, and may never be, attained?

What is the relationship of shame to guilt? Are they fundamentally the same phenomena? Is one "worse" or "more primitive" than the other, or do they, in fact, interact in parallel and significant ways? Since shame relates to passivity and dependency, is it primarily an emotion of women (as some authors have claimed)? Is this view rooted simply in an outmoded concept of "genital inferiority" and "penis envy," or do other character traits emphasizing intimacy and attachment (which have been associated principally with women) create this impression? If the latter is so, are not men also subject to such concerns and yearnings? What is to be made of shame-related emotions – anger and rage, contempt and envy, depression, humiliation? Are these to be seen as shame equivalents, or do they serve a defensive function against the actual experience of shame? Finally, what really is the relationship of shame to narcissistic phenomena? Does shame play a role in all experiences of narcissism and vulnerability of the self?

These are indeed perplexing questions. Having thought hard about shame during the writing of this book, I am convinced of the central importance and significance of shame as an affective experience – for each of us, as for our patients. Shame is, by its very nature, confounding. What can be more immediate and clear than the piercing shame one suffers in the recognition of failure in a project long struggled with? That piercing shame might be both defense and affect; the failure that produces shame might be defensive against success and castrating retaliation or the direct experiential registration of defect and inferiority; it might represent a sense of public humiliation with respect to an act and private failure regarding a personal, internal goal or ideal.

I am also convinced that, so long as shame or its manifestations are fundamental and experienced strongly, it is fruitless to proceed with dogged interpretations or clarifications of conflictual or genetic factors. That is, any attempt to bypass shame in favor of underlying explanatory factors will be unsuccessful and counterproductive and will cause patients to feel misunderstood or criticized and attacked. As Lewis (1971) noted, the continued bypassing of shame represents one of the major sources of the negative therapeutic reaction.

A POTENTIAL SCENARIO

In this Epilogue, I want to offer a more personal and impressionistic view of shame. Having presented or summarized throughout the book clinical examples from patients, let me spin out a yarn with many shame implications from my own potential experience. Let us say that I had poured much of my own effort and conviction into a particular work – for instance, a psychoanalytic critique of a particular novelist's fictional writings. No doubt, much of my own self-esteem would have been invested in that project – both that it should adequately reflect my own particular vision, my personal ideal which that project sought to express; and that it should meet with external approval (I guess I also mean acceptance), success in the eyes of my readers. I think I would be particularly concerned about the opinions of my professional colleagues, who have helped to shape that aspect of my ideal self which this particular project might attempt to express. The project would be an expression of my self and hence would lay that self vulnerable to observation, judgment, and approval or rejection.

So, the project, an expression of my vision and understanding of a particular body of writing, would contain within it representations of my own self and the shape of its aspired-to ideal. Such a project would not simply represent my own private, internal aspirations, for I would probably seek a publisher (a ready-made selfobject potentially available for mirroring). A letter expressing reservations and criticism from the future publisher might come as a shock and might well generate feelings of despair and anger. After all, I might have allowed the project to carry for me some tempered representation of my own grandiosity, some fantasy that this would be a major contribution integrating a unique view of literature and analytic theory. I would not be keeping this particular personal vision private and internal, but I might also be seeking to exhibit my contribution to colleagues, risking the possibility of their disapproval.

And then, with a thud, that critical letter would have arrived from the reader/publisher. My first reaction—disappointment and rage, followed by depression—would, on closer examination, no doubt contain a fundamental underpinning of shame. This shame would reflect the critical appraisal by the esteemed, external reader; the jolting recognition of personal hubris (grandiosity) that went into the "greatness" fantasy; and the private, internal (and, perhaps, hidden) realization of personal failure to attain my goal or ideal. My personal capacity to weather this disappointment and deal adequately with my shame and its intensity would depend on my own strength, security, and self-cohesion—all products of my own developmental experiences (and the success of my own personal psychoanalysis!). However, I think the presence of some shame manifestations would, indeed, be inevitable.

I have not yet dealt in this book in any detail with positive alternatives to shame. Let me give my work fantasy a different twist and suppose that a letter arrived praising my project and offering a contract for publication. I would not then have to face the dashing of my hopes and would not be confronted with a sense of excessive grandiosity, failure, or self-defect—all ingredients of potential shame. What might I feel instead? Excitement certainly, probably exhilaration, a feeling of self-affirmation and justification for the commitment of parts of my ideal self into this project. An extreme example, were my self-cohesion less firm, my vulnerability to narcissistic disruption greater, might be flight into manic excitement, the merging of actual and ideal selves (as described by Freud, 1921). More likely, there would be a feeling of satisfaction with the results of my work and an accompanying feeling of pride and pleasure, an absence of shame. Healthy pride has occasionally been noted as the opposite of shame (Nathanson, 1987), but I think that this view somehow fails to encompass fully the affective impact of the absence of shame, especially to someone familiar with its ponderous effects. To healthy pride, then, must be added a representation of the feeling of well-being that accompanies the absence or reversal of shame–something approaching euphoria.

To return to my hypothetical project, an encouraging letter from the publisher might eliminate my readiness to feel shame and generate in its place an experience of healthy pride and well-being–feelings familiar to the relatively well-adjusted among us. My achievement and competence strivings, my ambitions, would be in relative harmony without significant conflict; I would be feeling adequately mirrored and appreciated and in good empathic resonance with my relevant selfobject. But such absence of shame (the healthy pride and well-being) is, in fact, transitory and evanescent. The work might be published, but I would then face a series of reviews, discussions at professional meetings, and so on. These might be reasonably accepting and positive, or any one could be severely critical, again subjecting me to the loss of that sense of well-being and reintroducing the elements of shame and public humiliation by now well-known to you, the reader.

Another matter not clearly developed so far in this book has to do with the potential for dealing with shame in an adaptively mature and useful manner. Clearly, we cannot aim at the total elimination of shame. How does one learn to accept potential shame through life, to live with it without experiencing self-devastation, despair, and mortification? I will not make of this book a "how-to" manual, but certain relevant points can be made. First of all, we can consider the energy invested in secrets–in hiding and concealing facts and feelings about the self–which might be modified. It need not be so terrible, embarrassing, or humiliating to reveal certain secrets to selective others. Second it is possible to turn more frequently inward, to oneself and to affirming selfobjects, for the nod of approval or acceptance about ourself or our efforts–to grant less judgmental and critical power to the public, viewing audience. Finally, through that inward gaze, we can attempt to transform the harshness and severity of the ego ideal into a more accepting, attainable ideal self. I grant that these (rather simply stated) efforts to ease the pain of shame are not easily achieved. I am reminded, however, of the points suggested by Kohut (1966) for the transformation of narcissism into wisdom, a sense of humor, empathy, and acceptance of mortality. These points appear to resemble, and to be relevant for, easing the prominence of the subjective experience of shame.

How might these points be applied to the potential disappointments and blows to my project? I might think about not concealing my high hopes and expectations for the project, my eagerness that it meet with success, and my disappointment if it were uniformly rejected. I might even risk sharing the fact that my commitment to the project derived in part from my own early interest in, and fantasy of, writing fiction. Then I might think about how important critical reviews, even if positive, were in determining the worth of my efforts. Certainly, editors, colleagues, even family members might not have agreed with what I had been saying. Of course, this would be unfortunate (the common phrase is "a shame"), but wouldn't it have counted that I had devoted time, thought, and energy to something that I considered significant and worthwhile? I had remained with my interest, tried to develop it as best I could, and the process, as well as the product, would represent something valuable of myself. Having worked devotedly at my project, I would have finished it to my own relative satisfaction and, finally, would have relinquished it and let it/me "go public." These feelings would be separate from those evoked by the public response to my project and would themselves have been worthwhile sources of self-esteem and contentment.

This turning inward of my own self-evaluation and judgment would represent, in my opinion, a big step in my capacity to deal with shame. I think that public, external shame and sensitivity to ridicule is probably the more primitive form of shame, the one that has given shame such bad press in relation to guilt. Turning the potential control of shame inward is an important developmental step – in a sense, the "transmuting internalization" of a selfobject mirroring function into the creation of firmer self-structure. This internalization might then allow for a firmer establishment of and control over sources of self-regard and shame than were possible with the previous emphasis on external forces. With regard to my project, to the degree that I was able meaningfully to turn inward in trying to deal with my shame, I might have reminded myself that another's opinion of my work was not necessarily the last word in assessing its value, that I continued to consider my project worthwhile and that creation of the product itself had been a useful process.

I might also have reflected on the therapeutic understanding I had gained about my tendency to assess myself in terms of achievements; to berate myself when I felt that I fell short of some goal or ideal, especially a goal defined by another; to set uncompromisingly exact and harsh standards for myself, which might then be unattainable and lead me to seek distractions against the painful reappearance of shame; and, finally, I might recall what I had learned about the developmental determinants of my own shame – my childhood wishes, longings, and parental roles in shaping my self-image.

It must be amply clear that many elements of my "hypothetical project" bear striking resemblances to the process of writing this book. As I review this scenario of shame with regard to the project, I think again about the familiar questions raised at the beginning of this chapter. My shame, were I to feel bad about the outcome of my work, would certainly be a deeply personal, direct affective experience. Would it also be a defense? I think so, for external criticism (or my own dawning doubt) would remind me of my own grandiosity, hubris, at hoping – even, from time to time, thinking – that my project contributed a major new link between literature and psychoanalytic thinking. Shame, then, would defend against my exhibitionistic, grandiose wishes and aggressive or competitive urges, which I might then try to deny or disavow.

Does a psychological perspective on the self – particularly that developed by Kohut and his followers – help in understanding such a potential shame experience? I think it does; it offers a useful framework from which to conceptualize the potential limits to, or disintegration of, my self-cohesion – through senses of failure, inferiority, infirmity. The empathic failure of my fantasied editor/selfobject to mirror and fully accept the expression (and hence representation) of my self would likely lead to some intensification of shame, depending on the degree of my narcissistic vulnerability. However, does this mean that classical conflict theory plays no role in my shame? I think not. My wish to succeed might reflect a tormented battle against success prohibitions, or fears against displaying my project/self emanating from internal oedipal/ negative oedipal conflicts. My shame might even reflect a sense of "smallness" and weakness from a self-imposed regression from, or loss in, an oedipal struggle.

Would my shame reflect external or internal factors? I think it is clear, from the foregoing discussion, that it would have both external and internal sources. It is too facile, it seems to me, to attribute shame solely to public, interpersonal elements. Rather, the interaction of both public and private (internal) sources seems more likely, and I have suggested that internalization (and personal ownership) of the source of shame presents a potential for personal growth and for success in modifying and controlling the shame experience. This internalization of subjective responsibility for, and control over, shame differ, incidentally, from the unremitting, pervasive quality of primary internal shame in narcissistic conditions.

Finally, what would be the relationship of my shame to narcissism? I have noted that this shame, should my project fail, would reflect a puncturing of grandiose, exhibitionistic wishes, of hubris, and, thus, of manifestly narcissistic elements in my character structure. I suggest that similar wishes are there for each of us and therefore need not be deeply pathological. However, I think that the extent of my shame – evident in defensive rage and retribution, concomitant depression and despair, or thoughtful contemplation would be a useful indicator of the degree of my narcissistic vulnerability. Failure and severe resultant shame would indicate that I felt anything but special in the community of scholars; that I had lapsed irrevocably from my ideal; and thus that my deep yearning for reunion and merger with my fantasied parental ego ideal (or idealized, sustaining selfobject) would feel forever unrealizable. Here, shame and severe narcissistic pathology would go hand in hand. Alternatively, tempered shame might emerge with a vision of other works yet to be attempted, other aspects of life that would bring satisfaction, a more forgiving ego ideal and less formidable ideal self, and the greater narcissistic resilience of healthier character functions.

OTHER FACTORS

Another matter not yet addressed has to do with the role of shame in contemporary society. Did the lack of attention to shame until recently echo its relative irrelevance to personal experience, or did such inattention represent a historical artifact relating to therapists' difficulty in acknowledging their own shame? To the degree that shame is deeply embedded in narcissism and narcissistic phenomena, this historical question must be broadened to include narcissism and its current significance in contrast with earlier epochs. I believe that, with broadening guidelines about acceptable behavior and increased encouragement for personal expression, narcissistic phenomena have come to play a larger role in the spectrum of psychopathology than during previous periods. I am here in accord with Lasch (1978) and other commentators on the "me" generation of a decade or so ago. I suspect that this societal change parallels a certain degree of interpersonal disengagement (witness increased divorce rates, later marriages, and so forth), which may now be changing yet again. The recent increase in narcissism, then, would be apparent in the growing attention to shame as a manifest emotion, as the self becomes relatively more significant than previously in comparison with the "other." It seems to me that one manifestation of this change might be the increased incidence of diagnoses of narcissistic personality disorder instead of the familiar diagnosis of borderline pathology.

Alternatively, others believe that narcissism has always been prevalent but that recent theoretical and diagnostic sophistication has led to an increase in its recognition. This same argument can be made about shame, which only recently was teased apart from guilt and which currently is gaining broader appreciation. I believe that this viewpoint about shame is accurate, deriving principally from Freud's relative disinclination to investigate shame. I alluded to this earlier (see chapter 2) by suggesting that several of Freud's references to guilt pertained more appropriately to shame. It is also my impression that Freud had reason to avoid shame and move toward oedipal guilt because of the relevance to narcissism and shame of Jung's, and particularly Adler's, interests (inferiority feelings, masculine protest, and bisexuality/passivity).

However, I think most significant in Freud's inattention to shame may be – like that of many of his followers – his own shame sensitivity and disinclination to experience and examine his shame. I lay no claim to expertise on this matter, but evidence for this impression might be found in Freud's feelings about his own Jewishness in turn-of-the-century Vienna; his dream of his father's passivity when his hat was knocked into the gutter by Cossack soldiers (perhaps a projection of Freud's own passivity and shame); and his feelings about a series of disappointing relationships with male colleagues (the revenants). The most pertinent of these relationships probably was his kinship with Fliess, who played a seminal role in Freud's development of psychoanalysis. Freud's dramatic silence about Fliess after the end of their relationship, as well as his probable reaction to Fliess's surgical ineptitude with Freud's patient Emma Ekstein, suggests that Freud may have experienced shame over this relationship, as well as over his misguided male friendships in general. These thoughts about Freud's shame sensitivity are speculative, but the evidence is clear in his later written works that shame played a relatively minor part in his theoretical and technical contributions. Knowing what we do about the evolution of psychoanalytic history, it is not surprising that it has taken so long for interest to arise in an area that Freud ignored.

So, does shame play a significant role in contemporary society? I have no doubt that it does. In addition to its multiple manifestations in individual psychology, shame is also a major factor in social interaction, socialization, and other sociological phenomena. Cultural anthropologists have written—earlier, and more extensively, than psychoanalysts—about shame, especially calling attention to "shame cultures" (for example, many oriental, and some African, societies) as opposed to "guilt cultures" (principally, Western civilization). These anthropologists (for instance, Benedict, 1946; Singer, 1953) emphasize the role of guilt and shame as motivators and instruments of social control. In our own country, there is little doubt that the relationship of social class and racism to shame is among the most potently destructive influences on our society, having led to severe social upheaval and destruction. Gilligan (1976) has convincingly argued that shame arising from racism, social prejudice, and poverty is a major source of rioting and other organized aggression and retaliation against a repressive society. Similarly, much of the rage in the nation's ghettos, leading to violent crimes, assaults, and murders, is a response to an underlying sense of shame and helplessness—particularly a lack of access to sources of power and economic stability—which have provoked retaliatory outbursts. This response is a societal manifestation of Piers's (1952) guilt-shame cycle, representing an assertive response to the passivity-related shame imposed by that society. A remarkable result of the civil rights movement was the experience of competence and effectiveness in altering society, transforming shame into pride and a sense of relative well-being for many blacks in this country (e.g., "Black is beautiful" as a new rallying cry).

On the other hand, the fear of shame itself serves an important and normative function in socialization. As described earlier, shame is one of the earliest, manifest infantile affects, readily observable in response to a failure to elicit an expected parental response (Broucek, 1982; Tomkins, 1987). Parental use of active shaming to influence the developing infant's learning, control, and self-image is inevitable, particularly during the phases of toilet training and bladder control. Reciprocally, the toddler experiences and expresses shame at failures to meet parental expectations or defiantly responds by withholding or lashing out – perhaps the earliest manifestation in human development of Piers's (1953) guilt–shame cycle. During this early phase of development Erikson (1950) noted the identity correlates of shame and doubt.

SHAME AND SUICIDE

I believe that one dire manifestation of shame, still underappreciated in clinical practice, is the danger of suicide. Evolving from Freud's (1917) view of depression, suicide has traditionally been considered to be a manifestation of rage directed at an ambivalent or abandoning internalized object (leading to guilt), or a response to the loss of a beloved object. Certainly, these dynamics are present in many instances of suicide, but I believe that shame – reflecting a sense of the self as unworthy, failed, discovered, or defective – plays as important a part in suicide as the guilt delineated by Freud. In fact, it is possible that shame, stemming from the narcissistic issues now attaining prominence, may be the more frequent stimulus to suicide at this time.

This relationship between shame and suicide has been recognized by cultural anthropoligsts in their studies of so-called shame cultures (for example, Singer, 1953) and has been noted in several clinical studies of shame (Wurmser, 1981; Kaufman, 1985). It seems to me, however, that the centrality of shame in many suicides has been ignored and that shame ignored in therapeutic work with depressed patients may be the precipitant in many suicides. Greater attention to shame in work with suicidal patients can become a useful tool in effective therapeutic suicide prevention. Kohut (1977) recognized this relationship when he spoke of the connection between mortification and "nameless shame" and overwhelming failure, which may lead to suicide in later life (see chapter 5, this volume). Shame seems to have played an important part in the suicide of a patient whom I had treated several years prior to his death. An elderly man in his seventies, Mr. L had been living alone and had recently suffered major financial reverses that had left him feeling isolated from the social and business community in which he had previously held a prominent position. When I was treating him, the allure of suicide as a solution to his pain was great, and he was plagued by feelings of humiliation, especially after the suicides of his wife and his favorite son. His isolation and shame had formed major foci of our therapeutic work together, but he left treatment in a euphoric flight after marrying a woman whom he saw as his salvation and the solution to his deep despair. I learned subsequently that shortly before his suicide his second wife had abandoned him, leaving him feeling again humiliated, hopeless, and alone. No doubt rage at abandonment turned inward played a significant role in his suicide, but this rage defended in part against his tenacious self-doubts and self-loathing. He had finally succumbed to despair over his lifelong humiliation and failures.

One does not have to present clinical data from the consulting room to establish the relationship between shame and suicide; newspaper headlines and televised events often make the connection plain enough. For example, network television reported a news conference called by a state official who had been accused of playing a central role in a public scandal. In front of the rolling camera, he stepped to the podium and reached into his inside pocket. Instead of the speech the assembled officials and press expected, he pulled out a pistol, held it to his head, and shot himself to death. Such a public self-excoriation could only be interpreted as a means of publicly wiping out the devastating humiliation and mortification that had accompanied his sordid exposure, as well as expressing his rage at the public source of his humiliation.

Other examples of shame-induced suicides of prominent figures include the public suicide of the aging Japanese author Yukio Mishima, who killed himself with his samurai blade, again in front of cameras, and following an elaborate Japanese pageant of death with a corps of his younger colleagues. In New York City, Donald Manes, a well-known political leader, was found near death in his automobile, the victim of a major suicide attempt, shortly after public disclosure of his participaton in a parking meter scandal. He died shortly afterward, as the extent of his involvement in the scandal was reported in the media. Similarly, a story in *The New York Times* (August 21, 1988) began with the headline, "Judge Kills Himself After Sex Misconduct Reports." The article reported that the judge had withdrawn into a "deserted hallway" and shot himself minutes before the local newspaper began printing an expose of his sexual activities with young male defendants and students. An acquaintance commented that the judge's feeling of "disgrace" had driven him to suicide. In this example, his withdrawal into social isolation and the timing of his suicide in relation to public exposure seem relevant.

A final example of a tragedy linking homicide and suicide – a not uncommon pairing – illustrates the role of shame and public humiliation as a stimulus to violent destruction. Another *New York Times* story (September 1, 1987) headlined "Six Deaths Linked to Fear of Shame," reported that a Vietnamese immigrant had shot and killed five people (four of whom were relatives) and then committed suicide out of "a fear of lost honor" following the accusation by relatives that he had stolen money from a family member's bank account. He had apparently called the relatives together to discuss the problem and then began shooting in response to what one relative described as "loss of face," a major personal trauma and manifestation of shame in Vietnamese culture.

These examples of shame-related suicides contain several separate issues. First, the public forum of several of the suicides (and murders) is striking: Mishima, surrounded by his officers corps and cameras; the state official, in front of a videotaped news conference; the Vietnamese man, in the context of a family discussion. All suggest the need for an audience in front of which to seek expiation for failures, humiliations, and self-defects, and to express rage over public exposure. The shame in these instances represents public humiliation and disgrace for immoral deeds that fall far short of the apparently high standards and ideals to which these individuals aspired. Each had apparently sought high achievement and at least an image of ethical righteousness; each had come instead to a tragic denouement. Perhaps, instead of producing expiation, the public nature of these suicides was intended to impose even further disgrace and self-debasement, as well as a forum for the expression of overwhelming rage.

Of course, not all shame suicides are public, external expressions requiring the presence of an audience. Suicide may also be a very personal, private, and solitary statement. Mr. L, whom I described earlier, feeling publicly disgraced for business failures and abandoned by his recent wife, committed suicide by taking pills in the privacy of his office; his body was not found until several days later. Manes had driven alone to a quiet street at night, where he mortally wounded himself. The judge sought a deserted corridor in which to end his life. For these people, shame was apparently solitary and internal; they seemed to remove themselves from public view, to go into hiding, in order to wipe out their sense of unworthiness and disgrace.

These suicides, and the one related homicide, suggest the potential lethalness of shame and humiliation. Such examples suggest the violent extremes to which the experience of shame can push vulnerable persons, especially those forced to face enormous disparities between ideal and manifest public images, between perfectionistic/ideal and flawed selves. Shame suicides are consequences of what Chasseguet-Smirgel (1985) has called "the malady of the ideal." Shame is a frequent, and often overlooked, cause of suicide and suggests a possible approach to suicide prevention. Where shame is deep and pronounced, especially when coupled with other indices of identified suicidal risk, the danger of suicide is strong. Intervention should include inquiry about, and identification of, shame and its manifestations (such as hidden secrets) and should be directed at uncovering and sharing the details of shame in the patient's immediate circumstances. Such an inquiry should form a part of the evaluation of suicide risk, and, once that connection is established, concentration on shame should be part of the acute treatment of the suicidal patient.

SHAME MANIFESTATIONS IN OTHER WRITINGS

Shame has been more clearly recognized and discussed within the fields of philosophy, theology, and anthropology[1] than it has been in psychology and psychoanalysis. Sartre (1943) considered shame extensively in *Being and Nothingness*, drawing on Hegel's elaboration of the "dialectic of master and slave." Nietzsche deliberated on the ravages of shame in great detail in *The Genealogy of Morals* (1974) and in *Beyond Good and Evil* (1966).

As Schneider (1977) noted, the Old Testament abounds with references to shame but tends to neglect guilt. A striking example of shame occurs in the book of Genesis, with Adam and Eve, naked, cast out of Eden for tasting of the fruit of knowledge. Among the several examples noted by Schneider is one from the Book of Ezra (*The New English Bible*, 9:6–7): "My God, I am ashamed, I blush to lift my face to you, my God. For our crimes have increased, until they are higher than our heads, and our sin has piled up to heaven."

Interestingly, in this quote, as in many others from the Old Testament, shame refers to "sin" and "crimes" –a usage more customarily associated in psychoanalytic writings with guilt (that is, transgression and violation of a boundary). Shame is aptly equated with blushing, a minor indiscretion; but sins are piled high. There is no hiding these transgressions from God–forgiveness is the only remedy, the only antidote to guilt. This is an interesting reversal of Freud's attribution of guilt to feelings more appropriately associated with shame (for example, inferiority; see chapter 2).

Major works of fiction have depicted shame as well as guilt. Dostoyevsky's *Notes From the Underground* and *The Possessed*, Hawthorne's *The Scarlet Letter*, Eliot's *Middlemarch*, Kafka's *The Trial* and

---

[1] For more extensive discussions of the place of shame in philosophy and religion, see Wurmser (1981) and particularly Schneider (1977).

Metamorphosis, are but a few of the great novels in which shame is a major experience of their characters. More recently, Roth's *Portnoy's Complaint* immersed the reader in its hero's shame and humiliation.

As our review has attempted to demonstrate, shame is a major element of human existence. Shame permeates the Old Testament, although it tends to be replaced by guilt (after the murder of Jesus) in the New Testament. Cultural anthropologists have long noted distinctions between "shame" and "guilt" cultures. Why is it, then, that shame has for so long been ignored in the psychoanalytic literature? I return to one of the guiding questions of chapter 1 that launched this inquiry. Any answers will be speculative, but I believe that, besides the historical factors noted earlier, the explanation lies in the nature of clinical interaction, the source of psychoanalytic inquiry and theory.

FURTHER CONSIDERATIONS

While philosophical, anthropological, and biblical writings, as well as fiction, may involve subjective reflection and introspection, they are primarily creative expressions of intellectual, observational, or literary investments. Authors may, and in fact must, distance themselves from the sources of their contemplation and creativity. When based on subjective experience, these works represent intellectual abstractions from introspected knowledge or projections and displacements into fictional characters. This distancing allows the author to treat the product as "not-me" and usually enables the shame experience to be observed from a position more remote from the self.

I have suggested throughout that the shame discerned in a patient by a clinician inevitably involves a confrontation with the therapist's own shame—there can be no awareness of a patient's defenses against, and experience of, shame and humiliation without recognition of similar feelings and memories in oneself. The patient's shame jogs the therapist's memory, reminds him of his own shame experiences and invokes the same tendency to hide and conceal that cloaks the patient's experience, leading so often to the collusive ignoring of shame noted in earlier chapters.

In essence, because of this collusion, shame for the most part has remained unanalyzed and untreated in the therapist's own personal therapeutic experience and hence has persisted unrecognized in the treatment of patients. I have suggested that Freud moved away from, and ultimately ignored, the role of shame as a focus of his attention, along with his fading interest in narcissism and the ego ideal. As noted, this trend may have grown out of the political realities of Freud's disputes with Adler and Jung; his investment in guilt, intrapsychic conflict, and the structural model, which did not lend themselves to a study of shame; and, very possibly, his own shame sensitivity. Thus, the tone was set for the subsequent avoidance of work with shame by analysts and therapists until the more recent consideration of narcissism made such avoidance impossible.

Shame has been considered in philosophy, cultural anthropology, theology, and fiction, then, because it was correctly recognized as a central human affliction by observers who could establish in their works some distance from their own subjective experience. In psychoanalysis, beginning with the teachings of Freud, such remoteness was impossible because of the inevitable intersubjectivity between the shared experiences of analyst and patient. Recognition of the tendency to collude in ignoring shame should help the therapist to attend to, and deal with, this crucial affect.

Another guiding question about shame raised in chapter 1 has to do with passivity and femininity. Passivity as a quality of the self has been shown to be central to shame, a defense in response to aggressive and libidinal drives in the guilt–shame cycle, and a manifestation of subjective dependence and need. The relationship of passivity to femininity is complex. While certainly not innate, cultural and biological factors have conspired to instill in women feelings of passivity and inferiority, which frequently engender a sense of shame. Freud (1933) stated that shame is "a female characteristic par excellence" (p. 11). Lewis (1971) observed greater field dependency, passivity, and shame in women than in men.

While shame is by no means gender dependent and is equally an experience of men, some have argued that shame depressions predominate in women (for example, Anthony, 1981). An interesting paper by Bodin, Hunt, and Kassoff (1987) assesses aspects of shame in women, presenting convincing clinical examples of women's body shame, shame over competitive feelings with men in career advancement, and shame about intellectual achievement. In my own clinical experience, I have found that women tend to be particularly sensitive to matters of dependence, need, affection, and unrequited desire. This sensitivity can be understood to be the result of failed selfobject responsiveness and attunement to earlier expressions of need and desire and to assertiveness and competence. Recall that such a woman in analysis said, "Humiliation is the worst feeling I have ever experienced."

It is a mistake, however, to overemphasize the presence of shame in women. Men too feel shame over dependency and unmet needs. I think, though, that men tend to feel shame particularly about failure to achieve an ideal or goal. Body shame is, of course, important for men too, but most frequently in relation to failure to attain an ideal of phallic or athletic prowess. Shame in men, then, most frequently reflects failure, inadequacy, or inferiority in the face of an ideal of competence in work, phallic assertiveness or performance, or in intellect. While this difference does not constitute an absolute distinction in shame between men and women, it does suggest that women's shame relates more to intimacy, affectionate ties (as suggested by Lewis, 1987), and failure in selfobject mirroring, whereas men's shame relates more frequently to achievement, performance, and failure in idealized selfobject function.

CONCLUSION

In this Epilogue I have returned to the explicit questions from the introductory chapter that have informed our study of shame. In general, answers to these questions are not definitive, but tendencies have emerged that indicate how complex and important a problem shame is and how closely shame touches many of the issues that are at the cutting edge of contemporary psychoanalysis and psychotherapy.

First, is shame primarily a defense against exhibitionism/grandiosity, or is it principally an affective experience? Certainly it can be experienced as either defense or affect, but I have tried to show that the affective experience of shame predominates. Even when shame serves as a defense, the affective, experiential nature of shame must be understood and acknowledged. When the shame experience is ignored, underlying genetic factors cannot be adequately investigated.

Must a perspective on the self and its deficits be added to classical structural psychology to make possible a complete understanding of the meaning of shame? While structural theory–and its contributions regarding the ego ideal, object relations, and narcissism–is central to the dynamics and development of shame, the importance of a broad, comprehensive viewpoint on the self to a thorough understanding of shame has been demonstrated.

Can shame be understood to arise in isolation as an internal, intrapsychic phenomenon, or does it occur only in a social, public, external context? The answer to this question depends, I believe, on the status one gives to the developmental elements of ideals, selfobjects, and self-regard. Shame, seen as humiliation and embarrassment, clearly occurs in response to public exposure and provocation, but I have tried to show that shame may also be a response of the viewing, experiencing self alone to internal need and failure– "the eye turned inward" (Morrison, 1987). Here, the subjective quest for selfobject attunement and responsiveness, and the response of shame to repeated selfobject absence or failure, complicates the matter of shame as an internal or external (relational) response.

What is the relationship of shame to guilt? While this has not been a primary focus of this study, I have tried to show at various points that, while related, these two affects are distinct in important and meaningful ways. Much of the literature on shame has concerned itself with these differences (e.g., Piers, 1953; Levin, 1967; Lewis, 1971; Thrane, 1979; Wurmser, 1981). Hartmann and Loewenstein (1962) alone argued that no significant psychoanalytic difference exists between shame and guilt.

Is shame a manifestation of passivity and dependence, and thus a singularly female affect? I believe that shame certainly is strong in women, but is by no means unknown in men. Some gender differences in shame have been noted in this chapter.

What is the relationship of shame to anger/rage, contempt, and envy? I believe that these function with regard to shame primarily as defenses and thus, implicitly, that shame elicits defenses more frequently than it defends against drive elements (for example, aggression or desire). Depression tends, by contrast, to parallel experiences of shame regarding hopelessness, inferiority, and failure to attain ideals. What relationship does narcissism bear to shame? I have come to believe that shame, in some form, is always present in narcissism and its various manifestations. These manifestations include what I have called the *Dialectic of Narcissism,* in which autonomy, self-sufficiency, and isolation may be an ideal/goal of the self, the response to object pain and disillusionment, or to selfobject failure. Alternatively, object idealization, dependency, and quest for selfobject merger may represent attempts at reunion with the lost ego ideal. Oscillations in these states seem, to me, always to involve shame and to sustain the categories of "egotistical" or "dissociative" narcissist delineated by Broucek (1982).

THE PSYCHOTHERAPY OF SHAME

In this book, I have tried to portray shame as a genuine human affliction that requires acknowledgment and treatment. My basic thesis has been that shame is a major problem for patients, one that has frequently been overlooked in treatment because it is concealed and because it inevitably reverberates with shame experiences in the therapist, who may collude with the patient to keep these feelings unrecognized and unexamined. Shame is, nevertheless, ever-present in the therapeutic encounter; and, unless it is adequately understood and considered in treatment, genetic and transferential interpretations will frequently seem to be criticisms or even irrelevant.

Shame presents in various ways, often very subtle. Seldom will a patient speak explicitly of shame, but may speak instead of feeling foolish, ridiculous, pathetic, insignificant, invisible, or worthless. It is important that the therapist become familiar with the language of shame in order to recognize and probe for underlying shame feelings and experiences. Sometimes shame will be suggested by externalization or projected defenses against the experience—anger and rage, contempt or envy—or by depression. Again, familiarity with the defensive maneuvers to protect against underlying shame will facilitate penetration and exploration of shame feelings. At other times, shame itself will be manifest as passive defenses against other phenomena (for example, oedipal competition or longing, or feared anger); in these cases, exploration of the conscious shame will prove fruitful in leading to repressed conflictual elements.

Shame will have different significance in the treatment of different diagnostic groups. For neurotic patients, it will tend to be circumscribed and will frequently relate to failure in action, often reflecting defensive passivity against oedipal aggression, competition, and desire (the guilt–shame cycle). For patients with primarily narcissistic patterns, shame will tend to be more totally pervasive and will lead to the core of all aspects of narcissistic vulnerability. Defenses against underlying shame will tend to be more active and primitive, representing, in particular, manifestations of projective identification. Psychotherapeutic efforts with patients suffering from manic-depressive illness will frequently lead to shame sensitivity and narcissistic vulnerability. The shame of borderline and schizophrenic conditions has not been explored in this volume.[2]

From a self-psychological perspective, shame may represent self-object failure in mirroring, in which case shame sensitivity and anx-

---

[2]Shame about psychotic disintegration often is felt by the patient during periods of reintegration, when they look back on their helplessness, delusions, intense hatred, object need, and the like. Since this seems so specifically about self-states of fragmentation, I have not reviewed them in this work (with the exception of manic-depressive illness). For further study of shame and borderline and schizophrenic conditions, see Fisher, 1985; N. K. Morrison, 1987; Will, 1987; O'Leary and Wright, 1988.

iety will reflect concern about the detailed empathic attunement of, and attachment to, significant objects who function as selfobjects. This will frequently be the case in work with narcissistically vulnerable women. On the other hand, the shame from selfobject failure in idealization, frequently present in men, may be revealed through feelings of failure, worthlessness, and inadequacy with regard to idealized, external or internalized objects. These differences are illustrated in the cases of Lily and Cristophe in chapter 9. In either case, shame may be experienced as humiliation or embarrassment with regard to an external object (the humiliator) or to an internalized object or function (the ideal self). These different manifestations of shame should be explored in an elaboration of the shame experience for each particular patient.

So, shame itself may be hidden, while at the same time it functions as a central concern and experience that must be identified and explored, frequently before useful work can proceed in the interpretation of underlying conflicts and genetic issues. This is not to suggest that shame is primary and supersedes the interplay of dynamic conflicts, but, rather, that it is frequently of great significance and may be of primary conscious importance, to patients. This concern must be recognized, accepted, and addressed, often before the patient's interest and access to dynamic conflictual issues become available for consideration and interpretation.

A sequence has evolved in my clinical work in which I try to remain sensitive to shame in all of its presentations. I attempt to identify and delineate the patient's particular shame experience, convey my acceptance of, and interest in, the patient's shame, and then work in depth with the patient on the precipitants and manifestations of his or her shame. As this sequence progresses, the therapeutic emphasis shifts from the exploration of shame to the investigation and interpetation of other genetic and dynamic factors.

I have attempted to demonstrate in this book that work with shame is an essential part of the psychoanalytic and psychotherapuetic endeavor and that, without attentiveness to this issue, the therapeutic task will often remain incomplete.

References

Abraham, H. C. & Freud, E. L., ed. (1965), *A Psycho-Analytic Dialogue: The Letters of Sigmund Freud and Karl Abraham, 1907–1926,* trans. B. Marsh & H. C. Abraham. New York: Basic Books.

Abraham, K. (1911), Notes on the psychoanalytic investigation and treatment of manic-depressive insanity and allied conditions. In: *Selected Papers on Psychoanalysis.* London: Hogarth Press, 1927, pp. 137–156.

_____ (1913), Restrictions and transformations of scopophilia in psycho-neurotics. In: *Selected Papers on Psychoanalysis.* London: Hogarth Press, 1927.

Adler, A. (1907), *Study of Organ Inferiority and Its Psychical Compensation,* trans. S. E. Jellife. New York: Nervous & Mental Disease Monograph Series, No. 24, 1917.

_____ (1912), *The Neurotic Constitution,* trans. B. Gluck, & J. E. Lind. New York: Moffat, Yard, 1917.

_____ (1929), *Problems of Neurosis.* New York: Harper & Row, 1964.

Alexander, F. (1938), Remarks about the relation of inferiority feelings to guilt feelings. *Internat. J. Psycho-Anal.,* 19:41–49.

Anthony, E. J. (1981), Shame, guilt, and the feminine self in psychoanalysis. In: *Object and Self: A Developmental Approach,* ed. S. Tuttman, C. Kaye & M. Zimmerman. New York: International Universities Press, pp. 194–234.

Basch, M. F. (1976), The concept of affect: A re-examination. *J. Amer. Psychoanal. Assn.,* 24:759–777.

198

Benedict, R. (1946), *The Chrysanthemum and the Sword.* Boston: Houghton Mifflin.

Bibring, E. (1953), The mechanism of depression. In: *Affective Disorderes,* ed. P. Greenacre. New York: International Universities Press, pp. 13–48.

Bion, W. (1959), *Experiences in Groups.* New York: Basic Books.

Bodin, R., Hunt, P. & Kassoff, B. (1987), The centrality of shame in the psychology of women. Presented at Conference of the Association of Women in Psychology. Denver, CO, March.

Boris, H. N. (1986), The "other" breast. *Contemp. Psychoanal.,* 22:45–59.

Brenner, C,. (1974), On the nature and development of affects: A unified theory. *Psychoanal. Quart.,* 43:532–566.

Broucek, F. (1982), Shame and its relationship to early narcissistic developments. *Internat. J. Psycho-Anal.,* 65:369–378.

Bursten, B. (1973), Some narcissistic personality types. *Internat. J. Psycho-Anal.,* 54:287–300. Also in: *Essential Papers on Narcissism* (1986), ed. A.P. Morrison. New York: New York University Press, pp. 377–402.

Chasseguet-Smirgel, J. (1985), *The Ego Ideal.* New York: Norton.

Cohen, M. B., Baker, G., Cohen, R. A., Fromm Reichmann, F. & Weigert, E. V. (1954), An intensive study of twelve cases of manic-depressive psychosis. *Psychiatry.,* 17:103–137. Also in: *Essential Papers on Depression* (1986), ed. J.C. Coyne. New York: New York University Press, pp. 82–139.

Coyne, J. C. (1986), Toward an interactional description of depression. In: *Essential Papers on Depression,* ed. J.C. Coyne. New York: New York University Press, pp. 311–330.

Curtis, H. (1984), Clinical perspectives on self psychology. *Psychoanal. Quart.,* 54:339–378.

Demos, E. V. (1988), Affect and the development of the self: A new frontier. In: *Frontiers in Self Psychology: Progress in Self Psychology, Vol. 3,* ed. A. Goldberg. Hillsdale, NJ: The Analytic Press, pp. 27–53.

Dinnerstein, D. (1976), *The Mermaid and the Minotaur.* New York: Harper & Row.

Emde, R. N. (1980), Toward a psychoanalytic theory of affect: II. Emerging models of emotional development in infancy. In: *The Course of Life, Vol. 1,* ed. S.I. Greenspan & G. Pollock. Washington, DC: NIH, pp. 85–112.

Erikson, E. H. (1950), *Childhood and Society.* New York: Norton.

Feldman, S. S. (1962), Blushing, fear of blushing, and shame. *J. Amer. Psychoanal. Assn.,* 10:368–385.

Fenichel, O. (1945), *The Psychoanalytic Theory of Neurosis.* New York: Norton.

Fisher, S. (1985), Identity of two: The phenomenology of shame in borderline development and treatment. *Psychother.,* 22:101–109.

Freud, A. (1936), *The Ego and the Mechanisms of Defense.* New York: International Universities Press.

Freud, S. (1892–1899), Extracts from the Fliess papers. *Standard Edition* 1:175–280. London: Hogarth Press, 1966.

_____ (1895), Project for a scientific psychology. *Standard Edition*, 1:283–397. London: Hogarth Press, 1966.

_____ (1896), Further remarks on the neuro-psychosis of defense. *Standard Edition*, 3:159–185. London: Hogarth Press, 1962.

_____ (1898), Sexuality in the aetiology of the neuroses. *Standard Edition*, 3:261–285. London: Hogarth Press, 1962.

_____ (1900), The interpretation of dreams. *Standard Edition*, 4 & 5. London: Hogarth Press, 1953.

_____ (1905), Three essays on the theory of sexuality. *Standard Edition*, 7:125–243. London: Hogarth Press, 1953.

_____ (1908), Character and anal eroticism. *Standard Edition*, 9:167–175. London: Hogarth Press, 1959.

_____ (1914), On narcissism: An introduction. *Standard Edition*, 14:67–102. London: Hogarth Press, 1957.

_____ (1917), Mourning and melancholia. *Standard Edition*, 14:243–258. London: Hogarth Press, 1957.

_____ (1921), Group psychology and the analysis of the ego. *Standard Edition*, 18:67–143. London: Hogarth Press, 1955.

_____ (1923), The ego and the id. *Standard Edition*, 19:3–66. London: Hogarth Press, 1961.

_____ (1930), Civilization and its discontents. *Standard Edition*, 21:57–146. London: Hogarth Press, 1961.

_____ (1933), New introductory lectures on psycho-analysis. *Standard Edition*, 22:3–183. London: Hogarth Press, 1964.

Friedman, L. (1980), Kohut: A book review essay. *Psychoanal. Quart.*, 49:393–422.

Galatzer-Levy, R. M. (1988), Manic depressive illness: Analytic experience and a hypothesis. In: *Frontiers in Self Psychology: Progress in Self Psychology, Vol. 3*, ed. A. Goldberg. Hillsdale, NJ: The Analytic Press, pp. 87–102.

Gilligan, C. (1982), *In a Different Voice*. Cambridge, MA: Harvard University Press.

Gilligan, J. (1976), Beyond morality: Psychoanalytic reflections on shame, guilt, and love. In: *Moral Development and Behavior*, ed. T. Lickona. New York: Holt, Rinehart & Winston, pp. 144–158.

Greenberg, J. & Mitchell, S. (1983), *Object Relations in Psychoanalytic Theory*. Cambridge, MA: Harvard University Press.

Grinker, R. R. (1955), Growth inertia and shame: Their therapeutic implications and dangers. *Internat. J. Psycho-Anal.*, 36:267–276.

Grotstein, J. S. (1981), *Splitting and Projective Identification*. New York: Aronson.

Hartmann, E. (1939), *Ego Psychology and the Problem of Adaptation*. New York: International Universities Press.

_____ (1950), Comments on the psychoanalytic theory of the ego. *The Psychoanalytic Study of the Child*, 5:74–96. New York: International Universities Press.

_____ & Loewenstein, R. (1962), Notes on the superego. *The Psychoanalytic Study of the Child*, 17:42–81. New York: International Universities Press.

Hazard, P. (1969), Freud's teaching on shame. *Laval Theologique et Philosophique*, 25:234–267.

Jacobson, E. (1954), The self and the object world: Vicissitudes of their infantile cathexis and their influences on ideational and affective development. *The Psychoanalytic Study of the Child,* 9:75–127. New York: International Universities Press.

_____ (1964), *The Self and the Object World.* New York: International Universities Press.

Joffe, W. G. & Sandler, J. (1967), Some conceptual problems involved in the consideration of disorders of narcissism. *J. Child Psychother.*, 2:56–66.

Kaufman, G. (1985), *Shame: The Power of Caring.* Cambridge, MA: Schenkman.

Kernberg, O. (1975), *Borderline Conditions and Pathological Narcissism.* New York: Aronson.

Kinston, W. (1980), A theoretical and technical approach to narcissistic disturbance. *Internat. J. Psycho-Anal.*, 61:383–394.

_____ (1983), A theoretical context for shame. *Internat. J. Psycho-Anal.*, 64:213–226.

Klein, M. (1946), Notes on some schizoid mechanisms. In: *Developments in Psychoanalysis.* London: Hogarth Press, pp. 292–320.

_____ (1957), *Envy and Gratitude.* New York: Basic Books.

Kohut, H. (1966), Forms and transformations of narcissism. *J. Amer. Psychoanal. Assn.,* 14:243–272. Also in: *Essential Papers on Narcissism* (1986), ed. A.P. Morrison. New York: New York University Press, pp. 61–87.

_____ (1971), *The Analysis of the Self.* New York: International Universities Press.

_____ (1972), Thoughts on narcissism and narcissistic rage. *The Psychoanalytic Study of the Child,* 27:360–399. New Haven, CT: Yale University Press.

_____ (1977), *The Restoration of the Self.* New York: International Universities Press.

_____ (1984), *How Does Analysis Cure?* ed. A. Goldberg & P. E. Stepansky. Chicago: University of Chicago Press.

_____ & Wolf, E. S. (1978), The disorders of the self and their treatment–an outline. *Internat. J. Psycho-Anal.*, 59:413–425. Also in: *Essential Papers on Narcissism* (1986), ed. A.P. Morrison. New York: New York University Press, pp. 175–196.

Kris, A. (1985), Resistance in convergent and divergent conflicts. *Psychoanal. Quart.,* 54:537–568.

Lasch, C. (1978), *The Culture of Narcissism.* New York: Norton.

Levin, S. (1967), Some metapsychological considerations on the differentiation between shame and guilt. *Internat. J. Psycho-Anal.*, 48:267–276.

_____ (1971), The psychoanalysis of shame. *Internat. J. Psycho-Anal.*, 52:355–362.

Levin, S. (1982), The psychoanalysis of shame, unpublished.

Lewis, H. B. (1971), *Shame and Guilt in Neurosis.* New York: International Universities Press.

_____ (1981), Shame and guilt in human nature. In: *Object and Self,* ed. S.

Tuttman, C. Kaye & M. Zimmerman. New York: International Universities Press, pp. 235–265.

_____ (1987), Shame and the narcissistic personality. In: *The Many Faces of Shame,* ed. D. Nathanson. New York: Guilford, pp. 93–132.

_____ ed. (1987), *The Role of Shame in Symptom Formation.* Hillsdale, NJ: The Analytic Press.

Lowenfeld, H. (1976), Notes on shamelessness. *Psychoanal. Quart.,* 45:62–72.

Lynd, H. M. (1958), *On Shame and the Search for Identity.* New York: Harcourt Brace & World.

Mack, J. E. & Ablon, S. L. (1983), *The Development and Sustaining of Self-Esteem in Childhood.* New York: International Universities Press.

Mahler, M., Pine, F. & Bergman A. (1975), *The Psychological Birth of the Human Infant.* New York: Basic Books.

Miller, S. (1985), *The Shame Experience.* Hillsdale, NJ: The Analytic Press.

Modell, A. (1975), A narcissistic defense against affects and the illusion of self-sufficiency. *Internat. J. Psycho-Anal.,* 56:275–282. Also in: *Essential Papers on Narcissism* (1986), ed. A.P. Morrison. New York: New York University Press, pp. 293–307.

Morrison, A. P. (1983), Shame, the ideal self, and narcissism. *Contemp. Psychoanal.,* 19:295–318. Also in: *Essential Papers on Narcissism,* ed. A.P. Morrison. New York: New York University Press, pp. 348–371.

_____ (1984a), Working with shame in psychoanalytic treatment. *J. Amer. Psychoanal. Assn.,* 32:479–505.

_____ (1984b), Shame and the psychology of the self. In: *Kohut's Legacy,* ed. P. E. Stepansky & A. Goldberg. Hillsdale, NJ: The Analytic Press.

_____ ed. (1986a), *Essential Papers on Narcissism.* New York: New York University.

_____ (1986b), On projective identification in couples' groups. *Internat. J. Group Psychother.,* 36:55–73.

_____ (1987), The eye turned inward. In: *The Many Faces of Shame,* ed. D. Nathanson. New York: Guilford.

Morrison, N. K. (1987), The role of shame in schizophrenia. In: *The Role of Shame in Symptom Formation,* ed. H.B. Lewis. Hillsdale, NJ: Lawrence Erlbaum Associates.

Murray, J. M. (1964), Narcissism and the ego ideal. *J. Amer. Psychoanal. Assn.,* 12:477–511.

Nathanson, D., ed. (1987), *The Many Faces of Shame.* New York: Guilford.

Nietzche, F. (1966), *Beyond Good and Evil,* trans. W. Kaufman. New York: Random House.

_____ (1974), *Genealogy of Morals and Peoples and Countries.* New York: Gordon Press.

Nunberg, H. (1955), *Principles of Psychoanalysis.* New York: International Universities Press.

Ogden, T. H. (1979), On projective identification. *Internat. J. Psycho-Anal.,* 60:357–373.

O'Leary, J. & Wright, F. (1988), The role of shame and guilt in the borderline patient, unpublished.

Panel, (1981). The Bipolar Self. *J. Amer. Psychoanal. Assn.*, 29:337–394.

Piers, G. (1953), Shame and guilt: A psychoanalytic study. In: *Shame and Guilt*, G. Piers & M. Singer. New York: Norton, pp. 15–55.

Rapaport, D. (1967), Should Edward Bibring's theory of depression be restored? In: *The Collected Papers of David Rapaport*, ed. M. Gill. New York: Basic Books.

Reich, A. (1953), Pathological forms of object choice in women. *J. Amer. Psychoanal. Assn.* 1:

_____ (1960), Pathologic forms of self-esteem regulation. *The Psychoanalytic Study of the Child*, 15:215–232. New York: International Universities Press. Also in: *Essential Papers On Narcissism*, ed. A.P. Morrison. New York: New York University, pp. 44–60.

Rothstein, A. (1979), Oedipal conflicts in narcissistic personality disorders. *Internat. J. Psycho-Anal.*, 60:189–200.

_____ (1984), Fear of humiliation. *J. Amer. Psychoanal. Assn.*, 32:99–116.

Sandler, J., Holder, A. & Meers, D. (1963), The ego ideal and the ideal self. *The Psychoanalytic Study of the Child*, 18:139–158. New York: International Universities Press.

Sartre, J. P. (1943), *Being and Nothingness*. New York: Philosophical Library, 1956.

Schafer, R. (1960), The loving and beloved superego in Freud's structural theory. *The Psychoanalytic Study of the Child*, 15:163–188. New York: International Universities Press.

_____ (1967), Ideals, the ego ideal, and the ideal self. In: Motives and thought. *Psychological Issues*, Monogr. 18/19. New York: International Universities Press, pp. 131–174.

Schecter, D. (1974), The ideal self and other. *Contemp. Psychoanal.*, 10:103–115.

_____ (1979), The loving and persecuting superego. *Contemp. Psychoanal.*, 15:361–379.

Schneider, C. D. (1977), *Shame, Exposure and Privacy*. Boston: Beacon Press.

Shane, M. (1985), Summary and discussion of Kohut's "The Self Psychological Approach to Defense and Resistance." In: *Progress in Self Psychology*, Vol. 1, ed. A. Goldberg. New York: Guilford Press. pp. 69–82.

Singer, M. B. (1953), Shame cultures and guilt cultures. In: *Shame and Guilt*, G. Piers & M.B. Singer. New York: Norton, pp. 59–100.

Socarides, D. D. & Stolorow, R. D. (1984–85), Affects and selfobjects. *The Annual of Psychoanalysis*, 12/13:105–119. New York: International Universities Press.

Sohn, L. (1985), Narcissistic organization, projective identification and the formation of the identificate. *Internat. J. Psycho-Anal.*, 66:201–213.

Spero, M. H. (1984), Shame: An object-relational formulation. *The Psychoanalytic Study of the Child*, 39:259–282. New Haven, CT: Yale University Press.

Stein, M. H. (1979), Review of "The Restoration of the Self" by H. Kohut. *J. Amer. Psychoanal. Assn.*, 27:665–680.

Stepansky, P. E. (1983), *In Freud's Shadow*. Hillsdale, NJ: The Analytic Press.

Stern, D. (1985), *The Interpersonal World of the Infant.* New York: Basic Books.
⸺ (1988), Affect in the context of the infant's lived experience: Some considerations. *Inter. J. Psycho-Anal.,* 69:233–238.
Stolorow, R. (1986), On experiencing an object: A multidimensional perspective. In: *Progress in Self Psychology, Vol. 2,* ed. A. Goldberg. New York: Guilford, pp. 273–279.
⸺ & Lachmann, F. M. (1980), *Psychoanalysis of Developmental Arrests.* New York: International Universities Press.
⸺ ⸺ (1984–85), Transference: The future of an illusion. *The Annual of Psychoanalysis,* 12–13:19–37. New York: International Universities Press.
Supplement (1983), Defense and resistance: historical perspectives and current concepts. *J. Amer. Psychoanal. Assn.,* 31.
Thrane, G. (1979), Shame and the construction of the self. *The Annual of Psychoanalysis,* 7:321–341. New York: International Universities Press.
Tolpin, M. (1978), Self-objects and oedipal objects: A crucial distinction. *The Psychoanalytic Study of the Child,* 33:167–183. New Haven, CT: Yale University Press.
Tolpin, P. H. (1985), The primacy of preservation of self. In: *Progress in Self Psychology, Vol. 1,* ed. Arnold Goldberg. New York: Guilford Press, pp. 83–87.
Tomkins, S. S. (1962–63), *Affect/Imagery/Consciousness (Vols. 1 and 2).* New York: Springer.
⸺ (1987), Shame. In: *The Many Faces of Shame,* ed. D. Nathanson. New York: Guilford, pp. 133–161.
Vaillant, G. E. (1977), *Adaptation to Life.* Boston: Little, Brown.
Will, Jr., O. A. (1987), The sense of shame in psychosis: Random comments on shame in the psychotic experience. In: *The Many Faces of Shame,* ed. D. Nathanson. New York: Guilford, pp. 308–317.
Winnicott, D. W. (1965), *The Maturational Process and the Facilitating Environment.* New York: International Universities Press.
Wolf, E. (1980), On the developmental line of selfobject relations. In: *Advances in Self Psychology,* ed. A. Goldberg. New York: International Universities Press, pp. 117–130.
Wurmser, L. (1981), *The Mask of Shame.* Baltimore, MD: Johns Hopkins University Press.

Author Index

Subject Index